DIAMONDS
IN THE ROUGH

CHAMPIONSHIP GOLF ON
THE SENIOR PGA TOUR

DIAMONDS
IN THE
ROUGH

CHAMPIONSHIP GOLF ON
THE SENIOR PGA TOUR

MARK SHAW

BALLANTINE BOOKS • NEW YORK

A Ballantine Book
Published by The Ballantine Publishing Group

Copyright © 1998 by Mark Shaw

http://www.randomhouse.com

Library of Congress Cataloging-in-Publication Data
Shaw, Mark, 1945–
    Diamonds in the rough: championship golf on the Senior PGA
Tour / Mark Shaw.—1st ed.
        p.   cm.
    ISBN 0-345-41745-3 (alk. paper)
    1. Senior PGA Tour (Association)   2. Golf—Tournaments—United
States.   I. Title.
GV969.S46S43   1998   97-52665
796.352'66—dc21

Manufactured in the United States of America

First Edition: May 1998
10   9   8   7   6   5   4   3   2   1

Dedicated to
Chris Roark Shaw,
for her love and support of an eccentric,
and to
Kimberly, Kyle, Kevin, and Kent,
for putting up with one

And

To the memory of Larry Gilbert,
a true gentleman,
a great golfer

"Golf is the greatest game in the world. It is frustrating. It is rewarding. It is humbling. It is exhilarating. It can send you to the depths of despair. It can rocket you into an orbit of incomparable satisfaction and joy ... It puts a man's character to the anvil and his richest qualities—patience, poise, restraint—to the flame."

—BILLY CASPER
Great Moments in Golf

Contents

Acknowledgments   *xi*

Introduction   *xiii*

Prologue: The Field   *3*

BOOK I: The Doctor Is In   *9*

BOOK II: Hale and Hearty   *79*

BOOK III: Chicago Swampland   *109*

BOOK IV: One for the Club Pros   *135*

BOOK V: Hale Versus Gil   *205*

Bibliography   *277*

Index   *279*

Acknowledgments

DIAMONDS IN THE ROUGH HAS TRULY BEEN A COLLABORATIVE EFFORT, and I am thankful to a great many people for their assistance in making this book possible.

Without belief in me by literary agent Richard Pine, a gem of a man with a taste for literary excellence, my idea for a book chronicling many of the great golfers in history would never have been born. His link up for me with Judith Curr, the effervescent publisher at Ballantine Books whose love for the game shone through from our first meeting, sealed the assignment. I thank Judith for her confidence in me throughout the writing process.

Doug Grad, a learned editor at Ballantine, certainly deserves praise, as do copyeditor Jeff Smith, Joe Luigs, an official with the United States Golf Association, Tom Nettles, a gifted correspondent at The Golf Channel, and John "Spider" Miller, former U.S. Mid-Amateur champion, who thoroughly reviewed drafts of the book. My beloved wife, Chris Roark Shaw, constantly supported my efforts, as did our friend and colleague Becky Howard.

Officials at the PGA Tour, including Commissioner Tim Finchem, Phil Stambaugh, Dave Senko, Denise Taylor, Dave Combs, Julie Cordes, and Brian Henning, assisted me at every turn. Tom Meeks and Craig Smith of the United States Golf Association were also most helpful, as were Jami Roggero and Julius Mason of the PGA of America and broadcasters Jim Kelly, Andy North, Frank Beard, Mike Tirico, and Robert Wrenn of ESPN.

Along the tournament trail, I thank Tony George, Lee Gardner, Rollie and Jeff Schroeder, Connie Baines, Jeff Kleiber, Mike Popcheff, Bill York, Paul Furimsky, Larry Bianco, Pete and Alice Dye, Jim Ferriell, Mike Stipher, Mike Horri, Jerry Aiken, Verne Boatner, Jack Lupton, Tom Hartley, Jan Gaylor, Tanya Benson, Davis Szena, and Solon Weiner, among others.

Special thanks go to Toni Billie, who assisted me most capably with research for the book, Mark Huber, a gentle man with a great zest for life whose insight into professional golf was most revealing,

Fred Roark, my father-in-law, who shared his love for the game, Senior Tour wives Gail Murphy, Marcia Colbert, Carolyn Summerhays, and Willye Dent, and new friends such as Sandy Jones, Willie Miller, Kyle Kenny, Mark Albus, and Todd Newcombe, who treated me with courtesy.

I also thank the professionals of the Senior PGA Tour for their cooperation and friendship. They are gentlemen who play the game at the highest level. And respected journalists such as Jerry Potter, Richard Mudry, Jim Bohannan, Michael Arkush, Gary van Sickle, Phil Richards, and Thomas Bonk, who covered the Tour on a regular basis.

Thanks also go to my children, Kimberly, Kyle, Kent, and Kevin, for their continued support. And to my canine pals Bach, Peanut Butter, Snickers, Reggie Miller, Shadow, and White Sox for their companionship at five in the morning.

Above all I thank the Good Lord for my continued blessings. Writing *Diamonds in the Rough* was an unforgettable experience, one I shall treasure for many years to come.

Introduction

THE PUTT ON THE EIGHTEENTH HOLE WAS A SLIGHTLY DOWNHILL ten-footer that barely moved left to right. By high-stakes gamblers' standards, it meant little, but I knew the consequences if I missed would be high.

To my right stood Jim Colbert, 1995 and 1996 Senior PGA Tour Player of the Year. I had been his guest in a three-on-three match at the Bighorn Golf Club, which bordered his palatial home in Palm Springs, California. For seventeen holes, I had played like a duffer, barely getting the ball airborne on the front nine. At one point, after a blue darter of mine ricocheted off the rocks directly in front of us, Jim, who had taken me as a partner, said under his breath, "Mark, don't you think you should tee the ball a little higher?"

Even before that shot, which nearly killed a golf club employee standing nearby, my confidence was at a low ebb. I had been on a Big Ten championship team at Purdue as a collegian and continued to be a low handicapper through most of my life. Whenever someone asked what kind of golfer I was, I simply replied, "I parred the Road Hole at St. Andrews."

At the first hole at Bighorn, Colbert had announced me as a six handicap, but his voice was quivering when he said it. Moments before, I had embarrassed myself by failing to strap my brand-new shiny-black Callaway golf bag filled with brand-new shiny Callaway woods, irons, and putter, which Colbert had loaned me, onto the golf cart. As we headed up the path toward the tee, the bag fell off with a thud and clubs scattered like toothpicks across the asphalt.

All this ran through my mind as I sized up my ten-foot putt. Nobody on the opponent's team had made birdie, and with a shot, my four would square up the match, a godsend at that point despite our having Gentleman Jim on our team. More important, I knew that many of Colbert's fellow Senior PGA Tour compatriots would be hearing about Mark Shaw the golfer in the coming weeks as I continued to write *Diamonds in the Rough*. If the ten-footer went in, Jim might say, "Well, he can't play a lick, but he came through in the clutch," which would save my credibility. A miss, though, and "He can't play a lick, nearly killed someone" would be my rep.

Fortunately, my brand-new shiny Callaway putter hit my brand-new Titleist just right, and the ball fell in the right lip of the hole. Colbert and I exchanged high fives, and I marched off the green wiping my brow and feeling as if I had just won the U.S. Open.

Later in the 1997 Senior PGA Tour season, the announcement would come that Jim Colbert had prostate cancer. That was just one of the unbelievable developments during a year that produced enough thrills, spills, and heartbreaks to cover a lifetime.

I must credit John Feinstein's superb book, *A Good Walk Spoiled*, as being the inspiration for *Diamonds in the Rough*. After reading his text for the hundredth time, the idea came to me to chronicle a year on the Senior PGA Tour. I felt that many of the great players in the game, especially those who competed on the PGA Tour beginning in the 1950s, might very well be winding down their careers in 1997. That proved to be the case.

Ballantine Books publisher Judith Curr, a golf-savvy Australian lass with a twinkle in her eye, shared my vision, and I began my cross-country trek in January to Senior Tour events, unsure where the story would lead. Each week, whether I attended the tournaments in person, watched them on television, or talked with research assistants directly after the event, I wrote the account as it happened.

Diamonds in the Rough unfolds in dramatic fashion as the over-fifty gang faced challenges involved not only with winning and losing, but family problems, health concerns, financial woes, and myriad others. For many, the professional golf mulligan known as the Senior Tour, a new chance at fame and fortune, was filled with ecstasy, while others labored through a year they would rather forget.

After a season of tournaments, certain images remain crystal-clear. Most vivid is a conversation on the practice tee at the Comfort/Brickyard Classic with Arnold Palmer, whose displeasure late in the year with his golf game didn't dampen his love for the sport. He had read my aviation book, *Forever Flying*, and talked about his own adventures in the air. "I started flying because I was scared to have others in control," the pilot with more than 15,000 hours in the air admitted. I was mesmerized by his every word, aware that Palmer might very well be playing his final complete season of competition.

Other images ran rampant. I chatted with Chi Chi Rodriguez about "Little Bertha," a twenty-seven-inch putter that was guaranteed, he said, to cure putting ills. And watched him down a container of Bee Alive Queen's Nectar before a round. The tiny bottle is a souvenir that sits on my desk.

Watching ageless Sam Snead work on his bunker shots in the one-hundred-degree heat of Palm Springs proved scintillating. Talk about love for the game. Traipsing down the eighteenth fairway with Gil Morgan at The Tradition, which he won, was exhilarating, and following Jack Nicklaus, Ben Crenshaw, and Hale Irwin at the U.S. Open presented a past, present, and future look at the Senior Tour.

Observing Hale Irwin juggle golf balls while his daughter laughed along with the gallery gathered at the practice tee at The Tradition made me realize Hale, so often the serious one, had a light side. Watching his demeanor coming down the stretch drive at the PGA Seniors Championship proved to me he was as fierce a competitor as the game has ever known.

Learning that Larry Gilbert, who had climbed the mountain of his dreams in his fifth year, had inoperable lung cancer, brought a tear to my eye. Seeing Bob Duval, father of PGA Tour star David, fulfill the club professional's dream of gaining an exemption on the Senior Tour made me smile again.

Over the months, I found myself rooting for the underdogs and cursing those who didn't appreciate their good fortune. This book could fill a thousand pages, or more, for everyone competing on the Senior PGA Tour is a story.

In the final analysis, I learned a great deal from the sportsmen I covered, for they have lived a lifetime filled with incredible memories. They are true gentlemen who shared with me their tales, their thoughts about the game, and their impressions of those with whom they have competed in the latter half of the twentieth century. I thank them for their cooperation and trust that my words capture the true essence of these "diamonds in the rough."

DIAMONDS
IN THE ROUGH

CHAMPIONSHIP GOLF ON
THE SENIOR PGA TOUR

Prologue: The Field

THE PENCIL-THIN MAN IN THE WHEAT-COLORED STRAW HAT GLANCED down the practice range. Before taking a swipe at a brand-new crystal-white Titleist with a whiplash swing that nearly finished before it began, Chi Chi Rodriguez sized up the competition for the Royal Caribbean Classic, the first full-field tournament on the 1997 Senior PGA Tour.

To his immediate left stood sixty-year-old Bobby Nichols, the 1964 PGA champion who competed with two titanium replacement hips to match his titanium driver. Smacking practice balls beside him was Vietnam veteran Bobby Stroble, the black journeyman golfer three years removed from sleeping in his Chevy Impala, who'd won nearly $500,000 on the Senior Tour in 1996. Two spots down stood the stout, red-haired Englishman Brian Barnes, famous for wearing a kilt in a European professional event and marking his ball with a beer bottle.

Next to "Barnsey" was Hugh Thompson, better known as "Rocky." Three times a winner on the Senior PGA Tour, the Rock had more one-liners than David Letterman. Asked about his fifty-inch-plus Bumble-bee driver, he quipped, "When I hit it, it goes downtown. The only problem is I don't know which town." He added, "It's standard length—for Shaquille O'Neal."

Jack Nicklaus had taken one look at the yellow and black driver and commented, "It looks like a fly rod with a bobber at the end of it."

Chi Chi Rodriguez, jokingly accused by some Tour officials of being "undermedicated" due to his round-the-clock sparkling person-ality and never-ending energy, laughed to himself at the sight of Thompson, hit a ball toward a practice green seventy yards away, and then glanced to his right. Lee Trevino, twice a U.S. Open champion, was holding court, chattering nonstop, spilling out story after story about the days when he took unsuspecting pigeons for their pocket's worth playing with a pop bottle as a club on the public courses in and around Dallas. To his left stood Hubert Green. Having turned fifty in December of 1996, he was now a rookie on the Senior PGA Tour, the new kid on the block, armed with an abbreviated, quick-as-a-wink swing that rivaled Chi Chi's.

Practicing next to Hubert was Gary Player, still an Energizer Bunny at age sixty-two, beating balls with his stabbing swing and that famous walk-along-follow-through good enough to have captured three Masters titles, three British Opens, two PGA Championships, and the U.S. Open. Watching Player was the brash Jim Colbert, forced off the PGA Tour by back injuries, now resurrected through the use of magnets that alleviated his pain and permitted him to shock the golf world by dominating the Senior Tour in 1995 and 1996 as leading money winner and Player of the Year.

"It takes all kinds," the sixty-one-year-old Rodriguez thought to himself. "But I can still whip their butts, and that includes Arnie, Jack, and Raymond."

Chi Chi's high hopes for the 1997 season were based on a secret weapon, actually three of them, that he believed would bring his foes to their knees. Over the winter months, he had increased his dosage of lamb's hormone shots, which he swore blunted old age.

The Cheech had discovered the remedy when he was in Germany and found a doctor who promoted physical well-being through injections of frozen lamb embryo cells. "Over six million Germans had taken the treatment," Chi Chi proclaimed. "It's the Fountain of Youth. I told Trevino next time I go over there, I'm going to come back in diapers. He said, 'If you come back in diapers, I'll change them for you.' "

If the hormone shots weren't enough, Chi Chi had purchased a lucky multicolor cat's-eye ring in Bangkok. And he was playing a superior golf ball injected with a magical substance known only to the scientists who invented it. He loved the ball so much he bought the company. Well, part of it anyway.

Chi Chi's optimism to the contrary, there were nearly a hundred of the over-fifty professional golfing gang who believed 1997 would be *their* year. The January to December assemblage of forty-three events packed prize money totaling over $40 million, a far cry from the $250,000 offered in 1980, the $16.1 million up for grabs in 1985, and the $18.3 million offered as recently as 1990. As Senior Tour veteran Bruce Crampton, winner of nineteen events, said, "They're givin' money away every week, and I want my fair share."

The field for the 1997 Senior Tour ran the table. There were the Q-School qualifiers: Bob Dickson, David Oakley, Will Sowles, Mike

McCullough, John Morgan, Dennis Coscina, Buddy Whitten, and Dick Hendrickson.

Joining the qualifiers on the Tour would be Hubert Green and fellow rookie Leonard Thompson, who'd just crossed the over-fifty mark. In July, incandescent Johnny Miller, the California poster boy with twenty-four Tour victories, including the U.S. and British Opens, would make his debut on the Tour. Two months later, Larry Nelson, the quiet man with PGA and U.S. Open championship titles to his credit, intended to make his presence known as well.

The Senior Tour's sophomore class provided three genuine challengers for any tournament crown: former PGA champion David Graham, John Bland, and Vicente Fernandez. Fellow foreigners included Aussies Graham Marsh and Bruce Crampton, South Africans Gary Player and Simon Hobday, Japanese legend Isao Aoki, New Zealander Bob Charles, and John Morgan, the long-hitting Brit, figured to contend as well. Competing on a semi-regular basis would be South African Hugh Baiocchi and England's Tony Jacklin.

In the footsteps of black golf pioneers such as Charlie Sifford and Ted Rhodes walked Jim Dent, winner of ten Senior Tour events; cigar-chomping Walter Morgan, a twenty-year veteran of the U.S. Army who had caddied for Chi Chi in the 1966 Hawaiian Open; Lee Elder; Calvin Peete; and Bobby Stroble.

Joining Walter Morgan in the cigar-toting section were Larry Laoretti, Tom Wargo, and Larry Gilbert, three times the PGA Club Professional champion.

A fellow Gilbert, Gibby, no relation to Larry, hoped to be a factor on the 1997 Senior Tour by adding a sixth win. Achieving that number was also the quest of chain-smoking Bud Allin, the Bronze Star–decorated Vietnam veteran with five PGA Tour victories to his credit.

Besides Laoretti, Wargo, and the Gilberts, the former club professionals-made-good gang was headed by Jim Albus, Rick Acton, and Bruce Summerhays, the iron man of the Senior PGA Tour, who began the 1997 season having played in seventy-four consecutive events.

Former United States Amateur champions on the Senior Tour besides Bob Dickson included Jay Sigel, recognized as one of the top five amateurs to have ever played the game; Deane Beman; and Bob Murphy. Dave Eichelberger and John Schroeder would also be contenders each week.

Though Robert Landers, the soft-spoken farmer from Texas

who practiced the game in his cow pasture would be a part-time performer, the 1997 Senior PGA Tour would not lack for certifiable characters. Besides Chi Chi Rodriguez, Brian Barnes, Simon Hobday,
Terry Dill, Jim Ferree, and Rocky Thompson added spice to the Tour.
Thomas G. Shaw III, better known as Tom, recognized as one of the
real nice guys on the Tour; Homero Blancas, the rotund Texan with
the waddle walk and sleepy eyes who once shot 55-62 in an amateur
event; Butch Baird, the Carefree, Arizona, veteran in the Panama hat
representing Jelly Belly jelly beans; and Kermit Zarley, the devout
Christian dubbed "The Pro from the Moon" during his days on the
PGA Tour, were also certain to liven up the proceedings.

Among the other challengers were Dr. Gil Morgan; Frank Conner, one of only two men to have ever played in the U.S. Open in both
golf and tennis (Ellsworth Vines was the other); and Jerry McGee.
Also poised to strike were Mike Hill; Robert Fred "Bob" Eastwood;
Don Bies, or "Beez"; and Jack Kiefer. Larry Mowry, the first professional ever to Monday-qualify for a Senior Tour event and then win;
John Paul Cain; Bob Duval, father of PGA Tour professional David;
and DeWitt Weaver, continued their search for the pot of gold on the
Senior PGA Tour.

The over-sixty contingent for 1997 was headed by the studious
professor Bob Charles. His weekly Super Seniors challengers (competition for golfers sixty and over) included Ol' Sarge, Orville Moody; Bruce
Crampton; Jim Ferree; and "Mr. X.," Miller Barber. Contenders also included lean Texan Don January, Bruce Devlin, Jimmy Powell, Dale
Douglass, Dick Hendrickson, and Walt Zembriski.

Ex-officio members of the over-sixty group were eighty-four-
year-old Sam Snead, and Arnold Palmer, sixty-seven years of age, but
with the heart and zest for the game of a twenty-year-old.

Palmer was one of twenty-five golfers on the 1997 Senior Tour
with a professional Major championship on the PGA Tour in his
pocket. Jack Nicklaus, now fifty-seven; Lee Trevino, who matched
Jack's age; Hale Irwin, fifty-one; Raymond Floyd; and Billy Casper, had
all captured Major championships. Gene Littler; Al Geiberger, "Berger"
of 59 fame; Charles Coody; George Archer; Gary Player; Gay Brewer;
Orville Moody; Tommy Aaron; Don January; David Graham; Bobby
Nichols; and Tom Weiskopf also had at least one Major trophy on
their mantel. As did Bob Charles, Lou Graham, Hubert Green, Tony
Jacklin, Johnny Miller, and Dave Stockton. Larry Nelson would be
number twenty-six when he joined the Senior Tour in November.

In all, the contenders on the 1997 Senior Tour had won seventy-five Major professional championships among them, not including the fifty-eight won on the over-fifty circuit. With $40 million–plus up for grabs on what certainly could be labeled a "World Tour," the drama in 1997 promised to feature high-noon confrontation among many of the greatest names in the history of the sport as they battled for the opportunity to taste the thrill of victory one more time.

BOOK I

THE DOCTOR IS IN

1

THE 1997 SENIOR PGA TOUR BEGAN IN JANUARY, A MONTH THAT had blown into history like a Texas twister. In addition to the gala second-term inauguration of President William Jefferson Clinton, headlines covered stories focusing on Madonna's film portrayal of Argentinean leader Eva Peron, O. J. Simpson's civil trial, the death of Elvis Presley's guru Colonel Tom Parker, and the grisly murders of a seven-year-old aspiring beauty queen in Colorado and the only son of Bill Cosby.

By comparison, what occurred in the world of golf the first month of the year was mild, but it nevertheless provided excitement for those in need of relief from the hard, cold facts of life. First up were the Tournament of Champions for the PGA, PGA Seniors, and LPGA Tours. At La Costa, Tiger Woods added to his already legendary status at age twenty-one by beating Tom Lehman, Player of the Year for 1996, in a one-hole play-off.

Tiger's win, though impressive, shared the stage with a shocking announcement. During the dinner portion of the Tournament of Champions, Arnold Palmer announced he had prostate cancer that would require surgery at the Mayo Clinic. "That hit like a bullet," said Jim Colbert, there to receive the Arnold Palmer Player of the Year Award for his splendid performance in 1996. "I just kept shaking my head in disbelief."

The LPGA Tournament of Champions was won by Sweden's Annika Sorenstam, with two U.S. Women's Open crowns to her credit. Her closest pursuer was the LPGA's Karrie Webb, 1996 Rookie of the Year.

The Senior PGA Tour bowed in Hawaii, where the champions of 1996 tournaments squared off at a Jack Nicklaus course in Hualalai, where the beautiful lava formations and Alaskan whales performing in the crystal-clear waters of the Pacific challenged the players' concentration. The field included the elite of the Senior Tour. Notable absentees were Chi Chi Rodriguez and Gary Player, both winless the previous year.

In a rollicking first round, the wind blew near gale strength and the over-fifty crowd was dazed by bogeys and worse. Seventy-five became a good score for the day. Walter Morgan and Jay Sigel succumbed to Mother Nature, recording 86 and 80, respectively. "I couldn't even keep my cigar burning," Morgan quipped.

Morgan's start was especially disappointing after a 1996 season that saw him win twice and earn nearly $850,000. Quite a feat for a man who didn't pick up a golf club until he was thirty, after having survived the Vietnam War, dodging bullets in such dangerous places as Phnom Penh, Saigon, and the Ho Chi Minh trail.

Calmer breezes prevailed during the final thirty-six holes, producing a shoot-out between Hale Irwin and baby senior Gil Morgan, who'd turned fifty in September of 1996. Defending champion John Bland, the lively South African with the gift for gab, and prim and proper New Zealander Bob Charles contended, but the final round produced a one-on-one duel between the sharpshooting Irwin and Morgan.

Since many pundits felt the two would battle it out for the money title and Player of the Year honors, their head-to-head play produced a preview of things to come. The ebb and flow of the match brought the two men to the sixteenth tee dead even, but Morgan had the advantage since the next two holes demanded right-to-left shots to position the ball near the pin placements, something more difficult for Irwin, who played a fade. True to form, Morgan darted a mid-iron shot to within four feet at sixteen. A sound putt would provide a one-shot lead with three to go, but Gil's stroke, the Achilles' heel that kept him from winning a Major championship on the PGA Tour, broke down. The ball never hit the hole. Irwin still had a chance.

As ESPN commentator and former two-time U.S. Open champion Andy North said, "Hale Irwin plays conservatively until he gets a chance to snap at you, and then he will." And snap he did. At the par-three seventeenth, his approach shot was thirty-five feet right, but after Morgan missed a longer birdie try, nerves-of-steel Irwin drove the putt directly into the hole. When Morgan missed his short putt for par, it was point, set, match.

One for one in 1997, the bespectacled Irwin then ventured to the Mauna Lani Resort to join Jack Nicklaus, Raymond Floyd, and Lee Trevino in the Senior Skins' competition. Trevino was a late replacement, filling in for Arnold Palmer.

The Trevino-for-Palmer substitution made golf fans aware of the status of both careers. For Palmer, the battle with prostate cancer was the first serious illness confronted over his forty-plus years as a professional golfer. During that time, he had won seventy PGA and Senior PGA Tour events, seven professional Major championships, including four Masters titles, two British Opens, one U.S. Open, and a U.S. Amateur win. Only a PGA Championship had eluded him.

When Palmer turned fifty and began to play senior events in 1980, he brought them new life just as he had done with the PGA Tour in the 1950s. While Arnie's Army was a bit gray-haired, Palmer rallied them with expert shots reminiscent of the charging days of old. Even though he never dominated as he had on the PGA Tour, winning just nine times in his first six years, his magical presence prevailed and he excited the crowds and elevated the status of the Senior Tour like no one before or since.

The King could point to only one victory since 1986, and scores in the 76 and 77 range had become more common than not. He wasn't quite the braggart Sam Snead was, who, though seventeen years his senior, challenged friends to punch his hard-as-a-rock stomach. But Palmer was in good physical shape. Then cancer struck, and suddenly the sporting world realized even Arnold was mortal. At sixty-seven, questions arose as to whether golf fans had seen the last of Arnie, whether the magic moments might be a thing of the past.

Palmer's absence from the Senior Skins' game positioned Trevino in the spotlight, but Lee wasn't comfortable there. In 1996, nagging injuries had bothered him, and though he won once (the Emerald Coast Classic), the rest of the year presented just eleven top ten finishes in twenty-eight tries. The Senior Tour's all-time money winner ($6,715,649) was on the ropes, but over the winter months he promised to shed excess weight and begin 1997 with a trim physique and a fresh attitude that would once again make him a contender.

When Trevino entered play in the Tournament of Champions, however, he was still wide around the middle. Family illness and the desire to spend more time with his children had taken some of the zest for the game away from the Merry Mex. A twenty-eighth place finish at the Tournament of Champions wiped the smile off Trevino's face, but he vowed to play better in the Skins' game.

The competition was edged in controversy before it began. While Nicklaus, Trevino, Floyd, and Irwin were marquee players with records full of Major championship wins, many questioned the exclusion of Jim Colbert, Player of the Year on the Senior Tour in both 1995 and 1996. Certainly Hale Irwin, runner-up to Colbert, and Floyd, the defending champion three times running, were deserving, but neither Nicklaus's nor Trevino's play in 1996 measured up to that of the cocky Colbert, who clearly was the dominant player on the Senior Tour with five wins.

Initial selection of two players for the event belonged to Barry Frank of IMG and Howard Katz at ESPN. They chose Arnold Palmer and Jack Nicklaus, box-office names guaranteed to produce the desired television ratings. The defending champion, Raymond Floyd, automatically filled the third spot.

The fourth competitor was to be selected on the basis of ballots sent out in October and November to sportswriters and broadcasters. The clear winner was Hale Irwin, who was the number one player on the Senior Tour at that time. That changed when Jim Colbert made a late-season surge and nipped Irwin for Player of the Year honors.

The field was set until Palmer withdrew. Trevino's agent, Chuck Rubin, then lobbied the spot for his client. Frank agreed, while Katz thought Jim Colbert should be selected. Frank had the final say, and Trevino was chosen.

Jim Colbert took the news in a gentlemanly manner, but he was clearly disappointed, feeling that his championship play had earned him a place in the tournament. Especially when Trevino made it appear in a television interview that Arnie had personally called him and asked him to take his place. That was pure fiction, but Trevino fueled the story.

All four of the competitors in the Senior Skins' game entered the 1997 season with concerns for their golf games. Nicklaus was pestered at every turn with questions centered around comparisons with Tiger Woods and was still bothered by a balky hip and a bad back, injuries that had sidelined him from play at the Diners Club matches in December. Jack was coming off a 1996 season that was highlighted by his second straight Tradition win in Scottsdale and little else, save his sparkling performance in the U.S. Open at Oakland Hills and turn-back-the-clock rounds of 69 and 66 at the British Open.

Though Nicklaus was still formidable, his physical condition made him a question mark. "He can't beat the competition on one leg," remarked Andy North. Jack agreed, but hoped his inactivity over the winter months would heal his wounds and allow him to be competitive in 1997, the year he expected to play in his 149th and 150th straight Major tournaments at the Masters and U.S. Open.

Lee Trevino called 1996 "the year of the hook," dubbed by Willie Miller, Jim Colbert's longtime caddie, as "a ball that hits the ground with sneakers." A darting right-to-left shot caused by Trevino's too strong grip resulted in play that wasn't emblematic of the man who captured two U.S. Open crowns and twenty-seven tournaments on the Senior Tour, including three Majors.

The chatterbox admitted to lack of confidence in his game, but hoped a weaker grip would be his savior. "Lots of shots are going to go to the right for a while," Trevino warned.

Raymond Floyd called 1996 "a bad putting year," even though he captured the Ford Senior Players Championship. His goal, he said, "was to play less and play better. All my outside work, course design and so forth, takes time, but I need to focus more on my game."

Despite his opening-season win at the Tournament of Champions, Hale Irwin came to Mauna Lani unconvinced his game was on track. Pain in his knee caused by an old football injury at the University of Colorado reared its head, and compensating for that had caused Irwin to hurt his back. The result was a problem with fading the ball, a must for Irwin to be successful.

By the end of the competition, fifty-four-year-old Raymond Floyd was champion once more. He had prevailed in a format that suited his fancy. Playing to win specific holes and not worrying about total score wasn't for everyone, especially a player like Irwin, who admitted, "I'm not sure I have the formula for Skins. When you don't think about the score, that's against my training."

While Floyd's triumph at the Senior Skins garnered the headlines, the absent man, Arnold Palmer, wasn't absent from the hearts of both the competitors and fellow PGA professionals. Interviews with the King, mending at his home in Florida and missing his first Senior Skins' game in fourteen years, were conducted both days of the competition. Warm tributes from his friendly foes had to speed up the healing process.

"He epitomizes what golf is all about," Dave Stockton said, "respect and love for the game." Raymond Floyd added, "Palmer made the game what it is today." Jack Nicklaus commented, "He's been a friend and foe for a long time . . . We've been beating each other's brains out for thirty-five years."

Even Tiger Woods got into the act, calling Palmer "my hero. Let's get down to Bay Hill and have that long-driving contest we talked about," he said to Palmer via taped message.

As for Arnie, he admitted that not playing was frustrating. "I miss the excitement," he explained, adding that he hoped to be back in shape and playing in six weeks. His fellow competitors hoped so, too, for the competition just wasn't the same without Arnold Palmer around.

"Golf without Arnie. I don't even want to think about it," said Gary Player.

Once the Tournament of Champions and the Skins' games were history, competitors on the Senior PGA Tour turned their attention to weekly competition. The main question on everyone's mind was: Could former Tour journeyman turned ESPN golf announcer turned Senior Tour prodigy Jim Colbert win another Player of the Year title? When Jim won four titles and the honor of being the best of the best in 1995, that was one thing. But back-to-back titles was astounding, especially against a field in 1996 that included Hale Irwin, Raymond Floyd, John Bland, Tom Weiskopf, Lee Trevino, Bob Charles, Jay Sigel, and Jack Nicklaus.

Exclusion of Colbert from the Skins' game made him more eager than ever to show the powers-that-be that he could whip the tails off everyone in 1997. "It's a challenge I'm looking forward to," Colbert professed confidently. "I can't wait to get started."

2

FIFTY-TWO-YEAR-OLD BRIAN THOMAS "BUD" ALLIN, A NEAR MIDGET of a man with a forehead full of wrinkles, stood over a fifty-foot sidewinding snake that was the most important putt of his life. Even though he had won five times on the PGA Tour in the 1970s, if he could get down in two, Allin would be the champion of the 1997 American Express Invitational, the fourth full-field stop on the Senior PGA Tour.

Allin's mystical sojourn to that point was the classical David and Goliath story. Just five days earlier he was not scheduled to be a competitor in the tournament at all. As first alternate in Sarasota, the final stop on the Florida swing, Allin had to sweat out the hours leading up to the deadline for qualified players to withdraw. If not for the sudden departure of Gibby Gilbert due to a knee injury at 4:55 on Tuesday, Allin would have been on the outside looking in.

Instead, the cagey veteran was a member of the standard PGA Senior Tour starting field of seventy-eight, which included the top thirty-one money winners from 1996, the top thirty-one on the all-time PGA Tour money list, eight survivors of the Q-School, four players with sponsors' exemptions, and four Monday qualifiers. Among them were former Tour player Rick Massengale; Robert Leaver, the former club professional from Oak Ridge, North Carolina; Texan Bob Rawlins, a former Senior Tour player affectionately known as "Cloud"; and Frank Grate, a casket manufacturer turned professional from Dubuque, Iowa, who survived a five-way play-off for the fourth spot. "Wow," he made it, wife, Gaye, exclaimed. "This is a dream come true."

Unfortunately, Grate's game wasn't in gear when the bell rang on Thursday. Though he used a new putter, dubbed "The Hog," he finished far down the leader board with 78-77-77, winning $792. Dan Devine of the *Sarasota Herald-Tribune* took one look at Grate's putter and said, "The Hog had a shaft like a fence post and a head like a two-by-four."

The casket manufacturer wasn't witness to the Tuesday Pro-Am featuring former major-league baseball stars. Though the jovial Irishman Bob Murphy and Hall of Famer Al Kaline defended their title by beating Jim Albus and former Baltimore Orioles pitcher Jim Palmer, the stars of the show were two of baseball's certified flakes, Mark "The Bird" Fidrych and Bill "Spaceman" Lee.

Banter between the two legendary eccentrics produced enough quotes to fill a three-volume set. Fidrych, who compiled a 19-9 record with the Detroit Tigers and was named Rookie of the Year in 1976, played golf the same way he pitched, muttering between shots and entertaining the gallery with offbeat remarks. Asked what he did for a living, The Bird explained, "Raise cows and sheep, but the farm is more for kids than animals," leaving those listening to wonder what the hell he meant.

Lee, the former Boston Red Sox pitcher who won 119 major-league games, provided curious onlookers with views on such varied subjects as communism, Zen Buddhism, how hoarding of wheat could be blamed for Earth's first war, and his famed television appearance with David Letterman, where his use of a four-letter expletive made the talk-show host flinch so badly his contact lens flew out.

When Lee and Fidrych retired to the sidelines, the professionals took the field. Arnold Palmer, recovering from cancer surgery, wasn't among them, but Miller Barber was. Most people figured his nickname, "Mr. X," came from his perpetual wearing of darkened sunglasses. Actually, it had been coined in the early 1960s by Dave Marr and other fellow professionals. "After I earned four thousand dollars for winning the '61 Seattle Open, we were headed to Bakersfield for the next tournament," Marr recalled. "Jim Ferree asked Miller, who was a bachelor at the time, to drive his car down there. I guess Miller got sidetracked 'cause he never showed up. A week or so later, Miller appeared at another tournament with Jim's car. Never would tell us where he was. Used to do that all the time, so we called him 'Mr. X.' "

The tournament entrants represented a wide array of ages from Hubert Green's fifty to Don January, sixty-seven going on sixty-eight. Many, such as Green and Gil Morgan, had experienced few injuries during their careers and had yet to notice the inevitable decline in their physical abilities. For others in the field, the years had taken their toll. Most agreed that at age fifty, the body began to disintegrate. Larry Ziegler, the fifty-seven-year-old crusty veteran with three Tour victories to his credit, said, "There are things in life you used to do, you just can't do. No use fighting it. It's a losing battle."

No doubt the heavy discussion of the ailings of old age had been brought on by the announcement of Arnold Palmer's prostate cancer. To the professionals, Arnie was still rugged and vibrant at age sixty-seven. "Hearing that Arnie's down makes us all think twice," one professional said. "It just doesn't seem possible. I figured Arnie would live forever."

One player who had Palmer on his mind was veteran Jim Ferree, known for wearing plus fours and dressing as if he were headed to a formal dinner. "Arnie can beat this," he told reporters, recalling his successful recovery from similar surgery in 1991.

Another was Gene Littler, who had been stricken with cancer in 1972. "Arnie will make it," Littler explained. "I know he will."

On the Senior Tour, agony with the body was a daily regimen. Richard Mudry of *Golf Week* said as much when he observed, "You have to have a medical degree to cover this Tour."

Many players spent off-course time either at a physician's office or in the Senior PGA fitness truck trying to soothe their nerve endings and stretch muscles laden with old age. Over the years, several players had dealt with a wide spectrum of serious injuries. George Archer and Bobby Nichols went under the knife to receive hip replacements. Lee Elder and Dick Rhyan fought heart trouble. Terry Dill had surgery to remove a tumor behind his right ear.

Floridian Bob Murphy battled a severe case of arthritis and then underwent surgery to remove a cancerous spot on his hand. Jim Colbert's bad back, the result of childhood injuries, nearly destroyed his ability to play at all, and only the saving grace of magnets to alleviate the pain rescued him. Jack Nicklaus's chronic hip condition also threatened his career, though the Golden Bear scoffed at reports he'd need hip replacement.

At fifty, most professionals agreed that lack of strength was their main restriction. "That's what separates the good players from the greats," Jim Dent, a tall, muscular specimen, said at Sarasota. "Lack of strength is the only thing that holds our Senior Tour players back from beating the younger guys."

Some, like Jay Sigel, the ex-insurance executive and great amateur player, didn't notice the age. "I really don't feel a lot different than when I was twenty-five," he said, provoking a sneer from two older professionals within hearing distance.

That was a 360-degree difference from players like Archer, who had spent nearly as much time in the operating room over the past twenty years as he had on the golf course. He had wrist, back, shoulder, and finally hip surgery, but still kept things in perspective. "I've never had the big C," Archer said. "Or heart problems. I just keep having flat tires."

Back problems were the most nagging injuries. "The back was not designed for golf," six-foot-tall Larry Ziegler pointed out. "You putt for an hour, it's hard to stand up."

Back pain had bothered Lee Trevino for years, so much that he had trouble practicing. "Trevino's living with a limited body," ESPN's Frank Beard explained. "It's coming to an end."

One professional who seemed to avoid physical injury and get better with age was Bob Charles, winner of more than twenty tournaments and $6.5 million on the Senior Tour. At sixty-one, he was sound physically. "I feel like I'm thirty," he stated. "And that I can win at seventy." His advice: "Do everything in moderation. No red meat. No sugar and fats. Eat vegetables, fruits, anything from the sea."

Charles and others such as Jimmy Powell (sixty-two) and Dale Douglass (sixty-one), still competitive, agreed with those who believed that golf skills for seniors became unglued at age fifty-six. "It's a big step from fifty to fifty-five and an even bigger step fifty-five to fifty-six," Powell said. "The skills somehow go south." He also said Senior Tour players didn't look too far ahead. "We don't even buy green bananas," Powell quipped, stealing George Burns's line.

The stats gave credence, since nearly ninety tournaments in Senior PGA Tour history had been won by players by age fifty-one. Only seven times had the winner been over the magic fifty-five mark.

A true exception to the rule was Gary Player, spry as a lightweight boxer at sixty-one. A true visionary in the 1960s who proclaimed the virtues of physical fitness, Player had kept himself in physical shape to be a contender in any tournament in which he competed. "Gary Player. He's not mortal," Don Bies chided.

At the American Express, Player and the other seventy-seven professionals took dead aim at defending champion Hale Irwin, certain they could steal his crown. Based on performance in the first three tournaments of 1997, there were many candidates ready and willing to succeed him as the sun rose on the 1997 Senior PGA Tour.

The first full-field tournament had been the Royal Caribbean Classic played at the island of Key Biscayne outside Miami, Florida. At the end of the first round, Chi Chi Rodriguez, armed with his hormone shots, a revolutionary golf ball, and lucky cat's-eye ring, stood at the top of the leader board.

Where else but on the Senior PGA Tour? While the leader board at what used to be called the Crosby (now AT&T) contained less-than-exciting names like Jim Furyk, Paul Stankowski, Brian Henninger, and Ted Tryba, the Royal Caribbean sported leaders that included household names like Chi Chi Rodriguez, J. C. Snead, Jim Colbert, and Tony Jacklin.

When play had begun on Friday for the standard Senior PGA Tour fifty-four-hole tournament, veteran Bud Allin was on the sidelines. The diminutive Vietnam veteran was the "bubble man" for the year, the first entry selected if one of the "exempt" players from the top thirty-one all-time money list withdrew. He was destined to travel from tournament to tournament, hoping to gain entry into the field.

"It makes it damn tough," Allin said with a sorrowful look as he stood watching his fellow professionals on the practice tee. "I feel like I've earned my way out here, but that's the way it goes. Maybe I'll get to play next week."

Defending champion Bob Murphy warranted the favorite's role along with Jim Colbert. Others expected to contend were Lee Trevino, whose 67 in the Pro-Am portended good things to come, Jay Sigel, and Gil Morgan, the most publicized optometrist in the history of his field to have never practiced a single day.

Though competitors on the Senior Tour referred to the player to beat as having a "bull's-eye" on his back, Jim Colbert, despite his Player of the Year awards, did not warrant that designation. That was reserved for Hale Irwin and perhaps Gil Morgan. Their play at the Tournament of Champions confirmed that the two recent additions to the over-fifty crowd would be the players to beat each week as the Tour progressed through forty-three events in twenty-six states.

Players recognized that though Irwin and Morgan were at the top of the heap, neither possessed the personality to be a crowd favorite. Irwin was "standoffish," as one player put it, "a real-know-it-all." Most players respected Irwin, but few were close friends.

Morgan, on the other hand, was a kindly sort, if certainly less than colorful. "Doc's just a damn good player who goes about his business," Bob Dickson remarked. "Nothing flashy, but he sure can play."

Irwin and Morgan, though newcomers to the Senior Tour, had been accepted into the "good ol' boy club." That exclusive group permitted entry based on an unwritten set of qualifications. Many people outside the game didn't realize that the Senior Tour contained a host of players who didn't just slide off the regular Tour into "over-fiftydom." In truth, the golfers on the Senior Tour created a caste system that either made the player welcome or someone who was shunted to the sidelines and treated with indifference.

The members of the elite club were those who had paid their dues, mostly by working their way up through the ranks of the PGA

Tour, having been club professionals who sweated their asses off cod-dling despicable club members for years, or who came from the busi-ness world looking for a chance to compete in the bigs after they turned fifty. True to the American way, the caste system made no dis-tinction between race, creed, color, or nationality for that matter, though there were those from the old school who were still not com-fortable around blacks.

What stood out with those on the "in" was that in the other play-ers' minds they had earned their Senior Tour card. Crybabies were avoided, and there certainly was no place for the pompous prick who thought he was holier than thou. Respect was the name of the game, and it didn't take long for the players to be divided into categories, those who warranted the friendship of the family and those who were known to be assholes.

Prior to the first round of the Royal Caribbean Classic, eight of the competitors played in the first edition of the Gillette Tour Challenge, a team competition that replaced the Merrill Lynch Shootout. The format was alternate shot, with play contested over holes thirteen through eighteen at the Crandon Park Golf layout, designated the number one public course in Florida.

The luck of the draw paired Jay Sigel with Graham Marsh, Wal-ter Morgan with J. C. Snead, Jim Colbert with Brian Barnes, and Bob Murphy with former U.S. Open champion Hubert Green, playing for the first time on the Senior Tour.

The levity on the first tee was worth the price of admission as the players kidded one another about the state of their respective games. "Did you winter well?" Barnes asked Morgan, a pipe dangling from his mouth. "Oh, you can hear this year," Jim Colbert kidded Marsh af-ter the Australian waved his hand for the crowd to quiet.

When Hubert Green teed up his ball for the monumental first swing as a senior golfer, Murphy promptly yanked it off and threw it toward the gallery. When a second ball replaced the first one, Colbert repeated Murphy's action as Green stood with a sly grin on his face. Green's caddie then tossed Hubert a third ball, but it went sailing when Morgan gave it the heave-ho. Finally, the fourth ball was left on the tee, and Green's buggy-whip swing sent it sailing down the middle of the fairway.

Barnes, all 6'2" and 240 of him, was next to hit. When he re-moved his pipe and teed up the ball, Colbert yelled, "Let's see some-one take *his* golf ball." The players backed away, laughing.

The good-natured banter continued through the match. "What a tank job," Colbert yelled at Sigel after he hit a three-footer so hard it ended up four feet past the cup. On one hole, Marsh was forced to hit a high fade from a position next to a palm tree over a tent toward the green. When he pulled it a bit, it hit the tent, prompting Murphy to exclaim in jest, "That's an interesting way to play the hole."

The relaxed mood suited Barnes—the jolly Englishman with the too tight golf shirt rolled up at the sleeves—to a T. At the tenth, as his caddie labored down the fairway with his bag, Barnes pulled out his fishing pole. He finally had a chance to use it in the pond behind the sixteenth green. While his partner, Colbert, putted out on the green, Barnes fished away, content as the other players shook their heads while loping by.

The caddies were not immune to the teasing between the players. Willie Miller, Colbert's longtime sidekick, was used to having a cart at his disposal since four screws in his left leg made it impossible for him to walk the full eighteen holes during a tournament. "You okay, Willie?" Colbert asked. "Gonna make it?" Murphy added as Willie displayed a full-faced grin at their jesting.

When the congenial group hit the eighteenth tee, Sigel/Marsh and Morgan/Snead were deadlocked at one-under par. Colbert/Barnes was a shot back and Murphy/Green out of contention.

After Sigel and Marsh made a bogey and Morgan and Snead a par, Colbert faced a thirty-five-foot sidehill putt for birdie to tie Morgan and Snead. No one doubted he'd make it, based on his propensity to do so with every important putt he'd had in 1996. True to form, the putt was dead center. "Might as well have given him that one," Murphy lamented. The effort produced sudden death, and a putting contest was set up to break the deadlock between Morgan/Snead and Colbert/Barnes. From just off the green, eighty-five feet away, Morgan managed to snug the ball within two inches of the hole. The Gillette Tour Challenge had its first champion, and the crowd had been treated to a special afternoon with eight of the best the Senior Tour had to offer.

Weather for the first round of the 1997 Royal Caribbean Classic was nasty. A thirty-mph wind that changed directions confused the players and sent the scores soaring. Sponsor-exempt player Herb Smith nearly threw up on the way to an 87. Lee Trevino, who'd proclaimed his chances as "excellent" after firing 67 in the Pro-Am, fired 39-42 for an 81. He blamed his poor play on unfamiliarity with new clubs and a Top-Flite Multi-Cover ball that flew fifteen yards farther than any he had used before. "I missed twelve greens, and on eleven of them, I was over the green. That sucker was hot," Trevino explained, his listeners wondering why he hadn't adjusted as the round progressed.

One player who wasn't intimidated by Mother Nature was the Cheech. Besides the seventy-dollar lamb's hormone cell shots he had flown to Europe for, the spiffy new Sutherland Sabre golf ball, and the cat's-eye ring, the Puerto Rican scalawag had changed his grip over the winter from overlap to interlock, à la Jack Nicklaus.

"My fingers become disjointed the other way," he remarked, his audience nodding their heads, though no one had any idea what he meant.

Armed with his new toys, extra energy, a new grip, what he called a "new frame of mind," and filled with motivation after he watched his fellow professionals compete on television without him in the Tournament of Champions, the sixty-one-year-old Chi Chi threw 32-35 at the field.

Most of the credit went to the golf ball. "It's the most perfect golf ball ever," he said proudly. "It's the first scientific golf ball ever made. It is injected."

When asked what it was injected with, Chi Chi whispered, "The scientists won't say."

The mystique of Juan "Chi Chi" Rodriguez began the day he was born, October 23, 1935. Witnesses to the birth swore Chi Chi was cracking jokes fresh out of the cradle.

Raised in Rio Redras, the ghetto area just outside San Juan, Puerto Rico, Rodriguez's family was dirt poor. "In my day, you drank milk with a fork," he explained. "You didn't want the glass of milk to run out. The biggest present I ever got was a marble."

One of five children, Rodriguez's father was a laborer. "He worked twenty-eight years in the fields, cutting sugarcane with a machete," Chi Chi said proudly. "Never made more than eighteen dollars a day." Despite the low pay, young Rodriguez admired his father. "He was the happiest man I ever saw," the Cheech recalled. "And he taught me so much. One time a guy came on our property and stole bananas from a tree. Dad and I hid out, and the next time the thief came, Dad caught him. He gave the thief the bananas and said, 'Why didn't you ask me? I would have given them to you.' "

Lessons learned from his father were ones Chi Chi never forgot. But that didn't mean he heeded all of his dad's advice, especially when it came to the game of golf.

"When I was a kid, I saw golfers at the nearby country club

[Rodriguez worked as a forecaddie at age eight]. I stomped out a tin can to use as the ball and tore off a branch from a guava tree for the club. Later I had a set of mixed clubs, and when I was seventeen I played well enough to finish second in the Puerto Rican Open. No matter, my dad thought I was crazy to be a golfer. 'How many Puerto Rican golfers have you ever heard of?' he warned. 'How many millionaires?' "

Baseball had actually been the young Rodriguez's first passion. He played on a sandlot ball club with future major-league pitcher Juan Pizarro. And a fairly good hitter named Roberto Clemente.

"Actually, Roberto was a pinch runner in Class A ball. Our manager must have been a genius. Roberto Clemente pinch-running for me."

When Rodriguez, who nicknamed himself "Chi Chi" after a rough-and-tumble Puerto Rican third baseman named Chi Chi Forres, turned nineteen, he joined the military and was assigned to Fort Sill, Oklahoma. When he returned to Puerto Rico in 1957, Rodriguez worked in a mental hospital for eighty dollars a month before joining professional Ed Dudley at the new Dorado Beach Hotel course as an assistant.

Chi Chi's intentions to be the assistant professional collapsed when he nearly wet his pants on the way to a nervous 89 audition round. Unimpressed, Dudley promptly hired him as a caddie master, Rodriguez's first real job in golf.

Two years later, Rodriguez got the break of a lifetime when Pete Cooper, who would later win the 1976 PGA Seniors' Championship, replaced Dudley at Dorado Beach. Cooper became Chi Chi's surrogate father and taught him the mechanics of the game and how to play like a gentleman.

"Pete changed my grip and made me practice," Rodriguez recalled. "He didn't care how hard I swung, just so long as I stayed back of the ball. There was a practice green, hard as Idi Amin's heart. Pete made me hit five thousand balls to it until my hands bled."

Those hands were crooked, the fingers bent as the result of a childhood bout with rickets. But ever the optimist, Rodriguez saw his physical handicap differently from most people. "If you look closely, when I close my hands, it's a blessing from God," he said, "because they form a perfect golf grip."

Armed with confidence from beating Pete Cooper every time they played during the winter season of 1959, Rodriguez yearned to compete on the United States Tour, which featured, among others, Arnold Palmer. "Chi Chi was just a good ol' country boy who showed quite a bit of personality," Cooper recalled. "He had a pretty good swing, and, after changing his grip, he was on the right track."

Rodriguez's financial benefactor was a Dorado Beach member, Laurance Rockefeller, one of the banking brothers. He advanced Chi Chi $15,000, and Pete Cooper and Cheech hit the road in Cooper's old Pontiac for the life of a nomadic golfer.

Times were lean, the competition stiff, and Chi Chi's inconsistent game left him far down the leader board. Only $4,406 was deposited in his bank account that year, and he thought of giving up. "I wondered if I could make it," Chi Chi recalled. "Those other guys were so *good*."

Worse than his performance on the golf course was the reaction of fellow players to his playful antics. "In the beginning, when I first did my thing, a lot of people looked down at me. They were used to the Hogan thing, wanting me to be serious like him."

The famous sword dance that became Chi Chi's calling card over the next forty years was born in Las Vegas after a round at the Desert Inn. Chi Chi made a sizable putt and placed his hat over the hole. Then he swerved his putter back, and the act began. "I pretended the hole was the bull. A birdie stopped the bull, so I drew my sword, stabbed it, wiped off the imaginary blood, and then thrust the sword back in the scabbard. People seemed to love it, especially after Lee Trevino began to liven things up a bit."

While Chi Chi, effervescent in bright-colored clothing, became a crowd favorite, his twenty-one-year career (1960–1981) on the PGA Tour produced mixed results. He won eight times, with the 1964 Western Open and the 1972 Byron Nelson his biggest triumphs. No Major wins came his way, his best finish a tie for sixth in the 1981 U.S. Open Championship.

When 1985 rolled around, Chi Chi was armed and ready for the Senior Tour. He won three events that year, including the Ford Senior Players Championship; seven the next, including the PGA Seniors, and a total of twenty-two as he headed into the 1997 season. Nearly $7 million in prize money had filled Rodriguez's coffer, a far cry from the impoverishment of his youth in Rio Redras. "When I write my autobiography, I've got the perfect title," Chi Chi explained. *"From the Sugarcane Plantation to Wall Street."*

Despite the lack of wins in recent years, Chi Chi remained the second most prized personality on the Senior Tour, a half step behind Arnold Palmer. The Panama hat, the quick wit, the trick shots, and the flamboyant nature of his game, combined with the famed sword dance, made him unforgettable. Especially to children. Though Rodriguez never had kids of his own (his wife, Iwalani, had a daughter,

Donnette, by a previous marriage), the Cheech gave his heart to disadvantaged youths across the world. "Kids and I have a lot in common," he explained. "We've all spent a lot of time in the rough."

Over the years, the Chi Chi Rodriguez Foundation had raised millions of dollars for children with little or no hope for the future. He was their hero, "Uncle Cheech," as they called him. At every tournament stop, kids of all ages swarmed to him like bees to honey, simply wanting to touch the man they loved.

After the first round of the Boone Valley Classic, Chi Chi hoisted a frail young boy afflicted with cancer into the air. And then took him for a ride in a golf cart. The lad's face was beaming. It was a moment he would never forget, especially when Rodriguez gave him and his parents passes for the weekend as the Cheech's special guests. "You have to take care of the kids," Chi Chi, named in 1994 to the World Humanitarian Sports Hall of Fame, explained. "It may be too late for us adults, but the kids still have a chance."

Chi Chi's sincerity was the key. Who could forget his words on television in behalf of the Senior PGA Tour: "Life is like a home. You put a good foundation on a home, it stays very stable. If you put a bad foundation, it breaks down. We try to give kids good foundations so they can become good people. When you do something for somebody else, especially a kid, you get an invisible trophy from heaven that is good for the soul."

One-liners attributed to Rodriguez over the years could fill a shelf full of books. Among the best were:

"I knew my Pro-Am partner might not be too good when I saw he had a new grip on his ball retriever."

"I'm so skinny I can drink a can of tomato juice, turn sideways, and look like a thermometer."

"For most amateurs, the best wood in their bag is their pencil."

"My accent is awful. I asked my caddie for a sand wedge, and he came back ten minutes later with a ham on rye."

"The winds in Scotland were blowing at fifty miles an hour and gusting to seventy. I hit a par-three with my hat."

"I was so small when I caddied, they used me for a tee marker."

And, of course, it was the Cheech who uttered those famous words regarding the greatest player who ever lived: "Jack Nicklaus has become a legend in his spare time."

In addition to the quips, the ever-present sparkling personality that lit up the cloudiest days and a zest for the game unparalleled among his contemporaries, Chi Chi Rodriguez was one of the greatest ambassadors golf has ever known. Lee Trevino said, "If everybody in this world were like Cheech, you wouldn't need borders or passports."

All told, Chi Chi Rodriguez will be remembered more for what he gave to golf than for what it gave to him. Longtime manager Eddie Elias summed it up when he said, "Chi Chi's biggest physical deficiency is that his heart's too big for his body. He gives everything away—money, clothes, his time. He says doing anything else would be betraying his mission on earth."

Bearing down on Chi Chi and his voodoo magic at the Royal Caribbean was Sam Snead's nephew J.C., whose 68 softened his feelings about a disappointing winter when he failed to kill his quota during the hunting season. "Them birds kept dodging my bullets," he told a friend.

Notable scores among the contenders after the first round included a one-under-par 69 from Jim Colbert, 71 for Isao Aoki, and 73 from defending champion Bob Murphy. Hubert Green, in his Senior Tour debut, shot 73 and headed for the practice range shaking his head and muttering to himself in disbelief at his poor performance.

Veterans Don January and Bruce Crampton, who signed incorrect scorecards, were on the sidelines as Gibby Gilbert, the Chattanooga, Tennessee, veteran with five Senior PGA Tour victories, assumed the second-round lead. His 66 vaulted him to the top of the leader board, but nineteen players were within five shots of his 136 two-round total.

One of the contenders was the irascible Mr. Green. After the 73, Hubert had one of those play-bad-score-well days, firing a 66 that featured eighteen putts, one off the Senior Tour record.

"I did some phenomenal things with my sand wedge today," Green said. "That was one of the best up-and-down rounds I've had in my career."

His short play was necessary since Green hit into *seven* greenside bunkers. "I felt like Lawrence of Arabia out there," he proclaimed. "That's a lot of sand to be eating. I had all three caddies raking bunkers. They were taking turns."

In all, Green hit only ten greens in regulation. He had six birdies and saved par *eight* times from off the green. Green had a putter's delight *twelve* one-putt greens and three greens with no putts, all thanks to two hole-outs from bunkers and a chip-in from the fringe.

Playing partners Calvin Peete and Buddy Whitten, a Q-School qualifier and former army medic who served in Vietnam with Walter Morgan, finally bent over in laughter when Green holed a thirty-five-yard shot at the seventeenth hole from a fairway bunker.

"I was laughing, too," Green said, "but I wasn't going to apologize for anything. The way I was hitting it, that could have been an eighty-five out there."

Joining Green in contention was Dave Eichelberger, the Waco, Texas, veteran marking his thirtieth anniversary on tour; Isao Aoki, nicknamed "Tower" by the Japanese press due to his being six feet tall; David Graham, winner of both the PGA Championship and the U.S. Open; and former quarterback DeWitt Weaver, who, ESPN's Frank Beard said, "would have won a basketful of tournaments if he could have holed a putt or two."

Lurking just three shots back was Jim Colbert, but only by the grace of God. A wayward pushed tee shot at eighteen found the mangrove trees, and a double bogey loomed large. But Colbert, dubbed "Bulldog" by his competitors, took a drop, launched a five-iron from 172 yards, and watched as it hit just short of the green and bounced onto the green and into the hole for a birdie as the fans roared their approval.

"Somehow I knew it was going in," he said while walking down the fairway grinning ear to ear.

Sure, Jim.

After Bob Charles won the thirty-six-hole MasterCard Championship (for players over 60) portion of the Royal Caribbean Classic in a playoff with Harold Henning after two rounds, Gibby Gilbert attempted to keep his lead and record a sixth Senior Tour title.

Mother Nature cooperated on the final day, as the sun burst forth to provide a warm blanket for the competitors. That contrasted with the final round of the 1996 tournament, when thirty-something temperatures sent the players scurrying toward winter garb. "We had the cart covered with a plastic shield, and we brought a propane heater with us," winner Bob Murphy explained. "I also wrapped a huge beach towel around myself between shots, so I didn't have to wear a lot of clothes. That permitted me to keep my swing free." And made him look like a kindly munchkin bundled up on a cold winter night.

Previous winners besides Murphy included Lee Trevino, who captured his first Senior Tour championship in 1990 despite putting problems that caused him to say, "Maybe I'll try a weenie on a stick and see if that works," and Don Massengale, the 1992 champion who charged from six shots back to beat Gary Player, who admitted he had "choked like a dog with a collar on." Player won in 1991 over a down-trodden Rodriguez, prompting the Puerto Rican flash to exclaim that "the ugliest words in the English language are 'if only.' The prettiest are 'next time.'"

Of that group, only Rodriguez made the leader board during the 1997 tournament, but there was a fistful of players ready to claim the crown by Sunday's end. Nineteen players were within five shots of C. L. Gilbert, Jr., "Gibby," the journeyman player from the PGA Tour with just three wins in seventeen years on the circuit. His best finish in a Major had come in the 1980 Masters, when the sensational Spaniard Seve Ballesteros beat him by four shots. "Seve wasn't so tough," Gibby recalled. "I should have beaten his butt."

Gilbert's professional career had been launched despite the fact that Gibby's mother wanted him to be a dentist. "My mom told me I should go to dental school, but I couldn't imagine a life stuffing my fingers inside someone's mouth," he recalled.

Gibby opted for golf, but after playing the PGA Tour with mixed success, he returned to Chattanooga, where he ran a pizza parlor and managed a golf course. When his fiftieth birthday came calling, Gibby sought the Fountain of Youth on the Senior Tour.

The golfer who during his PGA Tour days had set the course record (62) at revered Pinehurst No. 2 accumulated five victories in six years. One of those wins came in 1996, when Gibby chalked up nearly $500,000 in earnings to show for his efforts.

On the front side in the final round at Key Biscayne, Gilbert's worrywart opinion of his swing, honed in the winter months with respected teacher Jim McLean, began to crop up in his mind. By the tenth hole, nine players had crept to within two shots of him, including money machine Jim Colbert, whose swaggering walk and overwhelming confidence made him a threat every time he teed up.

"My golf swing was never one anyone would copy," Gilbert had admitted before the round while swiping at practice balls. "I know I was making too big a hip turn going back so that when I came back to the ball, my hips were too square to the ball. The key is the setup, and I believe I've solved the problems."

During the final nine holes, Gilbert kept his swing in check, producing shots that set up birdie putts galore. Though he finished fourth on the list for the tournament when it came to fairways hit, driving distance, and greens hit in regulation, Gilbert's putter was magical. He required just seventy-four putts over the three rounds to finish first in that category.

A birdie at nine jump-started his charge, and he recorded six more in the last ten holes. The pivotal one came at fifteen, when Isao Aoki, having crept to within two shots of Gilbert, missed from fourteen feet after Gibby drilled a twenty-footer straight into the cup.

The $127,500 first prize prompted Gibby to take Eileen, his seventy-four-year-old mother, who attended the entire tournament, to the restaurant of her choice for a victory celebration. "My son is *so* good to me," she said.

Despite the hormone shots, the perfect golf ball, the lucky cat's-eye ring, and the new interlock grip, Chi Chi Rodriguez finished twentieth. Lee Trevino, admitting that an off-season move from Jupiter, Florida, to Dallas and the heart-wrenching experience of his mother-in-law undergoing brain surgery had sapped his strength, added 70 and 71 to his 81 to finish fifty-second, and Gary Player, the only contestant from the Big Three contingent, managed a tie for twenty-fifth, though a final-round 69 portended better things to come. One fan from Alabama didn't care though, remarking, "I got to see Chi Chi's sword dance, Lee cracking jokes, and Gibby hugging his mother," she exclaimed. "The trip was well worth it."

3

OVER THE WINTER MONTHS PRIOR TO THE BEGINNING OF THE 1997 Senior PGA Tour, Hale Irwin had a recurring nightmare: the vision of Jim Colbert accepting the 1996 Player of the Year Award that he'd anticipated setting on the mantel above his fireplace in Missouri.

Though the rivalry certainly wasn't to be elevated to the Palmer/Nicklaus intensity level prevalent in the 1960s, Irwin/Colbert had caught the fancy of Senior Tour golf fans yearning for a good competitive fistfight.

When Irwin bounded onto the senior circuit as a rookie in 1996, Jim Colbert was the man to beat. His rags-to-riches story had propelled him from being completely out of the game in the mid-1980s to the number one position on the Senior Tour. The cocky former Kansas State football player had zoomed to the top by winning five times in 1996 and totaling a Senior Tour record $1,627,000 in earnings.

Colbert's achievement astounded the golf world, which had dismissed him as a viable player after recurring chronic back problems forced him to the sidelines in 1986. A successful business career, including ownership of golf courses, management of golf tournaments, evolution of a series of golf instructional clinics with his longtime guru Jimmy Ballard, and a three-year stint as a broadcaster on ESPN, had made Colbert a multimillionaire. But rarely had he traipsed to the golf courses in his home city of Las Vegas to try his hand at the game he loved.

As Colbert approached fifty in 1991, he itched to compete against the fellow professionals he had dueled with in the 1970s and 1980s, when he won eight times. With the full blessing of Marcia, his wife since high school days, Gentleman Jim worked with Ballard and plotted his return to big-time competition.

Despite the back problems that had forced him to become a twenty-two-a-day Advil junkie, Colbert burst into the winner's circle at the Southwestern Bell Classic and never looked back. He won three times, finished second on five occasions, winning nearly $900,000. "I was reborn," he said. "The Fountain of Youth blessed me."

Fans enjoyed seeing him back in business. "Colbert's fun to watch," one observed. "He's the one who flies the ball straight at the pin. The one with the balls out here."

Craig Gentry, a Hollywood set designer and Senior Tour aspirant, said it another way: "Colbert's a grinder whether he's first or last. The man's got eyes like an eagle."

If his Senior Tour competitors thought Colbert was a one-season fluke, they were dead wrong. The Bulldog in the turned-up-collar golf shirt and bucket hat won six more times in the next three years, all the while experimenting with ionic magnets designed to improve circulation in his back.

By 1995, Colbert, one of the mainstays of Team Cadillac, along with Bob Murphy, Jim Dent, Dave Stockton, Walter Morgan, Bob Charles, Jay Sigel, Lee Trevino, Tom Wargo, Larry Ziegler, George Archer, and Arnold Palmer, was ready to strike, and he did so with a vengeance. Four victories and more than $1.4 million in prize money made him the single most recognizable player on the Senior Tour. The man with the swaggering walk who tweaked his fingers at the gallery like a gunfighter after a successful shot became a favorite of the fans, who could relate to Colbert's never-give-up style and zest to win against the "big boys," the Nicklauses and Floyds competing on the Senior Tour.

Ironically, the turning point for Colbert to compete at such a high level came, according to Tom Hartley, his longtime financial partner, when Jim bought a jet plane. "Having a corporate jet made Jim realize he could play with all those others who had corporate jets," Hartley explained. "It really boosted his confidence, and he never looked back."

Colbert's days in the sun were expected to end in 1996 when Irwin, with his U.S. Open championships in tow, embarked on a Senior Tour career. Hale's impressive credentials spoke for themselves, and he was expected to dominate tournament play. "Colbert, who's Colbert?" Irwin thought to himself, certain that King Jim would melt into the background as the year went by.

All seemed according to plan for Irwin when the former University of Colorado defensive back swept through the first few months on the Tour. He won at Sarasota, then captured his first Major, the PGA Seniors' Championship. At one point, he led Colbert by more than $350,000 in earnings and had all but sewn up the money title and the Player of the Year honors that went with it. The Arnold Palmer trophy was certain to have his name on it.

Then rain clouds appeared. Colbert began winning, and Irwin couldn't. Slowly, the gambling man from Las Vegas scooted up the money list by recording five victories. Those included late-season wins at the Vantage and Raley's Gold Rush Classic. Suddenly, with the season-ending Tour Championship on the horizon, Irwin's once insurmountable lead wasn't insurmountable anymore.

The two combatants, linked by their football competitive spirit, squared off at the Dunes Golf and Beach Club in Myrtle Beach, South Carolina. Jay Sigel stole much of the thunder by winning, but the Irwin/Colbert tug-of-war came down to Colbert's final hole.

"Hale was ahead of me by a little more than $66,000. I knew Jay Sigel was walking away with the title, but I hung in there," Colbert recalled. "When Hale uncharacteristically played bad in the middle two rounds [75, 76], I knew I had a chance to catch him."

Irwin continued to play lackadaisically throughout the final round. On the back nine, Colbert said to himself, "I actually have a chance. Everything just became electric to me. That's what I live for, to be in that competitive moment. I wasn't nervous. I was charged up in a way only competitive golf can do for me."

After forty-plus tournaments, and more than nine thousand strokes with the golf club in 1996, the square-jawed, barrel-chested golfer faced his final one for the season, a tricky downhill sixteen-footer on the eighteenth hole for birdie three, unaware of exactly where he stood with his rival. Spying ESPN commentator Frank Beard in the distance, Colbert called him over.

"Where do I stand?" Jim asked. "Have I still got a chance?"

"Well, uh, you need to make that putt," Beard replied, stunned that Jim wanted to know what was at stake.

If Colbert made birdie, in all likelihood he would tie John Bland for third place. That meant $121,000. Irwin had earned $42,875 for a tie for eleventh. It didn't take an MIT graduate to figure the margin between third- and eleventh-place money was more than $66,000.

Beard's report made Colbert's eyes light up, and he smiled. "I'm still in the hunt," he said to himself, realizing that if he holed the downhill curler, he would polish off Irwin, whose nippy remarks regarding Colbert's gunfighter antics inspired him in the battle. For his part, Colbert regarded Irwin as a competent player, but told reporters, "Yes, there's competition between us, but we're completely different type of players. I enjoy this so much, but Hale never seems to be happy. I don't know, at least he doesn't show it. Gosh, if you don't like this, what would you like?"

After stalking the putt like a Bengal tiger, and eyeing it from every angle to stretch the suspense like the ending of an Alfred Hitchcock thriller, Colbert swaggered up beside the ball and positioned himself for the putt. He paused for an instant and then triggered the backswing, focusing on the putter head as it smacked against the back of the ball.

The white sphere tumbled at a snail's pace down the incline before picking up speed. It never wavered from its line and, with a plunk, fell gently into the hole. "I'd realized a dream," Colbert said later. "Making a big putt when you have to, to win it all."

For Irwin, suddenly all the U.S. Opens and memories of a great career that totaled twenty PGA Tour victories seemed a distant memory. The overwhelming favorite had been dive-bombed by the grinder, one not blessed with enormous natural talent like Irwin's, but by the true heart of a champion.

Irwin attempted to disguise his disappointment by pointing out that he had played in far fewer tournaments than Colbert, but the embarrassment was apparent. Everywhere he went, questions about Colbert followed him, and during the winter months of 1996–1997, Irwin vowed to get even.

The solid win at the Tournament of Champions, where Colbert finished fourth, put him right on schedule. Armed with a new strategy calling for caution instead of a full-force assault to birdie every hole, Irwin was determined to show Mr. Colbert there would be no chance to top him in 1997. True to his game plan, Irwin dominated at the LG Championship in Naples. Despite late final-round challenges from Bob Murphy, Vicente Fernandez, and David Graham, Irwin's rounds of 70-66-65 made him two for two in 1997. Colbert finished seventh, six shots back, telling reporters his putting was horrible. "My thirty-eight-year-old lucky streak I've had with the putter may be over," he lamented. "But I hope not."

Once again, Chi Chi Rodriguez, despite finishing seventeenth, kept things loose by revealing that he'd had silver fillings removed from his teeth. "I talked to a homeopathic dentist and told him I had a lot of pain in my shoulder," Rodriguez explained. "He said the fillings in my mouth were fifty percent mercury. All I was doing was sucking mercury into my system."

To cleanse his body, Chi Chi replaced the fillings with gold. "The pain has disappeared," he said. "I can finally swing away again."

One who swung away too many times on one hole during the championship was Dave Eichelberger, the Waco, Texas, veteran with four PGA victories to his credit. In the first round, Ike was on fast-forward, standing six under and leading the tournament when he approached the par-four seventeenth. A trip to the palmetto bushes on the right side produced a nightmare eleven when Eichelberger twice hit restricted-swing shots into the bushes and had to declare three unplayable lies. It was so bad that playing partner Vicente Fernandez said, "It wasn't even my nightmare, and I was feeling bad."

At the GTE Classic played at designer Bobby Weed's jewel of a course in Tampa, Jack Nicklaus made his 1997 debut. Though Arnold Palmer was still recovering from surgery and Chi Chi was taking a holiday from tournament play, Jack's presence and that of Gary Player and Lee Trevino made certain golf fans saw their favorite heroes.

The Golden Bear gained much of the pretournament attention, but David Graham, the native of Windsor, New South Wales, Australia, was lurking in the shadows. A solid fourth-place finish at Naples had placed him in a lighthearted championship mood, something he desperately needed.

Though Graham had amassed a fine professional record throughout the world (twenty championships, including the 1979 PGA Championship and the 1981 U.S. Open), Graham seemed to have a dark shadow following him from his early days in Australia. His decision to become a golfer (Graham played left-handed for two years before switching) so incensed his father that he refused to support him and booted David out of his life. "My dad was a heavy drinker," Graham explained. "He was old army and stubborn as could be. He and Mom never got along. My mother and I lived in the back half of the house, and my sister and Dad lived in the front. I rarely ever saw him."

Years passed with no contact, so David was surprised when his father showed up in Minnesota. "At the 1970 U.S. Open a marshal told me someone had asked to see me. When I walked over, it was my dad. Later he tried to explain things, but I told him he was a complete stranger to me and I didn't want to see him anymore. I never did. He died a few years ago. I haven't seen my mother for a long time either. Maybe one day I'll go back to Australia and see her. I don't know."

Two years after the fateful meeting with his dad, tragedy struck Graham. His wife, Maureen, delivered premature twin boys. Both died shortly thereafter. "That was awful tough to take," Graham said. "But then Andrew and Michael came along. What blessings."

Throughout his PGA Tour career, Graham won nearly $2 million. His last victory in the States came in 1983, though he won the Queensland Open in 1985.

As he approached fifty in 1996, Graham made preparations to play the Senior Tour. His length off the tee and shot-making ability somewhat offset an inconsistent putting stroke, and in nineteen events he managed to win nearly $300,000.

Graham hoped better play in 1997 would help him forget sour memories of an event he believed had severely damaged his reputation. That debacle occurred in the months leading to the playing of the 1996 Presidents Cup matches, a Ryder Cup look-alike featuring competition between professionals from the United States and a squad composed of international players.

Many pundits believed the competition had been conceived to showcase the wares of Greg Norman, ineligible for Ryder Cup competition. Graham had been named captain in 1996, as he had been in 1994. His team included Greg Norman, Steve Elkington, and Nick Price, among others.

Trouble for Graham occurred before, during, and after the 1994 matches. Players accused him of being uncommunicative and treating them like schoolboys. He had refused to let Steve Elkington leave a White House ceremony before it ended. He had alienated Ernie Els by writing him a nasty letter for refusing to play. Craig Parry was upset when Graham didn't back him for a Masters invitation. And Nick Price complained that the captain made him play when he was worn out.

Based on these incidents and others, Norman and the other players decided a change was in order. Graham's reputation was tarnished when the insurgents called for his resignation, citing the oft-used expression from the film *Cool Hand Luke*, "What we have here is a failure to communicate." Within hours of the abrupt announcement in Europe, Peter Thomson, the five-time British Open champion who'd blitzed the Senior Tour with nine victories in 1985 before his brand of Japanese golf ball was banned, became his replacement. Graham was left in the rubbish pile, much to the chagrin of fellow professionals, who considered him a true gentleman of the game.

His psyche in disorder, Graham revolted. He spouted out nasty words at Norman and promised legal action. Time tempered his thoughts, but the wound was severe. "It was ugly," Graham growled. "Very ugly."

Over the winter months, the stately Graham decided to invoke the old Bobby Jones adage, "Let your clubs do the talking." He practiced his golf game, analyzed it through videotapes taken at sponsor Callaway's test center in California, and readied himself for competition.

The fourth-place finish at Naples in the LG Classic proved Graham was on the right track. Even though Nicklaus was the defending champion and making a rare Florida appearance on the Senior Tour slate, Graham was supremely confident.

The same couldn't be said for Nicklaus. To hear him tell it, his game was securely in the toilet, a far cry from the finely tuned Jack who had won his ninety-ninth tournament at Tampa a year before. An opening-round 76 in 1996 had left him spitting expletives, but a Saturday 68 moved Nicklaus to within five shots of Isao Aoki. That lead had shrunk to one by the twelfth, but then the thin man from the Far East unraveled at the par-four thirteenth, producing a quintuple-bogey nine that caused his playing partner to say he "thought Aoki was playing hockey."

"All of a sudden I had been given a gift," Nicklaus exclaimed. "I was the chaser, and then I was the chasee." Never one to let an opportunity pass, Nicklaus pounded out solid pars on the final three holes, totaling 67 and beating J. C. Snead by one shot. "Winning is special anytime," Jack said while holding yet another trophy. "I don't care if you're ten, twenty, thirty, forty, fifty, or fifty-six. It's special."

Jack's win might have been in a play-off had it not been for the honesty of his playing partner, Bob Murphy, the Florida Gator alum born in nearby Mulberry. At the seventh hole in the final round, Murphy's tee ball plopped into a fairway bunker and skipped under the lip. Relegated to playing a sand wedge to the fairway, he blasted away, but the ball hit the lip, made a U-turn, and catapulted back toward Murphy. He ducked to shield his eyes from the sand, but felt a tick on his wide-brimmed trademark Panama hat. Believing the ball had careened off his hat, Murphy assessed himself a two-shot penalty and took a triple bogey on the hole. "It was such an odd circumstance," Murphy recalled. "Even Jack said he'd have trouble saying the ball hit my hat. He said he didn't think it hit me. But I've got to live with myself. Something hit my hat. Later, I thought it might have been the shaft of the club that brushed it."

Murphy's miscue made him intent on winning at Tampa in 1997. That was in contrast to Nicklaus, who told reporters, "I never really know from day to day these days about my golf game. It comes and goes. Hopefully, this week it will come."

Despite the fact that sunny skies and mid-eighties temperatures greeted the field in the first round, it was a Michigan Wolverine who stole the spotlight. Fifty-one-year-old John Schroeder fired a four-under-par 67 to lead Gil Morgan and J. C. Snead by one. The round was bittersweet for Schroeder, whose life was a roller-coaster in the late fall of 1996.

As August rolled around, everything seemed a perfect fit. John and his wife, Kathy, were basking in the sun financially thanks to a multimillion-dollar windfall from an inadvertent investment Schroeder made in Cobra Golf, the company Greg Norman made famous. Besides the sudden wealth, winnings on the Senior Tour had permitted Schroeder to escape from the NBC booth, where he provided commentary after leaving the PGA Tour with just one victory and barely $500,000 in winnings.

"My three daughters were out of the house, and Kathy was going to join me on Tour," Schroeder said. "We were empty nesters, and everything was great."

But it wasn't. A phone call to the Schroeders' San Diego home brought sorrow to their lives. Twenty-two-year-old daughter Patty, a recent graduate of the University of Michigan, had dived into a lake near Pontiac, Michigan, and struck the bottom, causing a severe spinal injury. Her fifth and sixth vertebrae were shattered; Patty would be a quadriplegic.

Suddenly, plans for Kathy to join John on the Tour were abruptly halted. His schedule was cut back, and his temperament suffered. "It's hard to understand things like that," he muttered, aware that his life had changed overnight.

The only place Schroeder found solace was on the golf course. "It's the only time I can put Patty's situation out of my mind," the dapper, gray-haired golfer explained. "That's because I have something to focus on and can have fun. A wedge for eagle is better than a psychologist's couch anytime."

Schroeder's upbeat attitude was a far cry from the depths of gloom he encountered after his daughter's accident. "Last year was the worst," he said. "At the end of the season, I had no fire. But you have to move on. I've dedicated myself to getting the most out of the year for my daughter. She's coping very, very well." Perhaps even better than her father, whose double-bogey, double-bogey finish 75 on Saturday and 74 on Sunday slid him well down the leader board.

Bob Eastwood's 65 and Ray Floyd's 66 highlighted the second round, but the man on a mission to win at Tampa was the Aussie Graham. After the second-round 68, he stood at 139, just three shots back. The golfer who Frank Beard had said "hit the ball like a rocket" was poised to challenge, ready to get back into the winner's circle after not having been victorious since the 1985 Queensland Open.

This was the same sure-shot David Graham who hit all eighteen fairways at vaunted Merion in 1981, firing a final-round 67 that won the U.S. Open crown. A PGA Championship had earlier graced his mantel when he defeated Ben Crenshaw on the third extra hole of a play-off in 1979 at Oakland Hills.

The only headline Graham had made since the 1980s was the fiasco with the Presidents Cup. To be sure, the experience had left its mark. "Those young kids, Norman in particular, cut a deep scar in me," he told reporters. "It still infuriates me that they conducted themselves in a manner not befitting professional golfers." Chi Chi Rodriguez, whose turned-up hat made one observer say he looked like Ed Norton of *The Honeymooners* TV show, said, "David didn't deserve to be treated like that. He's always been the consummate gentleman."

Though most viewed Graham's replacement as captain of the Presidents Cup international team as being caused by egos gone awry, Graham knew that headline-making golf scores would do much to displace all the talk about a sad chapter in his life. And in the final round at Tampa, seven birdies (including four consecutive on the back nine) and only one bogey propelled him to a three-shot win over Bob Dickson, the Q-School winner, former U.S. and British Amateur champion, and PGA Tour executive who admitted he couldn't break eighty three years ago.

Nicklaus finished ten shots back, Trevino six, and Rodriguez, despite telling reporters, "I've got a new grip that I invented where I take my thumbs off the club," finished third from the bottom. For David Graham, a broad smile and a gentlemanly bow at eighteen capped the victory. Winning $150,000 meant the biggest check of his career, the hope that fans would talk about his golf instead of the Presidents Cup, and a feeling that the best days were ahead. "We know how lucky we are," he exclaimed. "The Senior Tour is awesome. It's the most incredible thing I've seen in golf."

No sooner were those words out of Graham's mouth than controversy reared its head. On the Monday following the tournament, it was disclosed that his caddie, Steve Hulka, had violated PGA Tour rules by rolling balls from all directions surrounding the dot-marking hole locations on the greens the night before the final round. A spectator had noticed the infraction and told a media member, who in turn alerted Senior PGA officials. Faced with a decision as to whether to disqualify Graham for his caddie's infraction, the Tour decided not to, citing a rule that a player was not responsible for the actions of his caddie except during tournament play. Several competitors and caddies were upset with the ruling, believing Hulka's actions, tantamount to cheating, provided Graham a distinct advantage, but he remained champion. With his shaky psyche following the Presidents Cup, another blow might have sent him to a mental hospital.

While Gibby Gilbert, Hale Irwin, and David Graham picked up victories in the first three full-field tournaments on the Senior PGA Tour, Bud Allin waited patiently for his chances at the riches on the Tour. The DNP (did not play) at Key Biscayne was followed by a tie for seventeenth at the LG Classic and a tie for twenty-sixth at the GTE. Total money won was $22,344, a long way from what he had in mind for 1997.

And the money *was* important to Allin, for, unlike many of his Senior PGA Tour counterparts who had made millions on and off the golf course and flew their Lear jets to all the tournaments, Bud and his wife, Carol, still scraped to make a living, worrying about mortgage payments and such, all while Bud tried to escape haunting memories.

"Buddy went through many rough years before becoming eligible for the senior circuit," Jim Colbert noted. "He had to deal with all the Vietnam and the Agent Orange business. That's real pressure. And he stood up for his country, for everything. In my mind, he's a hero."

Colbert's remarks alluded to Allin's service in Vietnam for eighteen months in 1968–1969, when he was an artillery officer and earned four decorations, including the Bronze Star and Air Medal. "He was a forward observer," Colbert said. "One of those guys who flies out front in a little plane. You could shoot him down with a pistol."

That stint in the military preceded Allin's entry on the regular PGA Tour a year after he completed his studies at Brigham Young University, where a golf-team teammate was golden-haired Johnny Miller. He experienced mixed success on the Tour (five wins in five years) but was pleased with the results. "I was on a roll," he said. "I felt I could play with anyone."

Allin's prediction proved wrong when his game fell flat. He finally quit the Tour in 1978. "I was beating myself up financially and tired of all the travel and the financial insecurities," he lamented. "Some years we bought one Christmas present for all three kids," Allin recalled. "It was tough making a living out there."

A second shot at stardom in 1980 proved futile. The first of two operations for malignant lymphomas caused by chain smoking broke his 5'8", 130-pound body. "I spent a lot of time in bed. Worked on an instruction book and a putter that featured changeable weights in the club head."

A club professional job in California proved sound in the mid-1980s, but Bud Allin was no quitter, and he made it clear to his employers that when 1994 rolled around, he was Senior Tour bound. He even included an out clause in his contract. When that year came, Allin practiced until his hands blistered and then headed for the Senior Tour Q-School in Florida. Four rounds later the gritty Allin had earned his passport to the promised land.

Chi Chi Rodriguez was pleased to see him. When the tiny man with the crinkled skin and furrowed brow approached the tee, the Cheech shouted, "I'm glad you made it out here. Finally, someone comes along that looks older than me."

Displaying the guts of a lion, Allin found immediate success with his peers on the Senior Tour. The 1995 season produced a second, two thirds, and nearly $600,000 in earnings. Nineteen ninety-six proved less successful, and, worse, his $365,734 placed him just beyond the top thirty-one list, which meant he'd be first alternate for the 1997 season unless he qualified at the Q-School. He was unsuccessful there and entered 1997 with dimmed hopes of realizing a dream: his first victory on the Senior PGA Tour. Then he'd been odd man out at the Royal Caribbean Classic, a dismal way to start the season.

"You always wonder if you'll make it," Allin explained. "And I've always had something to prove. Golf is such a mental thing. The ball is just sitting there, not moving, and you have to make it go long and straight. That shouldn't be difficult, but it's the hardest thing on earth. Making a living out here is harder than fighting a war, because what you're fighting is your own mind."

When the Friday first round dawned on the American Express Invitational at the TPC at Prestancia in Sarasota, Bud Allin was not positioned in a marquee threesome. His 8:30 tee time included Bobby Stroble and Rick Massengale. Only a small gallery followed the group, but Allin caught their attention, throwing a 68 at the field that left him tied with Simon Hobday, Butch Baird, and Jim Colbert. Allin's score was even more impressive considering the chilly temperatures and a huff-and-puff wind that had golfers shaking their heads at well-intentioned shots gone awry. "I'm only 135 pounds," Allin observed. "I'd like to have another forty to play in this wind."

While Allin discussed the wind, Simon Hobday relished his tournament score. By his own admission, he'd played poorly in 1996, failing to win for the first time in four years. Despite that showing, Hobday, a native of Mareking, South Africa, was a crowd favorite wherever he went. He was arguably the best storyteller on the Senior Tour, though many times the stories were about himself.

Hobday's exploits around the world gave the word "eccentric" new meaning. While playing the European Tour, he accepted a five-pound dare from fellow golfer Sam Torrance and took off all of his clothes at a pub in Crans-sur-Sierre, Switzerland, during the European Masters. Other patrons stood gawking at him, but Simon continued drinking his brew as if nothing had happened. When the bartender asked him to at least pull on a pair of shorts, he agreed, pulling them over his head. That coincided with behavior at the Magnolia Inn near Pinehurst, where Hobday, recently crowned champion of the U.S. Senior Open, was told he needed to wear a tie before dining. Simon returned wearing one and not much else.

Hobday won that title despite nearly drowning after an opening-round 66. He went fishing, but too many brews forced a nature call. He stood up in the boat and unzipped his pants, but unsteadiness caused the boat to capsize. According to witnesses, Hobday began to flutter his arms in the water to stay afloat, only to discover that he was in two feet of water.

Hobday might have been better suited to play the Nudist Tour than the American or European ones. Gary Player recalled his behavior during a tournament in Sun City, South Africa. "It was hot as could be, and Sun City sits in a bowl," Player said while laughing. "Simon hit his ball on the green, took off his clothes and had a quick swim in the nearby lake, got out, dressed, and calmly putted out. He's the same guy who can swear using twelve different words, and they all sound the same."

On another occasion, Hobday refused lunch after an opening round of 76 at the 1995 PGA Seniors' Championship. "I'm not worth feeding," he responded.

Hobday's prowess with lifting his elbow in drink (a section of a bar in Puerto Rico was named after him) and causing a fuss in restaurants was legendary, but his real art was with swearwords. "I've always had trouble with the swearing," Hobday admitted while rubbing his mustache. "I don't like those sausage microphones. They can stand behind a tree fifty yards away and catch you whispering to your caddie. Or, in my case, spitting out something about a bad shot I've hit. That's gotten me in a lot of trouble over the years. Merely for talking to the ball. I should speak in Swahili or something. Then nobody would know what I've said."

That Simon Hobday was dubbed "Scruffy" by his fellow professionals was no surprise. "He looks like an unmade bed," one observed. Lee Trevino saw firsthand why Hobday's clothes were always on the wrinkled side. "We were going to dinner one time," Trevino said. "I slid by his room to pick him up. He yelled at me from the bathroom. I walked over there, and there was Simon. He had his shirts, socks, and shorts in the bathtub stirring them around with his putter. I said, 'Simon, how are you going to get the suds out?' He looked at me with those squinty eyes and said, 'I'll show you.' Then he took his driver and positioned it across the bathtub, hung the clothes on it, and turned on the shower. 'Let's go eat,' he said."

Hobday's 68 in the first round of the American Express was in contrast to a fellow fisherman, Bob Murphy, who straggled *fourteen* shots behind the leaders. Yes, fourteen, since Murphy was forced to sign a scorecard that included a snowman-plus-two, a *ten* on the par-five fifteenth. There Murphy, instantly dubbed "Tin Cup" by close friend Jim Colbert, drilled three shots into the lake stretching across the front of the green.

When the sun set on the second round, there was Bud Allin again, having fired a second consecutive 68 that provided a three-shot cushion over Jim Colbert, Graham Marsh, another globe-trotting Aussie, and former club professional Jim Albus, who confounded the golf world when he won the Senior Tour Players Championship in 1991. Albus was fighting back from a neck injury that harpooned the avid fisherman from competing at full strength in 1996. To ready himself for every round, he was forced to scrunch down his neck and pop it up, over and over, to relax his muscles. "I feel like a doggone ostrich when I do this," he said.

Hobday fell back as questions for leader Allin predictably focused on two dissimilar parts of his life, Vietnam and the state of his golf game while leading a tournament. Allin was blunt with his remarks about the first, quizzical regarding the second.

"My years in the army were the best three years of my life," Allin told reporters. "Vietnam didn't do anything but give me a sense of pride that I fought for my country. I just played the game of war, and I loved it. Vietnam did nothin' but strengthen me as a person." As for his prediction on Money Sunday, he said, "I can't say I have any confidence . . . I haven't ever teed it up with a three-shot lead, so I don't know how I'll feel. This morning when I washed my hands, I trembled a bit."

As he began round three, Allin recalled thoughts he'd had two weeks earlier: "Driving from Key Biscayne to Naples, I tried to think about how I used to play and feel when I competed years ago. I decided three things needed working on—my grip, the tension in my hands, and my setup. I watched a videotape of my swing and thought I was on the right track. I played fairly well there and then at Tampa, but the greens were awful and I didn't make anything."

Sarasota was a different story, and back-to-back 68s gave Allin confidence. They were good putting rounds, the result of Allin recalling a tip at the 1980 New Zealand Open he'd been given by Jerry Heard, a senior-to-be in May and purveyor of full-page newspaper advertisements proclaiming his new swing method as a cure-all for wayward golfers. "Jerry told me let the hands lag, move the club forward, like crackin' a whip. I made everything in both Pro-Ams this week, and that carried over into the tournament. Especially on Saturday, which is usually choke day for me."

Bud's wife, Carol, noticed her husband's positive attitude. "He told me we might not win this week," she said, "but he promised he'd win one for me one day soon."

Jim Colbert knew Allin, one of the most respected professionals on Tour, would be tough to beat. "We never say it publicly, but we know the pedigree of someone who's leading. Buddy's a thoroughbred," he observed, "tough to catch when he's out front."

Sunday's final round proved a worthy test of Allin's nerves. "I kept checking myself," he recalled. "Checking to see how I was holding up. To my delight, I was okay. It had been so long since I was in a position to win, but I felt okay."

The thirteenth and fourteenth holes were pivotal. "I had a twenty-five-footer at thirteen," Allin said later. "When I looked over the putt, I told myself, 'I can make this one.' And I did. At fourteen, I was left with a seven-foot downhill putt for par. I made it, but I said, 'No more of those.' "

At sixteen, a par-three, Allin's mettle was again challenged. "When I stood over the shot, I thought, 'If I can hit this six iron on the green, I can handle the rest.' I did, and even though I took bogey at seventeen, I felt good coming to eighteen."

By then, Jim Colbert had parred the hole to finish at ten under. "The pressure was a hundredfold more on Buddy than me," he said, aware that Allin was fighting for every dollar while he had won over $3 million in 1995 and 1996 alone and was financially set for life.

"My caddie, Buck, reminded me to pick a target," Allin remembered. "There was a tent in view by the green, and I focused just to the left of it."

Allin's tee shot was perfect, just 140 yards from the green. A bunker lingered to the right, and he wanted no part of it since he had not tested the sand all week.

A six iron was the chosen club, and Allin managed to plop the ball down on the front of the green, nearly sixty feet from the cup. Two putts meant $180,000, an exemption from qualifying for a year, and his first win since 1976.

Jim Colbert's mind-set was mixed as he watched Allin play eighteen. "I'd love to win, don't get me wrong," he commented, "but if I can't, Buddy's the one. He deserves it."

The sixty-footer looked like 160 to Allin, but he tried to remain calm. Carol stood next to the green, silent, her heart beating like an Olympic sprinter's. "No one knows what this is like," she murmured. "I'm praying by the second."

"The putt was up, up and over a rise," Allin discovered. "I knew I would need to hit it hard enough to get over the rise, or else the ball would come back at me. If I hit it too hard, there was a bunker only twelve feet past the pin."

After surveying one of the most significant putts of his life, Allin strode up next to the ball. Millions of ESPN viewers, thousands of fans around the green, and every golfer with a love for the underdog, the good guy, held their collective breaths.

"I don't even remember hitting the putt," Allin said later. "I don't know if I hit it well or not. But the ball ended up two feet from the hole, and I knew I was gonna win the golf tournament."

Once he plugged the ball into the hole, Carol came dashing out to congratulate him. They hugged like newlyweds and marched off the green with the world by the tail. The American Express Invitational had a true hero for a champion, a patriot, a man who'd risked his life for his country when others fled their duty.

"I knew this day would come," Bud said with a tear in his eye. "In this country you've got to believe it can happen before it will. As they say in the commercials, out here anything's possible."

4

THE FLORIDA SWING COMPLETED, THE SENIOR PGA TOUR PLAYERS set their sights on three tournaments leading up to The Tradition, the season's first Major. Gibby Gilbert, Hale Irwin, David Graham, and Bud Allin had emerged victorious in Florida, and the Toshiba Senior Classic, The Legends, and the BellSouth Dominion were scheduled through the first of April.

Arnold Palmer was still on the sidelines, and Jack Nicklaus was not competing until The Tradition. Gary Player, Chi Chi Rodriguez, and Lee Trevino carried the torch of "first-name" players, but Jim Colbert was the man on the spot.

In March, Colbert turned fifty-six, the mark that seemed to trigger a downswing in play. The 1995 and 1996 Player of the Year was winless in 1997 and could point only to the runner-up finish at Sarasota for encouragement.

Colbert admitted he was placing too much pressure on himself in search of a three-peat. "I just need to remember how I played before," he lamented. "Hit the ball, go get it, hit it again. And my putting—well, it hasn't been up to snuff."

As defending champion at the Toshiba in Newport Beach, California, Colbert was looking forward to the tournament. He'd blazed to a win in 1996, firing 68-65-68 to beat Bob Eastwood by two and his nemesis, Hale Irwin, by four. Colbert's play had been superb, and he saw no reason why win number one couldn't occur in Southern California.

In between tackling the Bermuda greens in Florida and the bent that would face them in Palm Springs at the Legends, the PGA Tour Seniors encountered mostly poa, as in *poa annua*, at the Newport Beach Country Club. The grass grew uneven as the day progressed, and putting became more luck than skill. Lee Trevino said it was like "putting on gravel roads." Other professionals were less kind.

Jim Colbert never could figure out which way the ball was rolling and finished far down the leader board. If he couldn't win, the next best thing would be for his close friend, Bob Murphy, to do so. Hale Irwin had bypassed the tournament, and the straight-driving Murph was a favorite along with David Graham, Gil Morgan, Lee Trevino, and Jay Sigel, whose mediocre Florida play was barely reminiscent of his overwhelming victory in the season-ending Tour Championship.

When the flag went up on Friday, three seasoned veterans mastered the *poa annua* and fired 65s. David Graham was joined by J. C. Snead and Bob Murphy, who shocked himself with his good play.

Murphy's reaction was based on a season full of what he aptly dubbed "bad play," the result of off-season finger surgery that scared the bejesus out of him. "I had a cancerous growth removed from my right index finger," he recalled. "And they went so deep it looked like a divot. It was ground under repair for over a month, and I couldn't practice."

When Murphy finally could play, the Tournament of Champions approached, but rounds of 78-75-71 followed by 73-76-74 at the Royal Caribbean made the Brooklyn-born golfer wonder if his game would ever come back. "Oh no," he thought, "it's 1987 all over again."

That was the year Bob Murphy's career as a professional golfer nearly ended. The nightmare began when the chipper Irishman stepped in a hole near a green at the Atlanta Country Club. He fell to the ground wincing in pain, believing he had sprained his ankle.

The left foot swelled like a balloon. Pain seeped into Murphy's knee and hip and finally into his hands, which puffed up so badly he couldn't hold a golf club.

Numerous attempts to diagnose the injury proved fruitless. Murphy endured the pain, which was especially acute when his feet, which normally fit into a size 10-D shoe, required an $11^{1}/_{2}$-EE.

"Watching Bob hurt all those years was tough," admitted wife Gail, a lovely lady with the patience of Job. "But Bob kept going until he just couldn't play anymore."

Not being able to compete drove Murphy nuts. He'd gone to the University of Florida on a baseball scholarship, earned through his prowess as a good-hitting first baseman who could also pitch. But hopes of becoming a big leaguer were dashed when Murphy hurt his pitching arm playing football.

Murphy had caddied for his father at an early age and decided to take a shot at golf. He contacted the legendary University of Florida coach Conrad Rehling. "Frank Beard and Tommy Aaron were on the team, but Conrad took the time to work with me," Murphy recalled. "He turned me from being a flaming hooker to fading the ball. He also said I'd never have a pretty swing, but to make the best of what I had. And to keep my legs as far apart as possible. 'You can always move them in,' he said."

And where did the famous pause at the top of Murphy's swing

come from? "I had a hesitation in my pitching motion. The coach said that batters would have a tough time picking up the white ball from my white uniform," he explained. "My way of hitting a baseball was to have a harsh, rushed, and violent action. That didn't work with the golf swing. Conrad wanted me to be 'quiet' at the top. I practiced in stages until I found just the proper pause. It helped me not to rush my swing. Some people say they hate it; others say it's beautiful. No matter, it worked for me, especially since it permitted me to start my forward swing at the same speed I finished my backswing."

Indeed, it did. Though Murphy failed to make the Florida golf team on his first two attempts (he shot 88-89 the first time), he did so with style in 1965, the year he won the U.S. Amateur Championship by one shot over Bob Dickson at Southern Hills. After adding the NCAA title in 1966 and playing on the Walker Cup team in 1967, Murphy bounded onto the PGA Tour in 1968 and won the Philadelphia Golf Classic. When injury finally sidelined him in 1988, Murphy had amassed five PGA Tour victories and more than $1.5 million in winnings.

The Floridian seemed destined to be a part-time player and television commentator with ESPN until a lucky day in 1989. That's when physician and family friend Al Kennemer spied Murphy's blotched and scaly legs.

"Where have *you* been?" Kennemer asked, wondering if his friend had been vacationing in the rain forests of Brazil.

"Nowhere," Murphy replied. "I have psoriasis."

Hours later, the doctor called Murphy. He'd decided Murphy not only had psoriasis but arthritis as well. Tests confirmed the diagnosis, and Murphy began taking methotrexate, a cancer drug that also alleviates swelling associated with arthritis. Instant results were produced, and Murphy returned to competition.

In 1993, when the Murph turned fifty on Valentine's Day, he was rarin' to go. Always known as a superb putter with a sound short game, Murphy exploded onto the Senior Tour, piling up prize money and winning both the Bruno's Memorial Classic and the GTE North Classic. Earnings of nearly $800,000 propelled him to Rookie of the Year honors. He became the first golfer ever to receive the award on both tours, having been Rookie of the Year on the PGA Tour twenty-five years earlier.

Entering the 1997 season, the former pitcher had won ten PGA Seniors titles and over $5.5 million. He'd given back to the game through his efforts with the Hook-a-Kid-on-Golf program, a project designed to make golf attractive to kids of all ages. "Our goals of having Little Leagues of golf is coming closer all the time," Murphy explained.

Though professional golf had been good to Murphy, his most favored memory was of the 1965 U.S. Amateur. "I'll never forget those days," he said with a grin. "Winning the championship was special. Amateur golf, too. One time on the way to an awards dinner in New York, I lost my luggage. When a bellman at the Waldorf Astoria asked me if I had any luggage, I handed him two *grocery* sacks full of underwear, socks, and golf shirts that I had just purchased. He looked at me like I was a homeless person."

Thirty years later, Murphy was anything but. The stock market aficionado's earnings secured a Lear jet and riches beyond his wildest expectations. But that didn't mean there weren't setbacks along the way. Besides the hand injury, Murphy learned early in the 1997 season that the lofts and lies on his Callaway clubs were bent. A visit to their testing center confirmed it, and corrections were made. "I had the worst tournament on the Senior Tour I ever had in Miami [Caribbean Classic]," Murph exclaimed. "My rhythm was just destroyed. When my finger got better and I could practice again and my clubs were in sync, my rhythm finally returned."

The opening-round 65 at the Toshiba had brightened Murphy's eyes, and he literally bounced to the tee for round two. He'd also led after round one in 1996, but forty minutes before teeing off for the second eighteen holes, he was informed his daughter Kimberly had given birth to his first grandchild. That brought back memories of the 1969 L.A. Open, where Murphy was leading on Saturday only to withdraw when informed wife Gail was giving birth to their first child. "My girls have bad timing," Murphy proclaimed.

This time the birth news produced a Saturday 70, which positioned Murphy one stroke back of David Graham heading into the final round. Lefty Bob Charles, who was dominating Super Senior play, was two strokes back, while Lee Trevino and Jay Sigel stood three behind.

Round three produced a battle for the ages. Several top players made runs at the lead, but by the end of regulation Bob Murphy and Jay Sigel, both at the top of their games with superb driving, excellent iron play, and clutch putting, were deadlocked at six-under-par 207.

The play-off between the two stocky competitors began at the eighteenth, where Murphy holed a pressure-packed seven-footer to tie Sigel's eighteen-inch tap-in birdie. Sixteen, seventeen, and eighteen were halved in match-play fashion as Murphy stood toe-to-toe with Sigel, whose outstanding amateur golf record made him one of the most accomplished match-play competitors in the game's history. And, arguably, the fifth greatest amateur player who ever lived, behind Bobby Jones, Jack Nicklaus, Tiger Woods, and Englishman John Ball, eight times British Amateur champion and the great-uncle of Errie Ball, still a fine teaching professional in Florida.

The sixteenth hole was again halved, as ESPN programmers in Bristol, Connecticut, shook their heads in disbelief. Their scheduled Stanley Cup hockey play-off game was interrupted several times as the two combatants tied seventeen and then headed for a record fourth time to the eighteenth. By then, Jay Sigel was joking that he'd played the holes so many times and had hit the ball in the same spot on each hole. "It reminds me of the film *Groundhog Day*," he retorted. Later, he added, "We'd gone around here so many times I was getting dizzy."

At the eighteenth, Murphy made a key putt that was a sign of things to come. With Sigel guaranteed a birdie from a foot, Murphy holed a testy fifteen-footer from just off the green. "It was the easiest putt I had all day," he said confidently. "I knew I simply had to make it. There was no other way."

When the putt dropped, Sigel shook his head, Gail Murphy nearly swallowed her tongue on national television, and ESPN, to its credit, stayed with the fight. When a return to sixteen resulted in pars, the round-faced Irishman and the smug, yet affable former stock-broker faced the par-three seventeenth. Murphy told himself he had to win now, for facing the long-hitting Sigel on the par-five eighteenth meant he might tempt fate one too many times.

Murphy's hopes were dashed when his pulled iron shot positioned the ball nearly eighty-five feet to the left and below the hole. Sigel was sidesaddled to the cup, twenty-five feet away. "I thought I had the clear advantage," he said later. "Murph's putt was tough, and even if he did two-putt, I thought I could make mine."

At that very moment, as Murphy stood over his ball, the tolling of the bell for Saint Paddy's day was just a few hours away. As the sun began sinking into the Pacific Ocean, just three Tiger Woods drives away, the majesty of the Irish spirit struck early when Murphy's lengthy putt snuck up the rise, around a curve, and dropped gently into the side of the hole. Sigel shook his head in disbelief, Gail Murphy's face nearly exploded, and *again* the ESPN programmers yelled, "Hooray." When Sigel's putt careened by the hole, Murphy's eyes lit up as if he'd just drunk a keg of green beer, and he tossed first his putter and then his Panama hat into the air for all the world to see.

The nine-hole play-off was the third longest in professional golf history, ranking behind Cary Middlecoff and Lloyd Mangrum's eleven-hole juggernaut at the 1949 Motor City Open (they were declared co-winners) and Jo Ann Prentice's ten-hole victory over Sandra Palmer in the 1972 Corpus Christi Open.

As for the marathon win, Murphy was full of piss and vinegar. "I wasn't weary at all," he said. "The adrenaline was flowing." Flowing just enough to can an eighty-footer!

5

THOUGH HE NEVER RECEIVED PROPER CREDIT, ARGENTINE LEGEND Roberto De Vicenzo started the Senior PGA Tour. To be certain, promoter Fred Raphael and the flamboyant golfer Jimmy Demaret conceived the idea of parading the legends of the game before golf fans, but it was the Argentine gaucho's superhuman play on April 30, 1979, in the Legends of Golf Tournament that is responsible for what became the Senior PGA Tour.

That year the fifty-six-year-old De Vicenzo, who should have won the 1968 Masters (he was penalized for signing an incorrect scorecard that caused him to exclaim, "Next time, I bring my lawyer to Augusta"), astonished the golf world and mesmerized NBC television audiences by birdieing seventeen and eighteen in the final round and then birdieing five of six play-off holes for him and partner Julius Boros in a dogfight finish with Art Wall and Tommy Bolt. Ratings for the match, the culmination of the second Legends of Golf Tournament, which carried over into NBC's prime-time schedule, were sky-high, and Raphael and Demaret knew that a Senior Tour concept for golfers over fifty could be a surefire success.

More than anything, the Legends concept provided a link between the PGA Tour for those golfers fifty and over who had "retired" from the Tour, the great players of the 1940s and 1950s, and the pioneers of the game. It was as if Old Tom Morris, Allen Robertson, Beatrix Hoyt, and Willie Anderson had passed the baton to Harry Vardon, James Braid, and J. W. Taylor, who, in turn, had handed it to Joyce Wethered, Walter Hagen, Bobby Jones, and Gene Sarazen. Those legends were the golf ancestors of Babe Zaharias, Sam Snead, Bobby Locke, Byron Nelson, and Patty Berg, who gave way to Cary Middlecoff, Gary Player, Billy Casper, Louise Suggs, and Peter Thomson. In turn, the baton was passed to Arnold Palmer, Mickey Wright, JoAnne Carner, Jack Nicklaus, Lee Trevino, and Raymond Floyd, who were succeeded by Tom Watson, Johnny Miller, Hale Irwin, Seve Ballesteros, Nancy Lopez, and Ben Crenshaw, all now either fifty, fast approaching it, or well past it. In the years to come, Nick Faldo, Greg

Norman, Ernie Els, and Tiger Woods would benefit from those champions' legacies.

While Raphael and Demaret knew they couldn't resurrect players like Vardon, Jones, or Walter Hagen or coax golfers like Hogan, Nelson, or Sarazen to compete, they could round up the best of the best of the over-fifty gang and provide them with a new opportunity to play against one another. That meant Sam Snead, Roberto De Vicenzo, Don January, Miller Barber, Kel Nagle, Gardner Dickinson, Art Wall, and the irrepressible Tommy Bolt could form the nucleus for a new golf venture to supplement the regular PGA Tour.

Until then, the only Major professional competition for senior citizens or seniors in general was the PGA Seniors' Championship, begun in 1937. Otherwise, the players over fifty either had stored away their golf clubs in the closet, played for fun with friends and family, or dabbled in a tournament here and there trying to keep a competitive edge.

In 1977, Raphael, the producer and director of *Shell's Wonderful World of Golf*, the benchmark for any televised event, had joined up with three-time Masters champion Jimmy Demaret. (Ben Hogan had said about Demaret, "He was the most underrated golfer in history. This man played shots I hadn't even dreamed of. I learned them, but it was Jimmy who showed them to me.") It was Demaret, the color commentator for the series, who conceived the idea for a better-ball format to feature the golden oldies of the game. The Legends of Golf premiered in 1978, and Raphael and Demaret produced a winner when Slammin' Sam Snead revived his magic play of old and birdied the final three holes, helping him and Gardner Dickinson beat the Australian duo of Peter Thomson and Kel Nagle.

De Vicenzo's heroics at Onion Creek Golf Club in Austin, Texas, followed the next year. "After I birdied seventeen and eighteen, Julie said, 'You play, you no need me,' " De Vicenzo recalled. Boros was right. De Vicenzo was hotter than a Palm Springs summer day, and his superb play continued when he birdied fifteen, the first play-off hole. And the sixteenth, and the seventeenth, all the while sparring with Tommy "Thunder" Bolt.

"We kept pointing fingers at each other, me and Tommy, having fun," Roberto explained. "At eighteen in the play-off, I had a long birdie putt. Julie was away, but he said, 'You putt. You kill 'em.' I drilled it, and then Bolt made his. He looked at me, smiled, and said, 'F___ you.' "

The first four holes of the play-off tied, the teams hit the fifteenth again. "I had a downhill break right to left," De Vicenzo remembered. "I didn't expect to make it, but I did. I glanced over at Tommy and said 'F___ you.' He had already made birdie and had even taken his glove off. His face was beet red, he was so pissed."

At sixteen, De Vicenzo nearly knocked himself out of the hole. "I hooked my drive on the dogleg to the left over into fifteen fairway, but I had a shot," said De Vicenzo, who won the very first U.S. Senior Open in 1980, at Winged Foot. "I hit a wedge a foot from the hole, and we won."

De Vicenzo's hot streak, Bolt's antics, and Julius Boros's easygoing manner aside, what the superb effort by all the legends proved was that the golf gladiators of old could still really play the game. It was one thing for the magical names to simply reappear, but with a huge television viewing audience, one of the largest ever for a golf telecast, viewing great golf, Raphael and Demaret and several of the senior players knew they would be receptive to tournaments featuring the legends of the game. And they wouldn't be stopped by comments such as the one uttered by Jack Nicklaus to Bob Goalby: "You're over the hill. Nobody will watch you." Wrong, Jack.

"That was really smart what Jimmy and Fred Raphael did," legendary teacher Bob Toski observed. "In the beginning, the guys hadn't played all that much. The four-ball format took all the pressure off. If they'd played badly, they'd have lost confidence and not come back. With the four-ball, they played more offensively than defensively, they could freewheel it, and it was like being reborn, like having a dream and then waking up to realize it was real."

The next step toward the evolution of a Senior Tour came in January 1980. Founding fathers Sam Snead, Gardner Dickinson, Bob Goalby, Don January, Dan Sikes, and Julius Boros met to discuss the concept for the proposed Tour. All agreed eligibility would be based on the all-time money list and that a pro-am format where amateurs could play with the heroes of the game would be the key to the Tour.

The fifty-man field was composed of the top twenty from the all-time victory list, twenty from the all-time money earnings list, six qualifiers, and four sponsor exemptions. Tournaments utilizing these figures were in effect at the Atlantic City International, where Don January won $20,000, and at Melbourne, Florida, where cigar-chomping Charlie Sifford beat the field.

"Don January's play in those first tournaments was important," said former Tour veteran Ernie Vossler. "Fans wanted to see good golf, and Don showed 'em he could still play like he had before. And that was damn good. He had more talent than anyone I ever saw. If he'd had the drive of guys like Arnold or the spirit of Hubert Green, there would have been no stopping him. But he was laid back, relaxed, a bit lazy, never planned ahead for anything. But he sure could play when the flag went up."

After the victories by January and Sifford, growing pains resulted with the format when Senior Tour hopefuls began appearing from across the globe. Seventy-six-year-old "Lighthorse Harry" Cooper, a Brit with thirty wins to his credit, ambled onto the tee, but it was clear that his game had rusted to the point where he couldn't beat his amateur partners. Sensing disaster, and insistent on keeping the level of play at a high level, the powers-that-be canceled use of the all-time victory list and designated the top thirty-six on the all-time money list as the qualification.

The 1981 Tour produced five more Senior Tour tournaments. Former Arkansas Razorback Miller Barber and his rickety outside-in swing joined the golf scene, and he became the first player to compete in an effective way on both the PGA and Senior PGA Tours. Wife Karen understood her husband's passion for the game well when she said, "The only thing that keeps Miller happy is to have a hotel key in his pocket."

Mr. X won the money title for the 1981 season with a little over $80,000, less than half the first-prize money for a single event in 1997. That year marked another turning point for the seniors when Arnold Palmer won the second U.S. Senior Open title. The realization that Palmer, at fifty-one, was indeed a senior, clicked with golf fans even though he had won the PGA Senior Championship in 1980, his first tournament.

"Arnie's win at the Senior Open in 1980 was significant," Bob Goalby recalled. "And, of course, his presence in any senior event gave us instant credibility."

In the early 1980s, the premiere event on the Senior Tour was the Legends. The year 1982 produced a classic when Sam Snead, who had invented a sidesaddle stance to cure his yips back in the 1960s, and his partner, Don January, cruised to a twelve-shot victory. When Sam holed putts that could only be measured with yardage figures on fifteen and sixteen, January chided him about being so far ahead. "Son," Snead replied, "you never know, somebody up ahead of us might be cheating."

Brian Henning, the former South African professional who was Commissioner Deane Beman's designee as the Senior Tour's first tournament director, remembered those early days well. "I was coordinating tournaments in South Africa before I came to the States.

There were fifteen events on what we called the Sunshine Tour. Gary Player, my brother Harold, Dale Hayes, Bobby Cole, John Bland, Hugh Baiocchi, all of them played. Then I persuaded a few Americans to come over, Lee Elder, Lee Trevino, Tom Weiskopf, Jim Albus, and others."

From that experience, Henning (nicknamed "Bruno"; his brother Harold is called "Horse") knew many of the players who would be eligible for the Senior Tour.

Early targets as hosts for tournaments were the cities that had no regular Tour events. "Reno, Lexington, Melbourne, Florida, Sun City, Arizona, where you couldn't build a home until you were a senior citizen, that's where I went. We needed a purse of $150,000. Didn't matter where we got it, but there were no sponsors then. We figured fifty golfers would play in two Pro-Ams. That's two hundred amateurs. Charge them $750 apiece and we're there."

The reception Henning received astonished even him. "I'd show them my list and they'd say, 'You mean Snead, Palmer, Boros, all those guys will come here? You mean Arnold Palmer will play?' Their eyes lit up when I said, 'Yes.' "

Ironically, television played a minor part in the Senior Tour's early success since the events weren't telecast the first few years. The big boost came when corporate America and ESPN discovered the Senior Tour in 1987. When Mazda partially funded production costs for the telecasts and provided a $300,000 players' bonus pool, everything changed.

Brian Henning realized what they were peddling was entertainment. "We had the greatest names in the game. Gary Player had come out in 1985, and Palmer's name was magic. Amateurs loved to play with their heroes, and the professionals couldn't have been more accommodating. I can remember Sam Snead and Lionel Hebert getting up on stage and playing the trumpet. And the stories they'd tell, we'd all end up crying they were so funny."

The year 1987 marked the evolution of the Super Seniors over-sixty competition and use of the advanced electric scoreboard. Format changes were made as well, with scores for the professionals in Pro-Am competition no longer being counted in the actual tournament. Also, the field was expanded to seventy-two players.

By 1988, the Senior Tour had grown to thirty events, something no one had thought possible. "We never had any idea that would happen," Don January recalled. "We just wanted a few events where the old guys could compete with friends."

The Senior Tour's entry into the 1990s was marked by the

reunion of Arnold Palmer, Gary Player, Jack Nicklaus, and Lee Trevino. Trevino found over-fifty golf to his liking and became the Senior Tour's first million-dollar man. The electric names were soon joined by a new breed of senior players, longtime club professionals such as Jim Albus, Larry Laoretti, Larry Gilbert, and a driving-range owner named Tom Wargo, whom country club golfers and public course amateurs could relate to. Bob Murphy, Jim Colbert, and Hale Irwin provided the spark in the mid-1990s as the Senior Tour continued its popularity. "We've got a great thing going," Brian Henning remarked. "And it's only going to get better."

6

THE ELDERLY MAN IN THE MILKY-BROWN STRAW HAT STOOD IN THE middle of the deep bunker. For nearly an hour, he had hit ball after ball in frustration in the near one-hundred-degree heat. Some never left the sandy surface; others were skulled across the practice green into heavy rough bordering the Arnold Palmer Course at PGA West in Palm Springs, California.

Exasperated, the eighty-four-year-old golfer peered up toward the sky as if pleading for divine intervention. Instead he heard the shrill words of his fifty-seven-year-old nephew, eleven times a winner on the PGA and Senior PGA Tour. "Your left side," the younger professional barked with a noticeable southern drawl, "your left side's breaking down."

"I *know* that," the older golfer replied. "Tell me how to fix it."

"I'm *trying* to explain," the nephew snorted, his tone echoing little reverence for an uncle who won seven Majors and more golf professional tournaments (dating back to 1936) than any player in the history of the PGA Tour.

Stepping into the bunker, the nephew demonstrated his point. "When the left side collapses, you lose your acceleration. Stay behind the ball," he explained.

The old man wiped his brow and glared at his nephew, who was never one to listen when his uncle tried to help him. "When I offer advice to my nephew," he'd said, "I put cotton in his ears in hopes it doesn't fly through his brain."

The two stubborn relatives continued to bark at each other as the legendary player resumed his position in the bunker. Four more practice shots produced two skulls, a flopper that went less than three feet, and another skull. The nephew, who once remarked, "With a name like Snead, you need to be able to play golf," shook his head, rose from his crouch, and headed toward the first tee mumbling to himself.

A half hour later, the sun having drenched his beige golf shirt, the old master continued to practice. By the time he handed his well-worn wedge to his caddie, Samuel Jackson Snead had hit six superb shots in a row.

The West Virginian's love for the game of golf was never more apparent than on that bright sunny day in 1997. Despite playing a limited schedule, Snead relished practicing his skills, ones honed during his sixty-one years as a professional golfer. His superb play and longevity earned him a position as the most revered man ever to have played the sport. Arnold Palmer certainly was the most popular, but no one enjoyed the enormous respect fellow professionals had for the man with the hoodwink smile.

Ernie Vossler believed he knew why. "Sam was always a kid," Vossler recalled. "Always the youngster. Acted like a child and people could relate to that. He wasn't cold-blooded like Hogan or Nicklaus."

Sam Snead was born on May 27, 1912, seventy-seven days before Ben Hogan. That year Woodrow Wilson was elected president, Jim Thorpe was named outstanding athlete at the Olympic Games, and C. K. Jung published *The Theory of Psychoanalysis*.

Jung would have had a field day with Snead. Born in the backwoods of West Virginia, he took to golf like most kids took to cotton candy. Introduced to the sport at an early age, Snead swung a golf club like the Good Lord Himself had given him lessons. By age ten, he was beating everyone within shouting distance, even when he played shoeless with a stick picked up in the woods.

Snead grew up to be a tall, willowy gent with an apple-cheek face and a southern drawl that drew words out as if they had never-ending syllables. His first professional victory was the 1936 West Virginia Closed Pro Tournament. He then won the Oakland Open in 1937, Snead's first year on the Tour.

For the next *five* decades, Snead played superbly. At one time, his career Tour victory count was up to eighty-seven. When officials deleted six wins from the record books, Sam retorted, "If they keep subtracting my wins, Nicklaus is going to go by me without even winning again."

While the victories were important, it was Snead's swing that will live for the ages. The great amateur Bill Hyndman said Snead's pass at the ball was "so good it was hard to believe. A true classic. He could hit a one iron straighter than I could hit an eight."

Snead said of the swing, "I try to feel oily."

Watching Sam hit practice balls, one writer said, "was like seeing a fish practice swimming."

"Sam Snead, I would imagine," Jack Nicklaus observed, "has

ripped out more long, straight drives and covered the pin with more approaches than any other golfer in the game's long history."

Snead stories were legendary. Before the first round of the 1956 U.S. Open, the one Major tournament that eluded him, Snead was asked by Merrell Whittlesey of *The Washington Post* his prediction of the winning score. "I'll take 280," Sam bellowed, "sit in the clubhouse, eat hot dogs, drink Coke, and fart." Three years earlier, Snead had entered the final round of the Open just one behind Ben Hogan, but a 76 doused his chances. Asked by Whittlesey, "Were you tight?" Sam responded, "Tight? I was so tight you couldn't a drove a flax seed up my ass with a knot maul."

"Sneadisms" stretch from one end of the earth to the other. Asked why he never bought anyone a drink, Sam replied: "Why should I help someone carry on a bad habit?" On comparing players of different eras: "How about a team of Hogan, Demaret, Nelson, Mangrum, and me. Who do you suppose could beat us?" Asked if he remembered any special shot more than another: "One time in Chattanooga, I hit a real pretty iron to the green. Halfway up in the air, it hit a bobwhite and knocked it to the ground, dead. The ball stopped a foot from the hole and I made two birdies on one hole." On his having a bad right eye: "Everything is wiggly and taller." Regarding his putting woes, he once quipped, "It's so bad I could putt off a tabletop and still leave the ball halfway down the leg."

When Sam Snead hit fifty in 1962, the Senior Tour was a decade and a half away. And he was still a bona fide contender on the regular Tour, winning the 1965 Greensboro Open at age fifty-two years and ten months to become the oldest champion in PGA Tour history. The largest purse he ever won: $28,000!

In 1963, Snead won the first of six PGA Seniors' Championships. He added four World Seniors' titles as well. At an exhibition prior to the Legends, he fired eight pars and a birdie, proving the sweet swinger could still play the game.

"My golf game comes and goes," he explained to a bevy of reporters yearning for his every word. "Problem is, I can't find anyone to play with. All my pigeons are dead. They stay away from my bailiwick."

Later in the year, at his eighty-fifth birthday celebration, Snead was asked to rate himself among the great golfers in the history of the game. "I come first, then Jack Nicklaus," Snead roared. "Then Ben Hogan and Arnold Palmer fought for third." Asked about Tiger Woods, Snead bellowed, "I like him. What he wants to do is win. He's like me that way. I wanted to win. I wanted to kill 'em all."

Though Snead's finest playing days were behind him, fellow professionals still watched him with awe. At the Legends, every player of stature, including Gary Player, Lee Trevino, John Bland, Dave Stockton, Jim Colbert, Don January, and Billy Casper, made it a point to pay their respects, shake Sam's hand. Then they stood there and shook their heads as he unwound that beautiful flowing perfect golf swing that every one of them envied.

Brian Henning watched Sam hit a few drivers and then remarked, "Isn't that the prettiest thing you've ever seen?"

Gary Player, standing nearby, added, "You know, Sam, if you'd just practice a little, you could really be good."

Sam Snead and every other American professional were descendants of John Shippen, the first American-born golf professional. While Charlie Sifford, Lee Elder, and other African-American golfers struggled with racial prejudice when they began playing the game, Shippen, the son of a black Presbyterian minister, encountered none when he entered the 1896 U.S. Open. Instead, a group of Scottish golfers objected to his competing, but Theodore Havemeyer, first president of the USGA, stood up for the seventeen-year-old Shippen, telling them in effect, "If Shippen doesn't play, you don't play." He competed, shooting 78 and an 81 that included an eleven.

John Shippen later became the head professional at Shady Rest in Scotch Plains, New Jersey, the first African-American club. "Shipp could do with a golf ball what Ella Fitzerald could do with a lyric," Earl Nettingham, a club member, told *Golf Digest*. "He was John Every Man; he ran the golf shop, he cut the greens, he was the caddie master."

John Shippen died in 1968 at age eighty-nine. He had grown up on the Shinnecock Reservation and helped build the original Shinnecock Hills Course in 1893. The first Open he competed in was played there, and every professional who followed in his footsteps owed him a debt of gratitude. Most, especially the younger players on the PGA Tour, didn't even know he existed.

But Sam Snead did. "John Shippen was the first," he recalled. "It all goes back to him."

At the 1997 Legends, Snead and his partner, Harvie Ward, winner of back-to-back U.S. Amateur Championships in 1955 and 1956, were joined by seven other four-ball teams.

Though not contenders, two of the more compelling names in the Legends field were Jack Fleck and Tommy Bolt. It had been forty-two years since Fleck beat Ben Hogan in a play-off for the 1955 U.S. Open crown at the Olympic Club in San Francisco, but in his mind he still carried the unfair stigma of being an unpopular champion.

"Because I was unheard of and kept Hogan from winning his fifth Open, my win was pooh-poohed all those years," Fleck said while hitting balls on the practice tee. "It was like I'd beaten God or something."

Tommy Bolt was also a U.S. Open winner, but became better known for his antics on the golf course. "Terrible," who beat Gary Player (then a rookie on the Tour) in the 1958 Open, was still lively and as quotable as ever at seventy-nine.

"Those stories about me being a roustabout are only ten percent true," the irascible Bolt, known to have owned over five hundred hats, offered. "I haven't lived long enough for all those stories to be true." This came from a man who wore hot-pink shoes and polka-dot pants and who favored color combinations like luscious lavender, lemon yellow, and a red brighter than a fire engine. When someone had the audacity to compare him with Doug Sanders, later to sport similar clothing, Bolt became indignant. "[Sanders] looked like a jukebox," he bellowed. "Even his feet. I, on the other hand, was simply being fashionable."

Bolt was among the most quoted golfers of his time. During a tournament at Hartford, PGA Tour Commissioner Joe Dey, a gentle-man with an air of dignity about him, heard that Bolt was on the first tee farting loud enough for all to hear. Dey approached Tommy and asked, "Are you passing gas?" Bolt stood stone-faced and replied, "Hell, everyone's trying to take all the color out of the game."

Though Bolt was a superb player for many years, he became known as the top club thrower in the history of the game. "Unfair," he spouted with a southern drawl while holding court with several on-lookers at the practice tee. "Sam Snead threw a lot more clubs than I ever did. Hell, he broke more putters than I broke clubs."

Jimmy Demaret disagreed, saying, "Tommy Bolt's putter has had more airtime than Charles Lindbergh."

At the Legends, Bolt decided another legend needed a bit of tu-toring. While sauntering by the practice tee, he noticed the great teacher Bob Toski holding court. "Your right hand is coming off," Bolt barked. Toski swung and hit a beauty. "That's it," Bolt com-mented. "Did I follow instructions?" Toski asked. "That's the way you used to swing forty years ago," Bolt offered. "Send me a bill," Toski laughed as Bolt continued by. "Maestro just got a lesson," summed up an observer.

Besides the presence of Snead, Fleck, Bolt, and Runyan, the remainder of the field for the 1997 Legends sparkled with magic. Bolt was paired with Fleck. Also competing were Roberto De Vicenzo; Mike Souchak, still a formidable player at age seventy; Bob Toski; George Bayer, the gentle giant, first of the long hitters from Bremerton, Washington, whose crew cut reminded Tour media official Dave Senko of television personality George Gobel; and Billy Casper, whose sizable paunch didn't prevent a sweet swing at age sixty-five. As Billy had put it, "Like a lot of fellows around here, I have a furniture problem. My chest has fallen into my drawers."

When Casper once blamed a poor round on having eaten pork sausage instead of buffalo meat for lunch, Miller Barber had quipped, "Yeah, pork sausage and a bunch of bogies will make anyone sick."

All these men were links to the past—to the great days when golf was more of a pure sport without all the fancy advances in technology. A time when the Great Big Bertha driver and the sixty-degree wedge were still years away.

Watching the legendary names of old on the practice tee was a treat, but onlookers cringed and had to look away when some hit shots reserved for twenty-five handicappers. Johnny Pott kept hitting one shot right, one shot left, causing him to remark, "I'm hitting the ball like a windshield wiper." Charlie Sifford, who admitted he hadn't practiced much over the winter months, hit several worm burners before getting the ball airborne. George Bayer could still hit the ball long, but on one occasion his club barely brushed it, hitting a missile dead right that sent a caddie in the practice-tee bunker scurrying for cover.

Defending champions Lee Trevino and Mike Hill headed the list of the current-day Legends. Chief challenges were expected to come from David Graham and Tony Jacklin, Bob Murphy and Jim Colbert, Hubert Green and Gil Morgan, and international stars John Bland and Graham Marsh.

For Marsh, affectionately known as "Swampy," the Legends was the first tournament after, as he put it, "three weeks off." Not vacation, mind you, but a whirlwind tour of golf courses he was designing in such diverse areas as Asia and northern Minnesota.

Whatever jet lag Marsh had didn't prevent him from playing like a champion in the first round. His ball produced three birdies while Bland, Rookie of the Year on the 1996 Senior Tour with four wins and over $1.5 million in earnings, threw four birdies and an eagle at the field. Their 63 was matched by a couple of oldsters, Gene Littler and Don January, who told the reporters he liked the better-ball format.

"If I happen to hit someone's house, I know Gene will be there," January said.

Littler wasn't so sure. He believed his game had never been the same since surgery for a broken arm in the mid-1980s. "They put a steel plate with nine screws in it," he explained, "and that absolutely destroyed my touch and with it my short game. I ended up with the chippin' yips."

Marsh and Bland took the second-round lead with a 64. Trailing them by one were Green/Morgan and Gibby Gilbert/J. C. Snead. Snead was fighting his game as usual, in addition to shouldering the burden of being Sam's nephew. "Comparisons have always been made, always will," J.C. lamented. "I've learned to live with that. To live with being compared with a legend. Right now though, I'm playing so bad I'm thinking about getting half drunk and see what happens."

Neither J.C.'s game nor his demeanor improved, and he and Gilbert faltered on Saturday. The final round at the Legends turned out to be a dogfight. Tour rookie Green and sophomore Morgan provided the chief opposition, but Littler, who had won the U.S. Open in 1961, and January, victorious in the PGA Championship in 1967, hung close. Those teams were aided by a strange turn of events at the fifth hole, where Bland and Marsh acted like two duffers from Dubuque. Two birdies on the get-go holes threatened to make them walkaway winners, but then they ambled up to the tee at the water-laden 207-yard par-three.

Bland and his caddie, brother Roy, decided on a two iron from a new set of Taylor Mades that had been delivered to Bland before the tournament—a club without the company insignia imbedded on the club face. That change was made because Bland believed the flight of the ball was altered by the imprint. He'd noticed a more reliable flight pattern the instant he'd tried the new clubs. Settling that issue had given him a bright outlook on the game, and he'd played his best golf in months during the first two rounds. Superb shots had continued during the first four holes of the fourth round, but then disaster struck. A dour swing produced an awful-looking shot that went kerplunk.

"Never mind," thought Graham Marsh. "I'll be there for you." He also chose a two iron, took a glance at the green, drew back the club, and, presto, hit a shot he later called "criminal." It veered to the left and then plopped in the drink.

The gallery gasp matched those of Bland and Marsh. Instead of playing like leaders charging toward a championship, they had hit shots like two high handicappers playing in the fifth flight of the public course four-ball.

By hole's end, a belligerent double-bogey five was penciled in on their scorecard. Bland/Marsh had hit the skids. Green and Morgan took the lead at 19 under.

Creeping into contention were Al Geiberger, "Mr. 59," assisted by adopted son/caddie Brent (the PGA Tour player), and Dave Stockton, who had hosted a pro-am to benefit the Bighorn Institute, a pet project preserving the longevity of bighorn sheep.

Geiberger and Stockton were a formidable team, as anyone who had watched the *CBS Golf Classic* in the 1960s knew. They were unbeaten in three consecutive years of competition against the best the world had to offer, despite having personalities that were poles apart. Stockton was the intense one, grinding away, looking as if he were down to his last penny and there was a nickel that still could be won. That contrasted with Geiberger, the calm and collected one, who always seemed as if he were playing a friendly game of checkers instead of competing for championships.

While most of the professionals had followed the yellow brick road, Geiberger had walked a crooked one filled with incredible ups and dastardly downs. The kindly California native, dubbed "Skippy" for his passion for the peanut butter sandwiches he munched during golf rounds, had ridden the roller-coaster of life, one that included eleven PGA victories, his famous 59, two failed marriages, one that ruined him financially, health problems that would have cut down a mere mortal, and the terrible loss of a son through a freak accident. Through it all, "Berger," as he was also known, had persevered, exhibiting a mettle that earned him the respect of everyone who crossed his path.

Geiberger's golf career began when his parents introduced him to the game at age five. Seventeen years later, he turned professional. Seven years after that, he possessed a coveted Major championship, the 1966 PGA Championship at Firestone Country Club.

Though Geiberger's career was dotted with victories, his image was frozen on June 10, 1977. That day he produced history of the proportions of Don Larsen's perfect World Series game, Roger Bannister's under-four-minute mile, and Wilt Chamberlain's 100-point game.

The site was the Colonial Country Club in Memphis, Tennessee; the tournament the Danny Thomas Memphis Classic. In the first round, with the temperature set at a sultry 103 degrees, the tall, willowy Geiberger jumped out of the gate on the back nine, which he played first, with 30. This included six birdies and three pars. He then eagled number one, birdied two and three, and stood ten under on the par-72 course with six holes to play. Two birdies at six and seven brought him to the brink of destiny as he approached the eighteenth hole. While seven golfers, including Sam Snead, had shot 60, no one had plunged into the fifties.

At his eighteenth hole, the normally conservative Geiberger decided to go for broke. "After my birdie at the sixth hole, people began to shout, 'Fifty-nine, fifty-nine, fifty-nine,'" Geiberger recalled. "By the eighth the crowd had grown; even some of my fellow professionals had come out. On the ninth, I hit a golf shot I would never have hit normally, a drive over a bunker that I had never carried before. It was like I was so pumped up, I could do anything I wanted to."

The humongous drive left Geiberger with less than 130 yards to the green. "I could have hit a hard pitching wedge, that's what you're supposed to do under those circumstances, play all out, but I decided on a nine iron, against my caddie's advice. I hit it flush to about ten feet. Jerry McGee and Dave Stockton were trying to stay out of the way. I remember Jerry rolled his putt to about four feet, and I asked him if he wanted to go ahead and finish, what with the crowd and all. But he didn't, and so I read the putt and got ready."

The next moments seemed to take forever. "I thought the grain came into me, and I read the putt to move left to right. I was afraid I would leave the putt short, so I smacked it, though I don't really remember too well, I was so nervous. Anyway, the ball just leaped off the club face, and darted into the hole slam dunk, like a basketball shot." At precisely that moment, "Mr. 59" was born.

"Berger came as close to getting excited as I ever saw him," Stockton, who kept the scorecard that fateful day and shot 76, *seventeen* shots higher than Geiberger, said. "He got his fist halfway clenched."

Geiberger's feat made him famous around the world. He won that tournament, and life was grand. Then the bottom fell out. Two marriages failed, his bank account dwindled to nearly nothing, and continued health problems threatened to destroy his golf career. Geiberger wondered if things could get worse, and then they did.

In 1985, Geiberger had found a new partner in life, Carolyn Springs. A year later, son Matthew was born, but in 1988, one year after Al had won three times on the Senior Tour, the toddler wandered away from the Geiberger home, fell into an unfenced wading pool, and drowned. "It was so hard," Geiberger lamented. "Matthew was very special. He touched so many people."

Feelings of guilt, unnecessary due to the freakiness of the accident, pervaded the Geiberger household and Al put up his clubs and took a month off. Then he returned to the Senior Tour, intent on playing in

Matthew's memory. "It took three years for me to win again," Al said. "But tragedies like that make you stronger, and you just have to keep going."

And Al did. Five more victories came in the 1990s, although his progress was hampered some in 1992, when he broke his big toe tripping over a blown-up Teenage Mutant Ninja Turtle Blimp belonging to son Allen, Jr. "You ever try to blow one of those up?" he chortled. "Liked to died trying and then tripped over it."

"Life is good though," he'd said early in the year. "I'm healthy and ready to play well. And I'll always have that fifty-nine."

At the Legends, Geiberger and Stockton forged a one-shot lead by the end of the tenth hole, but then faded in the final few holes when Geiberger's iron play was erratic and Stockton's magic wand on the greens was anything but magic.

When Morgan birdied the eleventh, he and Green had tied Geiberger/Stockton for the lead. Meanwhile, Bland and Marsh were attempting to regroup. Bland, a jolly gent with a ready wit, put things in perspective: "As we were walking to the next tee [after the double bogey], I said to Graham, 'We've made two birdies and we've dropped two shots, so we're back where we began. Now, we've got to start all over again.'"

If one shot decided the tournament, it came at the fourteenth. Bland had steadied the team with a critical birdie at the par-five eleventh and a nasty ten-foot curler for par at thirteen, but Marsh hit the par-five fourteenth in two and faced an eighteen-footer for an eagle.

With Green and Morgan looking on, the Aussie surveyed the putt he knew was makable. "I'd been in that same spot in the first round," Marsh recalled later. "John gave it a look-see, but I was confident I knew the line."

That settled in his mind, Graham crouched over the putt. His stroke was true, and the ball never wavered. The eagle catapulted the team back into the lead, and when Marsh followed with birdies at fifteen and sixteen, the game was over.

"That broke our backs," Green said. "We couldn't keep up. And Graham made birdies from outside where we were putting from." Hubert's quote didn't mean he hadn't fought until the very last putt dropped.

"If players like J. C. Snead and a few others had the spirit of the game in them like Hubie does," Ernie Vossler, mentor to Morgan, said, "they'd have won a lot more golf tournaments."

Despite Green's fire, the day belonged to John Bland and Graham Marsh, champions of the Legends. Ever humble, they acknowledged that their professional record didn't warrant the use of that term beside their names. "We know who we are," Bland said. "We're good players, but the real legends are guys like Jack, Arnold, and Sam Snead. Graham and I may have won the tournament, but my biggest thrill was watching Sam Snead hit balls on the practice tee."

7

WALKING OFF THE NINTH GREEN ON SUNDAY IN THE FINAL ROUND OF the 1997 Tradition, the Senior PGA Tour's first "Major" of the year, Dr. Gil Morgan held a six-stroke lead over the field. Only Isao Aoki and Arizona homeboy John Jacobs were within shouting distance. To catch the soft-spoken, shy Oklahoma optometrist, they needed to steal his contact lenses, kidnap his wife and children, and hold them hostage until Gil made five straight double bogeys.

The Tradition had become an overwhelming success on the Senior Tour within four years of its inception in 1989. The tournament instantly became a Major on the Tour by dedicating play to the great traditions of the game. Each year marked a gathering of the greats of golf, the over-fifty players with a Major championship to their credit on either the PGA or Senior PGA Tour. In 1997, invitations were accorded a vast array of players, including ninety-five-year-old Gene Sarazen; eighty-eight-year-old PGA champion Paul Runyan, aka "Little Poison"; Sam Snead, still slammin' away at age eighty-four; Jack Fleck, seventy-five, who set the golf world on its ear when he deprived Ben Hogan of a fifth U.S. Open title in 1955; and Terrible Tommy Bolt, the 1958 U.S. Open winner, rambunctious as ever at age seventy-nine.

Together the eighty-eight honorees had won an astounding *210* Major golf championships. That number included the 1996 Tradition victory by Jack Nicklaus, who was bidding in 1997 to become a five-time winner of the event. Jack Nicklaus added to his list of Major championships with a victory in the 1990 Tradition (his first since the miracle win in the 1986 Masters), when he birdied three out of the last five holes to beat Player by four shots. A forty-foot chip-in eagle on eighteen during Saturday's round propelled the Golden Bear into the lead, and birdies on three of the final five holes on Sunday cemented the victory in his first attempt at Senior Tour competition.

Though Nicklaus's propensity to portray Lazarus in Major tournaments and become a factor for the championship on Sunday was unmatched throughout his career, the 1991 Tradition provided a spectacular triumph unlike any before it. *Twelve* shots behind thirty-six-hole leader Phil Rodgers, Nicklaus bounded into contention with a third-round 66. A ninety-four-foot birdie putt at the fourth hole in the final round catapulted him to a 67, and he waltzed into the victory circle.

The 1992 Tradition provided a classic Jack Nicklaus/Lee Trevino confrontation reminiscent of their duel in the play-off for the 1971 U.S. Open title. The only thing missing was the rubber snake Trevino hurled at Jack prior to their showdown at vaunted Merion. Lee birdied fifteen and seventeen, sealing a one-stroke victory over Nicklaus when Jack's attempt at birdie at eighteen gently slid by.

The 1993 and 1994 Traditions produced champions in Tom Shaw and Raymond Floyd, but 1995 and 1996 saw Nicklaus back on top of the exclusive field. The four Tradition victories for Nicklaus had come at Desert Mountains, the resort community located outside Carefree, Arizona, east of Phoenix. Jack's ability to hit high left-to-right floating shots on the course he designed provided a distinct advantage for him, but seventy-seven other competitors, including Irwin and Dr. Gil Morgan, who was dominating the 1997 Tradition, stood determined to prevent Jack from "three-peating."

Scottsdale, Arizona, in the springtime. Eighty-degree temperatures, a balmy breeze flowing out of the west. Tourists flock to the desert water holes, traipsing around swimming pools in next to nothing, burning themselves silly. Sunscreen sales reach an all-time high.

Wrong! When the Senior PGA Tour brought its show to the home state of the NCAA basketball champion Arizona Wildcats, Mother Nature decided the golfers needed to add stocking caps, wool mittens, and parkas to their wardrobes. Forget the sunscreen, pull out the Ben-Gay for the aches and pains.

Being senior citizens made many contestants wish they had retired to a life of leisure in a tropical climate. The frigid weather caused the wildlife in the area, which included the mountain lion, desert tortoise, king snake, black-tailed jackrabbit, red-tailed hawk, and Great Plains toad, to scamper for cover.

One Tour veteran dubbed the event "The Alaska Open." Early first-round competitors were greeted with thirty-seven-degree temperatures. Those who laughed and counted their blessings that they had a late tee time were also greeted with thirty-seven-degree temperatures. The thermometer never rose above forty-five degrees that day, and a cold rain caused skin-and-bones players like American Express champion Bud Allin, who said he had no chance "because on this course you have to hit the ball long and high and I hit it short and low," to strike the ball eighty-one times.

Friday's second round produced similar weather. George Archer, his bulbous nose bright red from the cold, looked like a tall, blue icicle all bundled up in stocking cap and rain suit. Bob Murphy chose an outfit that included a wrap-around white beach towel that he clutched to his torso like a huge Band-Aid. Bobby Nichols swore his titanium hips needed a good lube job, and even fitness nut Gary Player was bundled up so much that he looked as if he actually had a paunch. Jack Nicklaus not only required a back rub from his caddie but did so many stretching exercises he looked as if he were in a morning aerobics class.

One former player who thought the over-fifty gang was worrying too much about the weather was CBS television announcer Peter Allis. "This is a midsummer's day back home in Scotland," he observed. "The dogs would be out romping about, and the elderly little ladies would be out having tea."

If anything, Saturday's third round was worse. As players jockeyed for position on "moving day," nobody could. Instead, they batted away the raindrops and tried to keep warm, hopeful they could catch a birdie or two and not pneumonia.

The cold conditions at the Jack Nicklaus–designed Desert Mountain Cochise Course near Phoenix virtually eliminated anyone from contention in the Senior Tour's first Major who wasn't (a) long off the tee, (b) packed with enough blubber to withstand the frigid temperatures, and (c) stricken with any type of physical ailment not workable in sub-fifty-degree weather. That meant players such as Jim Colbert, nursing a painful pulled muscle in his back, and Bob Murphy, whose arthritic condition made certain body parts unable to function without sufficient sunshine, were never in contention.

Colbert was also affected by personal problems off the course. His father had taken ill and later had to be placed in a nursing home. Jim's brother was then diagnosed with prostate cancer. His beloved wife, Marcia, was forced to have facial surgery when cancerous cells were discovered. If that weren't enough, Colbert's longtime caddie, Willie Miller, was missing, having remained in North Carolina to recover from the effects of medication taken after the sudden death of his sister. No wonder the best player on the Senior Tour two years running missed eleven putts under four feet, something unheard of for the gritty guy who completed the tournament when most others would have withdrawn. "Where I come from, we were taught to finish what we started," Colbert explained.

Contenders who emerged in the first three rounds included Gil Morgan, who easily won the best-dressed award by wearing a bright-red stocking cap with a white fuzzy ball on top; John Jacobs, the tall, likable veteran of the Asian Tour and champion of more long-driving contests than anyone since "Titanic" Thompson; and Isao Aoki, who broke every rule that said a slight golfer who hit the ball medium length couldn't contend in arctic conditions. They were joined by Terry Dill, known as "Space Cadet," the Tour's certified flake, who had carved out rounds of 67-67-71 to trail Morgan by six. That was one less than Jacobs and Aoki, who had to hope for a miracle screwup by the golfing doctor from the Oklahoma plains, who led by six after fifty-four holes.

Dill's third round had been marked by an incident that was indicative of the wacky week in the desert and, for that matter, in golf itself. What Dill added to the equation was a near birdie recorded from the depths of a swimming pool. Yes, that's right, don't change your dial. At the par-five fifteenth hole, the former Texas lawyer, who found himself in trouble with Senior PGA Tour officials when he called The Tradition "just another tournament" during a press conference, launched one of his prestigious drives with his fishing pole–sized driver into a swimming pool that bordered the golf course. "I was aiming down the right side trying to hit a hard hook and instead hit what I call a pop-up," Dill recalled. "The ball went high left, and I was afraid it was out of bounds."

Normally, that meant two shots and re-tee, but unlike 99 percent of the golf courses in America, Desert Mountain had no out-of-bounds. So Dill traipsed past the cactus and other desert shrubbery, all the while on the lookout for rattlesnakes that infiltrate the area, toward the houses of Desert Mountain residents who had escaped to Arizona seeking privacy only to have a national television audience inspecting their floor plan.

Dill and company searched in vain for his ball, only to discover that it had plopped into a swimming pool. Two spectators witnessed the dunking, as did ABC's roving commentator Bob Rosburg. Armed with that information, Dill entered the home of the already bedeviled residents and walked through their living room like an unwanted guest at tea time.

Later Dill described the situation during one of the most unusual Q & A's ever held in the Senior Tour press room.

Dave Senko (PGA Tour): So you went through their house?
Dill: Through the middle of the house, living room, den—nice house. Just a beautiful house.

Senko: Did you have coffee while you were in the house?

Dill: No, we couldn't do it. (Said in a serious manner—he didn't get the joke.)

Senko: Were they watching the tournament?

Dill: I didn't see their TV on.

Senko: Did they have carpet or just wood floors?

Dill: She had both.

Senko: But you had soft spikes?

Dill: Yes, the house was a southwestern design. Very nice. Kind of like you would see in Santa Fe.

Senko (rolling his eyes): Thanks, Terry.

Based on the sighting by the residents and Rosburg, Dill and caddie surveyed the pool. SuΩre enough, there was a golf ball positioned by the drain. Since everyone swore no golf balls had been dunked in the pool during the prior twenty-four hours, Tour officials bought the explanation and pronounced the submerged ball as Dill's. That left two choices. Dill could call for fins and snorkel and dive into the deep end to give the ball a whack or take a drop with no penalty. Despite being deaf in one ear, Dill heard the choices clearly and, using his law school logic, decided on the latter.

Deciding where the drop should occur took a bit of doing, but after depositing the ball on the sandy soil, he managed to avoid the prickly needles of a nearby cactus and spanked a shiny new ball back onto the fairway with a seven iron. "The pool was called an intervention," Dill said quite proudly, using a big word he probably charged fifty bucks for during his days as a lawyer. "I was intervened with, so I got the drop," he said. "One of the luckiest things I've ever had happen to me."

From his position in the fairway, Dill knocked a wedge shot to within twelve feet of the pin. Playing partner John Jacobs, no stranger to lunacy, sauntered over and said, "I'm trying to catch Gil and all that, but make that damn putt," realizing that a birdie from a swimming pool wasn't an everyday occurrence. Unfortunately, Dill yanked the putt, settled for a routine five, and headed to the next tee. "I've seen it all now," Morgan quipped later, tugging at his red stocking cap as he entered the press room yelling, "Ho, ho, ho."

By the end of that most unusual third round, the good doctor was in command. Lee Trevino, who seemed chipper despite the weather, could manage but two 74s and a 71 and was far back. Hale Irwin, the prohibitive favorite, who had treated fans to a display on how to shank a golf ball properly on the practice tee before the first round, found himself hitting too many errant shots during the tournament, firing a so-so 72-71-69 that left him thirteen shots behind leader Gil Morgan.

David Graham was expected to challenge after posting a second 1997 win at the Southwestern Bell Dominion a week before The Tradition when a final-hole eagle snatched victory away from John Jacobs. At that tournament, Texan Robert Landers, leader of the "Moo Crew" fan club, made an appearance, though noticeably absent were the hundreds of die-hard fans wearing black-and-white-spotted Moo Crew hats who followed the popular Landers when he burst onto the Tour in 1995.

That year ABC television was so taken with Landers's leap from practicing his golf game in a cow pasture trying to miss the curious animals to the Senior Tour that it broke away from coverage of the O. J. Simpson trial to cover his first putt on the Tour. Landers's stories about hitting balls into his homemade bunkers when the cows weren't lounging in them and dodging steaming cow patties while picking up practice balls made front-page stories, and he became the Walter Mitty of the sports world.

But Landers's golf scores didn't match his zest for the game, and putting woes prevented him from winning enough money to make the grade on the 1997 Tour. When a Q-School attempt went awry, Landers was forced to return to his lovable cows and practice his trade in front of them instead of a national television audience.

When officials at the Southwestern Bell Dominion offered him a sponsor's exemption, he grabbed it. Wearing his trademark tennis shoes, and with his ever-faithful wife, Freddie, carrying a bag full of clubs that had seen better days, Landers shot 73-71-74, tied for thirty-first, and won $5,520.

Landers went home to his cow pasture while Dominion winner David Graham prepared for The Tradition. He wasn't a factor, however, posting rounds of 72-74-71. Chi Chi Rodriguez, thrilling fans during a pretournament clinic with golf ball tricks, was far down the leader board after a ghastly 78 in the third round. "My bones are frozen," Chi Chi quipped. "I'm heading for the sunlamp."

When Sunday arrived, the tournament became Gil Morgan's to win or lose. The prayers of the Arizona Tourist Commission were answered as sunny skies and low-seventies temperatures greeted the golfers. Morgan discarded his Santa Claus hat but kept it safely tucked in his golf bag for good luck. Anything to help. He knew holding a large lead wasn't one of his attributes. Past experience made him hope history wouldn't repeat itself.

Haunting Morgan was the label that he was one of those players who had never quite lived up to his potential. Yes, he had won seven times on the regular Tour, and the golf world knew that Gil had a rock-solid swing, power to spare, and a deft touch around the greens. Having grown up on the plains of Oklahoma made him efficient in all types of conditions. He could score well whether the day was still or a fifty-mile-an-hour wind was blowing sand in his eyes. Dr. Gil was also known as a fighter, one who could squeeze every last ounce out of his ability.

The question marks arose regarding his lack of a Major championship, something that was a sore point for Dr. Gil. After three victories in the late 1970s, great things were expected from Morgan. He had also won the World Series of Golf in 1978, defeating Hubert Green in a play-off. Two more wins came in 1983, and another in 1990, but Morgan was never a real factor in a Major championship until the 1992 U.S. Open at Pebble Beach. There he became the first ever to reach ten under par in any Open championship. During the third round, he moved to twelve under and was on his way to a victory. With twenty-nine holes to play, he led by seven strokes. Then the nightmare began. He played the remaining holes twenty-one over par, carding a windblown 81 in the final round. "I kind of fell out of the sky," Morgan recalled. "It felt like my parachute had a hole in it."

Gilmer Bryan Morgan II's chances of winning a Major stopped right there. It had been a boyhood dream, ever since Gil was introduced to the game by his father at age fifteen.

When the prospect of competing with the over-fifty bunch presented itself as he approached his half-century birthday in September of 1996, Morgan began practicing his short game, especially putting, the Achilles' heel that prevented more significant finishes on the PGA Tour.

"I worked on a three-wedge system for the first time," he said. "I think I added a lot to my short game, and my putting really improved."

Brian Barnes, for one, still questioned Morgan's ability to gain status as one of the Senior Tour's premiere performers. "I don't think he'll find it all that easy," Barnes predicted before the 1997 season. "Unless you're a great putter, it's difficult to dominate on the Senior Tour, and I wouldn't put Gil in the class of great putters."

Former Tour player Ernie Vossler saw things differently: "Doc will show guys a thing or two. He's really a cool customer. And one with a very dry wit. Gil's got a great sense of humor."

Tom Nettles, the former professional golfer turned Golf Channel broadcaster, agreed: "When Gil's playing with someone he really knows, like Hale or Larry Nelson, he's quite entertaining, laughing all the time. That's why I nicknamed him 'Giggles.' "

When Morgan joined the Senior Tour in 1996, he felt much was expected of him. "There was a lot of stress to win," Doc said. "The guys on the regular Tour expected me to come out here and win. And I did, but then there was the question of the next one. I put a lot of pressure on myself."

That was something his playing companions did not do during the final round of The Tradition. For all practical purposes, the tournament was over after the first three holes. At hole one, the loquacious Aoki, who wore a wool sweater with a ferocious tiger on the front that must have been a Christmas present from someone attempting to be a friend, had a five-footer for birdie. Morgan was in the deep rough behind the green with what John Jacobs later called "a shot Houdini couldn't get up and down."

If Aoki made his putt and Morgan bogeyed, the game was on. But Dr. Gil proved his mettle with a plop shot (thanks to a sixty-three-degree wedge) that cuddled the ball within four feet of the hole. Aoki, armed with a new putter, pointed off the ground in the toe trademark fashion, then pulled his putt. When Morgan made his, Aoki was playing for second place.

John Jacobs encountered a similar situation at the third hole, but once again Morgan toughed out a pitch shot and made par. Hometown favorite Jacobs, who'd chastised a local reporter for calling him an "unknown," knew he'd missed his shot at Gil.

At the fifth, Morgan woke up his round with a birdie. The lead wavered between five and six all day until Aoki's birdie at seventeen cut the margin to four.

As if to prove his point that a Major victory, albeit on the Senior Tour, was now in his pocket, Morgan drilled a four iron to within twelve feet on the par-five eighteenth, then gunned it into the middle of the hole for an eagle. His twenty-two-under-par total broke the tournament record, causing Aoki, who spoke what reporters called "convenient English," to say while sipping a Michelob, "Too much good. He no come, I win."

Though Morgan clearly relished the win, he seemed more at ease in the press tent talking about his optometry degree and whether he would take classes to keep his license in Oklahoma "just in case my game goes down the tubes." In keeping with the weirdness of the week, reporters honed in on Gil's problems with surface vision, something that caused him problems reading greens. When the discussion turned to stories regarding eye examinations and his ability to see pigs and horses on charts, Dave Senko just shook his head. "This *is* a press conference about Morgan winning a Major golf championship, isn't it?" he thought to himself, aware that talk about lucky stocking caps, swimming-pool shots, and animals on an eye chart weren't the usual areas of interest on the Senior PGA Tour.

Morgan helped return things to normal just before leaving, however, when he was asked about the first-place prize money. "I don't know. What is it?" he asked a startled reporter, proving that his competitive spirit to win a Major championship was foremost in his heart.

BOOK II

HALE AND HEARTY

8

THE BARELY-OVER-FIFTY GOLFER WITH THE THREE-IRON BUILD AND the snappy wit tapped his practice ball gently with a six iron. Then he tapped it again, and the ball lifted just far enough off the ground so that he could slide under it and catapult the white sphere a few feet into the air.

As the early-morning golf fanatics who crowded around the practice range near the first tee at the 1997 PGA Seniors' Championship watched in wonder, the Joplin, Missouri, native with three U.S. Open titles to his credit ping-ponged the ball in the air like a waterfront juggler in San Francisco. Once, twice, three times, and then, as if to show off the athletic talent that made him an outstanding defensive back at the University of Colorado in the 1960s, he drew back his six iron, took a baseball swing that would make Tony Gwynn proud, and smacked the ball on a frozen rope toward the practice green one hundred yards away. The crowd oohed and aahed at the balancing act, and Hale Irwin, scoffed at by some for a lack of personality in spite of his prowess on the golf course, turned, smiled, doffed his cap, and bowed in appreciation.

The type of precise control of the golf ball that Irwin exhibited on the practice tee was a portent of things to come in the Seniors' Championship, played at the PGA National Champions Course in Palm Beach Gardens in April. The second so-called Major of the season had brought the best-of-the-best on the Senior Tour to the battle in South Florida. The field included fifty-five PGA club professionals from around the country, workaholics thankful for a respite from catering to the whims of country club members. They had qualified in the PGA Club Professionals Championship, earning a chance to tee it up with the finest players on the Senior PGA Tour.

The championship had a rich history. It began in 1937 at the behest of Bobby Jones, who believed the world needed a tournament where the finest professionals over fifty could compete on level ground. The first Seniors' Championship was held at Augusta National, where Jock Hutchison of Golf, Illinois, winner of the 1920

PGA Championship, emerged as champion by recording rounds of 76-75-72 to win by eight shots.

The first player to dominate the championship was Sam Snead, who won in 1964, '65, and '66 and then again in 1970, '72, and '73. That year, Snead, then sixty-one, astounded the golf world by carding four rounds in twenty under par at the PGA National East Course. Julius Boros finished fifteen shots behind the Slammer, whose side-saddle putting stance produced so many birdies that Boros called him "unconscious."

Through the years, notable winners were the Squire, Gene Sarazen, Roberto De Vicenzo, Charlie Sifford, Arnold Palmer, and Tom Wargo, the driving range professional from Illinois.

The 1997 PGA Seniors' Championship wouldn't be kind to Wargo, but it didn't matter to one fan. "He missed the cut," a cute forty-plus woman squealed in a voice reminiscent of Jack Nicklaus in his early years, "but he's got the best rear end in Palm Beach."

Irwin's win in 1996 made him the clear favorite in 1997, though Gil Morgan, winner of The Tradition, David Graham, twice a champion in the first few months on the Tour, John Bland, the jolly South African with the silky-smooth putting stroke, and the ever-present Jack Nicklaus, just returned from so-so play at Augusta in the Masters, figured to contend.

The Senior Tour welcomed Arnold Palmer back after his bout with prostate cancer. Palmer seemed genuinely moved by the attention, wiping away tears when the Senior PGA Tour Wives Association presented him with a $100,000 check, raised through sale of a needle-point rug with players' autographs woven in, to fight cancer.

Though a bit slow of foot, Palmer was his jovial self, especially with fans who flocked to see his every move. Arnie was back in his element, and he joked with admirers lined up beside the practice green behind the eighteenth hole. One spectator, in a Hawaiian flowered shirt and purple slacks, told Arnie, "I had that prostate cancer, and I'm feelin' great." Palmer shocked the onlookers by saying, "Yeah, and how's your sex life?" The startled man replied, "Uh, great." Palmer then turned around and said, "So's mine."

Nearby, Chi Chi Rodriguez, who had dazzled the practice-tee crowd by slashing through two golf balls, one with a hook and one with a slice so that they crisscrossed in flight, watched in awe of Palmer. "The fans love him," Chi Chi remarked. "Some guys out here put it on, but Arnie's the real thing." Then he added for no particular reason, "And remember Mother Teresa has nothing, but she has everything. Arnie would be like that, too. Even without the millions he's made, he'd still have everything."

Arnie's Army was in full force during the first two rounds of the tournament. They whooped and hollered at his play, groaned at every missed putt, and tried to look away when their god flubbed an easy shot. Absolutely no one cared about the score except Arnold, whose bold play produced several good shots but many that were emblematic of an old injured warrior battling to stay competitive.

A front-nine 37 on Thursday provided hope for Arnie and his followers, but two shanked shots from a fairway bunker that went out of bounds on the twelfth hole sent his score spiraling. An 84, and a second-round 82—marked by a nasty spat between Arnold and his caddie, who kept miscalculating distances—sent the living legend to the sidelines for the weekend.

Day one of the championship had seen John Bland, anxious to capture his first Major, assume control, firing a five-under-par 67. It came on the Champions Course, which had been doused with rain for days, causing Scott Tolley of *The Palm Beach Post* to label Bland the "head muck-raker" after opening day.

Bland's round came early in the day, before the weather turned downright nasty. A swirling wind and light rain shower made afternoon play treacherous. "Bland played early, when the tide was still in," kidded Bob Charles, a contender every week at age sixty-one, who shot 71.

Despite an opening round 69, Irwin was spooked by a sight he saw in the water bordering the sixteenth fairway. "We saw a water moccasin swimming along out there about like that," he exclaimed, holding his hands three feet apart. "We were all looking for fish, with Barnsey [playing partner Brian Barnes] being the fisherman, and [Dave] Stockton being the great huntsman. I was just the scout." Fortunately, none of the players hit the ball in the water, and Irwin gathered himself enough to roll in an eight-footer for birdie.

Bland's round was highlighted by a holed six-iron shot for eagle at the par-four ninth. "I've been aiming at that flagstick for some time." He laughed. "I finally hit it."

Another golfer hitting it close was Irwin, who blitzed the field with a picture-perfect 65 in the second round of the PGA Seniors' Championship. Four consecutive birdies beginning at number four etched him deep in red numbers and then a holed-out wedge shot for eagle at the thirteenth provided the coup de grâce.

At the end of the day, the field was frazzled. Club professional

Dana Quigley, the former PGA Tour professional returning to competition after a bout with alcoholism, played behind Irwin. "He's walking to the hole when the ball has not even gotten there, and on half of them he's beating the ball to the hole," Quigley exclaimed. "That's how dead center his putts are going. It's incredible. What a show."

Jack Nicklaus, whose second-round 72 left him at 143 and nine shots behind Irwin on a course he had designed, praised his foe's play, albeit in a way that irritated many of Jack's fellow competitors. When asked to talk about the course's difficulty, Nicklaus blurted out, "You're seeing a lot of old guys playing golf. If we were real sharp, we wouldn't be playing on this Tour. We're seniors. Give us a test that's fairly difficult, when you have to work around the greens with touch and the guys have a little trouble with it. Hale's the only one not having any trouble with it. He's still in diapers on this Tour."

First-round leader John Bland was bland indeed, and a fistful of bogies skyrocketed his score to a second-round 77. Bob Charles took over the runner-up spot seven shots behind Irwin, with Gibby Gilbert, winner at Key Biscayne in January, one more back. Gil Morgan was another shot behind. Jim Colbert shot 76 and 73 and barely made the cut.

Catching Hale Irwin was the call of the day for the survivors as the PGA Seniors' Championship entered round three. Someone suggested throwing him in the lake on sixteen and letting the water moccasin do the rest.

9

THIRTY-SIX HOLES OF THE PGA SENIORS' CHAMPIONSHIP REMAINED, and though anything could happen, Hale Irwin was blitzing the field like a battalion commander looking for a promotion. But in round three, Irwin's game suddenly went sour. His driving was erratic, his iron shots less than acceptable, and his putting, according to him, was "atrocious." That meant he was game for a challenge, but someone had to step forward and put pressure on the former U.S. Open champion.

Gil Morgan, Jack Nicklaus (limping less noticeably than during the first two rounds), and John Bland seemed the likely contenders, but none could mount a serious charge. Only one man stepped forward, Gibby Gilbert, who had captured the Royal Caribbean Classic in Miami in January.

Hole by hole, Gilbert chopped away at Irwin's lead. Gibby birdied the first three holes and four of the first six. At ten, he added another, and when Irwin bogeyed, the margin was but two strokes. "Hooray," shouted sportswriters looking for a story. "The game is on."

Gibby Gilbert had a bit of history on his side as well. In the final round at the 1996 Boone Valley Classic in Augusta, Missouri, Gilbert recovered from a disastrous quadruple bogey at the second hole and came from six shots down to tie Irwin at day's end. A play-off ensued, and Gilbert emerged the winner.

With the difference just two shots, Irwin stepped up his game, and when the pair reached the eleventh tee he led by three. Irwin's drive was fairway all the way, and then Gilbert began a twenty-minute nightmare that even five full boxes of Advil, the tournament's sponsor, couldn't relieve.

Gilbert's tee shot was a duck hook that darted into black, gooey muck bordering the hole. He slashed the ball back toward the fairway, but it scampered into the heavy rough on the par-four hole, preventing him from going for the green. Gilbert then hit a layup shot that positioned him with a wedge to the putting surface. He appeared hesitant about the shot, and the result was a fat, slobbering ball whose flight pattern looked like that of a wounded quail. The ball dive-bombed into more muck, this time in front of the green. Gilbert tilted his eyes toward the heavens in disbelief. "Is this really happening?" he thought to himself, his brain about to explode.

Once again, the would-be contender soled his shoes in the muck, and then hit a skulled shot that flew into the back bunker. Lying five, he now knew a big number lurked ahead. He just didn't know how big.

The bunker shot, with little green to work with, produced a ball that sped across the green. From thirty-five feet, the punchy Gilbert tried to steady himself, but his lag putt stopped five feet short. He then topped off the hole with a rimmed putt, tapping in for a nine. Gilbert walked off the green looking as if he needed a fresh supply of oxygen to clean out his head.

Irwin made bogey on the hole trying to avoid watching Gilbert's nightmare, but the four-shot swing terminated Gilbert's chances. Double-bogey at the next hole sealed his doom, and though Irwin mustered only an even-par round, his lead at the end of the day was seven, just as it had been when the Florida sun rose above the shimmering Atlantic.

One Gilbert replaced another in the runner-up spot, when Larry, the cigar-chomping troubadour from Fort Knox, Kentucky, with two senior victories to his credit, fired a third-round 70. John Bland was another two shots back, Jack Nicklaus one more behind Irwin.

Hale Irwin was born to golf at age four when his father cut down a set of clubs, using black electrical tape for the grips. That first set, encased in an old canvas bag, sat in the corner of Irwin's office in St. Louis, a reminder of the early years when he first learned the game.

Hanging on the bag was a dark-green towel with "Medinah" stitched on it. Another reminder—this one of Irwin's most revered championships, the 1990 U.S. Open.

In the time that passed between Irwin's use of his first set of clubs and that memorable championship in Chicago, Irwin had compiled a record filled with titles, many of them carved out on the toughest golf courses in the game. All this was due to a fighting spirit and will to win second to none.

Hale Irwin grew up in Baxter Springs, Kansas, one state removed from his birthplace of Joplin, Missouri. He was born in 1945, the year World War II ended. The meticulous Irwin would have made a great military officer, a field general perhaps.

To be sure, Irwin was a tough kid. Small for his age, he was the one under the pile when the football was fumbled. He came home with his face bloodied, then returned for more, unwilling to be a quitter despite his size.

Though Commerce, Oklahoma, the hometown of Mickey Mantle, was nearby, Irwin swore the man he most respected and tried to emulate was his father, Hale Irwin, Sr., an excavation contractor, who introduced him to the game of golf. He took his son to a nearby public course armed with a cut-down set of clubs. Irwin played the nine-hole layout as many times a day as daylight permitted.

Hale was a good player, but it was football that earned him his way to college. Coaches admired Irwin's toughness as well as his ability to withstand pain and ask for more. By 1965, Irwin was talented enough to be an All Big Eight defensive back for the University of Colorado Buffalos, a feat he duplicated the next year. Despite his honors, Irwin was extremely tough on himself when it came to returning passes he intercepted. "A lot of my runbacks looked like a drunk trying to run home," he recalled. "One time I had eighty yards of green grass in front of me and I dropped the ball."

The NFL didn't see a future for a six-foot-tall, 170-pound defensive back, but Irwin wasn't concerned. By 1967, his golf game had improved enough to win the NCAA Championship. Football became a thing of the past.

There was no doubt that Irwin would try his luck on the PGA Tour. He turned professional in 1968, but it took three years for him to hit the winner's circle. That title came at the 1971 Sea Pines Heritage Classic.

Irwin captured that same title two years later and was primed for bigger things. In 1974, he earned his first U.S. Open championship at Winged Foot. Irwin won that title again in 1979 at Inverness, and, in all, twenty victories on the PGA Tour, including the Heritage Golf Classic for the third time in 1994, at age *forty-nine*.

Along the way, Irwin gathered respect from fellow players as a gritty competitor, especially on the tough courses. But he was never considered to be a star. Most often he was forgotten when the so-called experts chose the great players of the day. Unlike foes Nicklaus, Trevino, Johnny Miller, and others, Irwin lacked a compelling personality and was reluctant to talk much about himself.

The bookish image Irwin projected also held him back. He looked like an English major from Princeton, a bank teller, or a computer wizard who just happened to be a superb golfer. Instead of possessing a flashy nickname like "Golden Boy," "The Bear," or "Super Mex," Irwin was indistinguishable. He could be spotted anytime fans saw a stone-faced golfer with steel-rimmed glasses strolling down the fairway.

Lack of charisma was a problem, too. Irwin had an icy demeanor, wasn't naturally funny, and didn't warm up to people. When he tried to be funny or show genuine interest in fans or competitors, he came off as plastic. Bob Murphy called Irwin's manner on the course "stingily serious, all business."

"Somebody needs to beat the shit out of him, lighten him up a little," offered another. "Though I wouldn't want to be the one to do it."

Johnny Miller, an opponent of Irwin's in the 1970s, said, "I don't think a lot of people really know him. Hale's a super perfectionist, can't tolerate anything that's not perfect. That's held him back at times, made him too tough on himself. But he's a great guy, really is, just misunderstood."

Miller also believed Irwin needed to work more on his demeanor than his golf game. "If I were caddying for Hale, I'd say, 'Hey, go out and have a little fun. Life's too short. Enjoy yourself.' But that would be difficult for him."

In defense, Irwin admitted that while he was a deep thinker engrossed in the game he played, it was necessary for him to compete at such a high level. "I've never had the greatest talent. I made up for it in other ways," he explained.

One way was to be one of the most competitive golfers to ever play the game. "Battling Hale Irwin is like fighting a pit bull," a Tour official explained. "I've seen his face when he's in the hunt. His eyes are hollow, and his jaw is jutted out. It's like he's saying 'Nobody is going to beat me.' And usually they didn't."

Longtime caddie John Sullivan described Irwin's feisty disposition and drive another way. "Hale gets upset when he misses five-footers, even in pro-ams." Brian Barnes added, "Irwin wouldn't be half the player he is if he didn't have that fire in him. Every putt is life or death."

Irwin's personality and his close friends on the Tour were emblematic of his approach to golf. Dale Douglass and Charles Coody, neither one a lively sort, shepherded Irwin through his early years. Like Jack Nicklaus, Irwin played the game in a conservative manner, close to the vest, which matched his keep-things-to-himself attitude toward life in general. Some players preferred not to play with Irwin because he said little. "I know I was short on conversation," Irwin admitted. "I never talked much during a round. That made some guys uncomfortable, but that's the way I am."

Playing to his conservative nature was a blessing for Irwin, as it had been for Nicklaus. Former Tour veteran Phil Rodgers said, "What makes great players is how close they play to one hundred percent of their personality. Jack was a methodical person. Very organized. Well planned. He never played a shot before he was ready. He played like he lived." The same could be said for Irwin, especially on difficult courses and in Major championships.

Hale Irwin's golf swing was self-taught. In fact, he shunned teachers. "I listen to all these coaches and what they tell players," he observed. "It blows me away. Like put a beach ball between your legs. I tried that and whiffed the ball."

Like Nicklaus, if Irwin believed something, he believed it, and it would take a mountain of evidence to convince him otherwise. "I'm not a wishy-washy type of guy. Not intimidated by anyone," he expounded. "Jack's like that. Strong-minded. That's why I admire him so much. And why we get along. We're a lot alike." Some saw that attitude as being offensive. "Like Nicklaus, Irwin's an expert on everything," a fellow senior member surmised. "The supreme know-it-all."

While Nicklaus had several images that defined his career, there was one that fit Hale Irwin more than any other. He might win more championships and bushel basketfuls of money, but forevermore, golf fans would link the thin man with the sharpshooting iron play to the 1990 U.S. Open at Medinah.

That tournament was indelible in his mind.

"I was walking down the eleventh fairway and saw on the leader board that I was one shot out of the top fifteen, who qualified for the next Open," Irwin recalled. "My goal was to play the final eight in one under. I figured that would make it."

Four straight birdies moved Irwin to minus 7 with one hole to play. "It was the most exciting one of my life," he would later proclaim.

The drama was set up by an average approach shot to the par-four final hole. "The putt was about forty-five feet, though it has grown to about sixty over the years," Irwin said. "It's become the longest putt in the history of man. Realistically, I was just trying to get down in two, but as the ball rolled toward the hole, I knew it had a chance. It was dead center with ten feet to go, dead center with five, and then the ball disappeared."

If Irwin had merely whooped and hollered or even emulated Chi Chi's sword dance, his date with history wouldn't have been solidified. But the Colorado Buffalo, the intense man with straight-A student looks, took off as if he were after a pass from the opposing quarterback. He raced around the green, all the while high-fiving an out-of-control, delirious gallery that didn't stop celebrating for half an hour.

"I don't know what happened," Irwin recalled. "I just wanted the gallery to be part of it. I know many people didn't know I could be that emotional, but I can. They just don't know me very well."

"The Putt," as it became known, launched Irwin to the eight-under-par total he sought. Tour journeyman Mike Donald tied that figure, and the two men were still dead even after Monday's play-off rounds of 74. Irwin then won his third Open title with a birdie on the first extra hole.

The image of Irwin on the eighteenth green at Medinah remains one of the most vivid in golf history. No wonder golf fans of the Senior Tour were excited when Hale hit fifty and announced he'd try his hand at winning more championships.

When 1997 began, Irwin was determined to be number one and win the money title, something he had never done. Early play took him to the top of the money list, and as he entered the final round of the PGA Seniors' Championship, he had already earned more than $380,000 in official prize money.

In addition, he had dominated the Senior Slam event held the first and second day of March in Mexico's Cabo San Lucas. Competing against Ray Floyd, Dave Stockton, and Jack Nicklaus, Irwin stormed to a nine-shot win.

Previewing things to come, Irwin had been the fodder for a sleight-of-hand magician named the "The Great Hondo" before the final round. Hondo performed "pick the right card," "make the foam balls disappear," and scintillating rope tricks, much to the delight of the players. Then Irwin followed up an opening-round 65 with a magical 66, during which TBS's television audience switched to a John Wayne film on HBO. "Irwin acts like he's in first and plays like he's in last," remarked commentator Bobby Clampett, trying to drum up some excitement. He couldn't. Irwin led by eight shots after the foursome had played the first six holes.

The only drama during the tournament was the long-driving contest held on the seventh hole. The winner would drive away in a BMW, and the four seniors stretched their backs and whaled away as if John Daly were in the competition. Clampett called it the "pass, punt, and kick" competition of professional golf. Ray Floyd, the slam winner in 1995 and 1996, won, edging Nicklaus.

Despite his third-place finish in the long drive, Irwin played like a sorcerer with a "trick a hole" up his sleeve. "I'd like to go home and bottle this feeling," Irwin said later. No one who watched the final eighteen holes of the PGA Seniors' Championship doubted that he opened the bottle and drank some of the magic potion he swallowed at the Slam just before he hit the first tee for the final round of the PGA Seniors.

With caddie John Sullivan proudly wearing a green ribbon symbolic of caddie Squeaky Medlin's fight with cancer, Irwin threw an eagle at the field on the par-five third hole and never looked back. On the back nine, the lead had grown into double figures, causing immediate comparisons with Woods's triumph at the Masters. "What are you going to call me? Pussycat?" Irwin roared at a reporter.

By day's end, the winning margin was twelve shots over Jack Nicklaus and Dale Douglass. Afterward, the Golden Bear chided Irwin, chortling, "We've got to get Hale out of diapers," a reference to his being just fifty-one and a "baby" Senior Tour player.

"That's Jack's new kick," Irwin replied. "He puts me in diapers. So I say, 'Get him a walker.'" Then he added matter-of-factly, "The tournament was mine to win or lose this week. And I opted for the former."

Dale Douglass put the best spin on the present state of Irwin's game. "Hale is our best player out here," he said. "He's so damn accurate."

"I was frustrated because I did not win more in 1996," Irwin concluded after the round. "My course management was a little suspect. I was determined to improve it. If I'm not comfortable with a shot, I don't try something that's not right for the moment. I'm playing more intelligently."

Twelve shots more than anyone else.

10

HALE IRWIN'S DOMINATION OF THE PGA SENIORS' CHAMPIONSHIP brought back images of Tiger Woods's phenomenal victory at the Masters a week earlier. But it was another image at that tournament that thrilled golf fans from one end of the earth to the other.

As Arnold Palmer approached the eighteenth green in the second round, the sixty-seven-year-old warrior's shoulders were noticeably slumped. His gait was abbreviated, and, though he waved his visor in the air for all to see, he was clearly distressed with his game. A smile greeted the well-wishers, but it wasn't the face-wide smile they had seen in years past.

For four-plus hours, Arnie had fought the demons at Augusta, attempting to muster a golf game that had seen him emerge four times as champion. In the first round, he'd come to the eighteenth, flubbed a chip shot, and ended with an 89. He'd called his playing an "embarrassment." "I came to Augusta to win," he said before the round. "I know I have little chance of doing that, but that's my nature, the only way I know how to play."

Unfortunately, tired bones still not fully recovered from a fighting match with prostate cancer surgery permitted only a two-stroke improvement in round two. After completing this round, scores of 89 and 87 positioned Palmer dead last in the field, forty-four strokes behind the second-round leader.

Despite his play, the boisterous crowd surrounding the eighteenth green cheered as Arnie made his way toward his third shot. Playing partner Ken Green looked on in awe as the noise crescendoed to a fever pitch when the King stepped onto the putting surface. Several in the gallery had tears in their eyes. At that special moment, nobody but Palmer cared about his score, for the masses were simply saying, "Welcome back to Augusta, Arnie. Welcome back."

Watching Palmer in all his glory was quite special. His reemergence at the Masters was the only thing that challenged what was otherwise known as "The Tiger Woods Show." From the outset, all the hoopla focused on the Immortal One, the man-child Earl Woods, Tiger's father, said had come to change the nature of the game and even, yes, life itself. And to provide a link with great African-American players of the past such as Senior Tour veterans Charlie Sifford and Lee Elder.

Tiger Woods's chance at immortality had been trailblazed by Sifford, the first black on the PGA Tour, at age thirty-eight, who joined the Tour in 1960 and became a full-fledged member four years later.

Sifford's road to the Tour had been a bumpy one even after he obtained his playing card, as racial discrimination plagued his attempts to compete. Bing Crosby finally invited him to the Clambake, but only after the NAACP picketed the tournament. Even then, Crosby couldn't find any white golfers to play with Sifford. Bing finally persuaded the three Mills Brothers to join him.

Sifford was never invited to play in the Masters, despite having a respectable PGA career. He won the 1967 Hartford Open and the 1969 L.A. Open when he defeated Harold Henning in a play-off. "I tried so hard to get the opportunity [to play in the Masters]," the seventy-three-year-old Sifford said in 1997. "I'm not angry about it. I kept fighting until they changed the rules in 1972, making it possible for every tournament winner to be eligible."

The first beneficiary of Sifford's efforts was Lee Elder, who joined the PGA Tour in 1967. He won four tournaments, the first being the 1974 Monsanto Open. Though he missed the cut in his attempt at Augusta, ground was broken. Elder returned to play three more times before leaving the PGA Tour in 1983. Eight victories followed on the Senior Tour.

In 1992, Charlie Sifford wrote his autobiography, *Just Let Me Play*. He discussed his disappointment at not being allowed to play in the Masters and Elder's performance, but his most shining words were prophetic ones that portended things to come: "What golf needs . . . is a black man with a great deal of personal magnetism and whale of a game who can demonstrate that blacks fit into the game. Maybe when the black Jack Nicklaus comes along and beats the pants off everybody and does it with a smile and a clear speaking voice and sound awareness of the media . . . maybe then we other black guys will get the recognition and acceptance that we've always thought we deserved."

At the time Sifford—who still remembered a day at the Phoenix Open in 1952 when he removed the flag from one hole only to find human excrement—wrote those words, Eldrick Woods was sixteen years old. Four years earlier, his father had taped a copy of Jack Nicklaus's record to Tiger's bedpost. When Tiger won the 1996 Las Vegas Invitational, he qualified for the 1997 Masters and his date with history was set.

It was sealed in the third round when Woods blitzed Bobby Jones's Augusta National with a seven-under-par 65. That gave him a nine-shot lead over Italy's Constantino Rocca, who admitted he and the field were playing for second place. Mr. Rocca was right.

The twenty-one-year-old Woods was the youngest player ever to pull on a green jacket, size 42 long. And it was left to Jack Nicklaus, whose final-round 79 left him twenty-nine shots behind Woods, to sum up the paradoxical, too-good-to-be-true Woods performance.

Jack, whose 147 rounds played at Augusta bettered Sam Snead's record, told reporters, "Bobby Jones should have waited until now to utter his famous 'He plays a game with which I am not familiar.' He should have saved it for Tiger."

Had the new black Jack Nicklaus arrived? A charismatic one just as Charlie Sifford had predicted? So it seemed, and within just two days of the fiftieth anniversary (April 15, 1947) of Jackie Robinson's breaking of the color barrier in major-league baseball. Even Tiger Woods was caught up in the irony, telling ESPN, "When I was walking up the eighteenth fairway, I thought of Charlie Sifford and Lee Elder, and, yes, Jackie Robinson. They all made it possible for me to have the chance to win the Masters."

Lee Elder saw the triumph a different way. "It's a payback. It was gratifying to see someone taking apart a tournament that had been so bad for the minorities who had tried to play there."

For all the senior players who had seen Sifford, Elder, and the rest of the black golfers suffer through the racial taunts of injustice similar to those Robinson experienced in baseball, the significance of Woods's victory was especially poignant. "Charlie and Lee paved the road," Jim Colbert said. Bob Murphy, who had befriended Elder when he first came on the Tour, added, "Guys like Lee deserve a great deal of credit. He and Charlie suffered, couldn't stay places or eat at certain places, it was awful. At Napa one year, they had to enter the clubhouse through the back door. But Lee stuck it out, and the game has always been better for guys like him."

Up in heaven, another black golfer, John Shippen, the first professional in the United States, must have smiled at Woods's performance and felt he had something to say about the transition from Sifford to Elder to Woods. Just as the great golfers of yesteryear playing on the Senior Tour were linked to their brethren who lit the candle in the 1940s, 1950s, and before, Tiger Woods now provided a link to the early days when black players struggled to find equality on the golf course.

*   *   *

Two weeks after the Masters, the Senior Tour hit gamblers' paradise—
the Las Vegas Senior Classic, played at the TPC at the Canyons
Course just outside the city. It had been designed by Bobby Weed, the
creative wizard from Jacksonville who earned his spurs toiling alongside Pete Dye. Aided by PGA player consultant Ray Floyd, the "Weed-
man" had dynamited out a pristine green golf course where only
barren desert calcite rock had appeared before.

The tournament was being played at TPC at the Canyons after a
two-year sojourn at the TPC Summerlin Course across the way. Before that, the Las Vegas Classic was set at the downtown Desert Inn,
where stories abounded about golfers slumbering down from their
hotel rooms to play while still feeling the effects of inebriation and all-
night bouts with the gaming tables. "Those were the days," reported
J. C. Snead. "Guys played with hangovers and in clothes they'd worn
the day before."

Defending champion for the 1997 classic was hometown boy
Jim Colbert, who had won in 1995 and 1996, the second year being
one for the Golf Hall of Fame archives. Coming to the fifty-fourth
hole, Colbert trailed Bob Charles by two and Dave Stockton by one.
Colbert faced an eighty-foot curler with little chance of survival, but
when he drilled it and Stockton two-putted, they were dead even.
Then Bob Charles, one of the most gifted putters ever to take club to
ball, did the unimaginable by three-putting. That meant a play-off,
which Colbert won with a par on the fourth extra hole.

Colbert returned to Las Vegas in 1997 with a golf game that was,
at best, a C+. He admitted to inconsistent play and speculated that
Hale Irwin, Gil Morgan, and John Bland, who had played well all season, had the edge.

Fifty-mile-an-hour winds on Thursday threatened to blow away
the PGA Fitness truck. The Pro-Am was canceled. Though Friday
and Saturday provided much calmer conditions, spurring Irwin to a
two-shot lead over Isao Aoki after the second round, Sunday's final
round produced body-bending forty-mile-an-hour winds that threatened to funnel the pencil-thin Aoki clear back to Japan.

Jim Colbert had crept up the leader board due to a scintillating second-round 66 that included six consecutive birdies, a round
played in the midst of an air show conducted at nearby Nellis
Air Force Base celebrating the fiftieth anniversary of the Air Force.
Images of the B-2 bomber and demonstration teams from seven

countries flashed by the golfers' eyes as they tramped along the Canyons Course.

Beginning Sunday's round, Colbert trailed by three, and superb play on the first nine holes cut the margin to two. A double bogey and a bogey at ten and eleven doused his chances for a three-peat, and the back nine became a duel between Irwin and Aoki, who swiped at the ball and fell back trying to keep his balance.

The shot of the day for Irwin was a punched seven iron at the thirteenth that stopped six inches from the cup. It came after a dastardly drive and a poor second shot. But par was his, and when Aoki made bogey, Irwin seemed to have the Classic wrapped up.

But Irwin putted like a twenty handicapper down the stretch, causing a match-play-like final stretch drive that was more interesting than Hale would have liked. He missed short putts on three consecutive holes, and by the time the competitors approached the green at the eighteenth, they were dead even.

Aoki was just off the putting surface, and the near winner of the 1980 U.S. Open jabbed his putt to within a foot. Irwin now had a twelve-footer to win, and he gently tapped the ball deep into the hole for his fourth win in seven tries on the 1997 Senior PGA Tour. The round of 72, quite remarkable under the gusting wind conditions, was his fourteenth consecutive at par or better. Aoki was second, with Colbert and J.J.—John Jacobs, the long-hitting former Californian—tied for third.

During the round, ESPN's Jim Kelly played a taped interview with Irwin. In reply to questions about his thoughts about golf in general, Irwin revealed an inner spirit for the game that was refreshing.

"The game is about realization of self," Irwin began. "What I've learned is that you can find out a lot about yourself, how to deal with pressure, how to deal with success and failure. With golf, you're hanging yourself out there, by yourself, no coach, no sports psychologist, just you against the golf course. And the question is, Can I get better? That's the challenge I love."

After the tournament win, which gave him nearly $750,000 in earnings over the first few tournaments of 1997, Irwin said of his victory, "I was leaking oil and throwing loose parts all over the place . . . it wasn't pretty."

All of his competitors at the Las Vegas Classic agreed. But it also wasn't pretty that they were finding themselves playing for second place in nearly every tournament Irwin entered.

One who wasn't surprised was Jim Colbert. "Hale's full of confidence, but then he should be. He's played even better than last year. He's always been a decent driver, but we don't have an iron player out here who plays as well as he does. When Jack is healthy, he is, but I'll put Irwin against those kids on the PGA Tour. He really knows the distances, and, right now, everything is ending up near the hole."

Hale Irwin's victory at Las Vegas was impressive, but he wasn't through. In a further attempt to achieve dominance over his fellow Senior Tour players, he contended at the Bruno's Memorial Classic held at the Greystone Country Club in Hoover, Alabama.

The course was designed by Bob Cupp and Senior Tour rookie Hubert Green, a native of nearby Birmingham, who had splashed onto the 1997 Tour with the same sort of flamboyance that earmarked his twenty-six-year career as a topflight performer on the regular Tour.

Known equally for the whiplash swing that sped through the ball at hummingbird pace and a sharp tongue that personified the phrase "Say what you think," Green accumulated nineteen victories on the Tour. A member of three Ryder Cup teams, his Major wins came at the 1977 U.S. Open and the 1985 PGA Championship, where he defeated Lee Trevino in a play-off. He also nearly garnered a green jacket at the 1978 Masters, missing a three-footer on the final hole to lose to Gary Player, who'd carded a final-round 64. That year, he lost the World Series of Golf Championship to Gil Morgan, who bested him in a play-off.

Images of Hubert Green abound, centered around two important characteristics: his propensity for being abrupt to the point of annoyance and the possession of an inner fire for the game unequaled in the history of golf.

Both resulted from Green's intensity as a competitor. He was looking for a fistfight the day he graduated from kindergarten, and the outlet for his passion became sports. "I played everything," Green recalled. "Tried baseball, but basketball was my game. But I was slow, and my vertical leap barely hit double digits."

To remedy Green's yearning for a life of sport, the Good Lord put a golf course, the Birmingham Country Club, between Hubert's house and school. "I had to walk across the course on my way home from high school," Green remarked. "I started to hit balls, practice or play. I found out I was pretty damn good."

And he said so. To anyone who would listen. And in a tone so direct it scolded the ears of the unsuspecting.

"Even at that age, I was a person no one really liked," Green remembered. "I was raised by a very strict father. I'm very honest—most people don't want to hear the truth. They'd rather be lied to. I always thought honesty was the best policy, but being that way caused me a lot of trouble."

Despite his ability to ruffle feathers, Florida State offered Green a golf scholarship. The zipity-zap, quick-as-a-wink pass he made at the ball wasn't impressive to the eye, but the kid could get up and down from bare dirt or on the downhill side of a grass bunker seventy yards from the green like few before or since.

Green's junior year produced his first significant victory, the 1967 Southern Amateur. Four years later, he won the Houston Champions International as a professional. Over the next thirteen years, Green won nineteen PGA Tour golf tournaments, three consecutively in 1976. Unfortunately, little publicity came his way since four other professionals named Nicklaus, Trevino, Miller, and Watson were performing heroics as well. In the 1970s, when Green won *sixteen* times, the Famous Four triumphed on eighty-six occasions. Adding Green's sixteen wins meant the five players won nearly 25 percent of all tournaments played in that decade. "We had some pretty good players back then," Green noted. "The competition was stiff."

Instead of getting his due, Green was labeled a rube, an oddball, the guy with the herky-jerky swing, a crouched putting stroke, and a ten-pound chip on his shoulder. He was Mr. Unorthodox, and the press had a field day, quoting his off-the-wall remarks, many that didn't endear him to the powers-that-be at the PGA Tour.

But one thing was for sure: The man could play. "What Hubert lacked with skill, he made up with heart," Ernie Vossler stated. "He just outgutted all those guys." "He could flat play," Lanny Wadkins said. "And everybody knew it."

While Green's 1985 PGA Championship win at Cherry Hills provided a sterling memory and the disaster at the 1978 Masters was his agony of defeat, it was the magical win in the 1977 U.S. Open that would be his legacy.

After three rounds at steamy Southern Hills in Tulsa, Oklahoma, Green led carrot-topped Andy Bean by a shot. Then the FBI received a phone call threatening Hubert's life. Someone (Green later joked that it was an old girlfriend) didn't want Green's name on the U.S. Open Championship cup.

As the slender, elf-faced contender from Alabama made his way off the fourteenth green, he suddenly noticed several dour men dressed in black suits. "I was told a woman called the FBI and said someone was going to shoot me on the fifteenth green. Here I am trying to make three-footers in the Open, and now I learn my life's on the line," Green recalled.

Hubert was given three options: withdraw, request play be suspended, or continue. Since Green's father didn't raise a quitter, he headed to the tee box at fifteen. Despite the pressure of a gun to his head and Lou Graham's late charge (four birdies in five holes), Green scrambled to par at fifteen. "I closed my eyes for a few seconds after I made that putt. Fortunately, there were no gunshots." He holed a birdie putt at sixteen and then made par at seventeen.

It took every ounce of energy Green had to finish play at the eighteenth. He needed a bogey to win, and after a poor approach shot, a weak bunker effort, and a lackadaisical first putt, he was left with a three-footer for bogey. "I tried to put everything out of my mind," Green recalled. "Fact is, I don't even remember hitting the putt. But it sure went in."

"If courage is grace under pressure, then no one has more courage than Hubert Green," the USGA's Sandy Tatum said after the incident.

Green's last PGA Tour triumph came in 1985, at the PGA Championship. "They thought I was dead, thought I couldn't play anymore," he chuckled, "but I showed 'em."

Between that victory and Green's Senior Tour debut in 1997, he became a lost child. Financial security made it possible for him to play regularly when his earnings dropped, but he was nonchalant about the game for the first time. "I hurt my shoulder, but even when it mended, I didn't practice much," he admitted.

That is, until the age of fifty came calling. Then Hubert hit the practice tee, invited a bit of advice, and began to sharpen a short game that had gotten rusty. All because he knew that the older golfers weren't going to let a young pup like him beat them.

But why was he still playing? "I owe everything to the game of golf," he said. "Where else could a guy with my IQ make a living?"

Coming to the Bruno's Memorial Classic in 1997, Green was less than pleased with his golf game as a senior. He played well in the first few events, winning nearly $140,000, but by his own admission that money had been the result of sharp chipping and superb putting, always a Green trademark.

"My game's in the C range," Green offered. "I'm up on the money board, but that's deceiving. I'm really not playing any better than I was during the last two years on the regular Tour, and we all know how bad a run that was."

The problem for Green was ball striking. "I'm working on

hitting the ball solid. The heck with those glancing blows. I'm not re-leasing through the ball as I should, and half-hit shots just won't make it out here. These guys can really play, and I'm ashamed to show them my game right now."

Though Green hoped to be a contender at the Bruno's Classic, he wasn't. His lack of length off the tee was crucial, and he fell back with rounds of 73, 76, and 70.

Nevertheless, Green's presence was a treat for the hometown folks. They'd warmed up for the event by witnessing a most unusual scene during the Pro-Am, the backbone of the Senior PGA Tour, that preceded tournament play. That occurred on the sixteenth hole at Greystone when former Heisman Trophy winner and current na-tional champion Florida Gator football coach Steve Spurrier threw a pass toward Rick Pitino, the Kentucky Wildcat basketball coach soon-to-be named head man of the Boston Celtics. Providing interference was none other than Hale Irwin.

Spurrier's pass never had a chance at success since he threw what Irwin described as a "dying duck pass." Perhaps the Gator coach should have hung around another foursome, one that included Green Bay Packer players Bart Starr and Brett Favre.

When the tournament started, the man who had no trouble find-ing his aim was Jay Sigel. Though Bob Murphy had beaten him in a play-off at the Toshiba Classic in Newport Beach in March, Sigel was tournament-tested-tough, a player who normally mowed down match-play opponents like a Lawn Boy.

In Sigel's amateur days, he was known as an intense competitor who bordered on being a curmudgeon while compiling an enviable record that included U.S. Amateur championships in 1982 and 1983, three U.S. Mid-Amateur titles, and the 1979 British Amateur crown. He was a member of *nine* Walker Cup teams and proved he could play with the professionals by being low amateur in three Masters, the 1980 British Open, and the 1984 U.S. Open.

Whether it was match or stroke play, Jay Sigel compiled a record that ranked behind Bobby Jones, Jack Nicklaus, Tiger Woods, and John Ball as the greatest amateur of all time. His achievements and love for the purity of golf made it very difficult to give it all up in 1994 when he decided to try his hand at the Senior PGA Tour.

"I didn't give it a lot of serious thought until I turned forty-nine," Sigel admitted. "Then everyone around me started talking about it. I decided to write down some questions in a notebook and do some thinking about them. My main concern was how my turning profes-sional would affect the amateur record I had compiled."

After consulting with several people, including Jack Nicklaus, Sigel decided to take the plunge. The results were immediate. Victory number one came when he rallied from ten shots back to tie Jim Colbert at the GTE West Classic and then won the play-off. That achievement, three top three finishes, and fourteen top tens earned him Rookie of the Year honors.

In the first round of the 1997 Bruno's Classic, Sigel fired a 68. Another reserved man, Gil Morgan, took the first-round lead with a sparkling 67. Hale Irwin produced an up-and-down 71.

Friday night's rain and swirling winds on Saturday made the course perfect for a charge from the slow-stepping Pennsylvanian, and he took the lead with 67. Irwin became his Sunday playing partner with a 68, four shots back.

A record Bruno's Classic crowd anticipated a great match-play finish between Sigel and Irwin, but Hale's game dropped to the D level. "There were no cookies left in the cookie jar today," he mused later in reference to a lack of intensity brought on by six consecutive rounds in the thick of battle. "I ran out of cookies."

Irwin's problem was a balky putter. "I'm going to shoe some horses," he lamented as he signed a scorecard that totaled 75. "I've got the touch of a blacksmith right now."

Sigel had none of those problems. "My game plan is to be as positive and aggressive as I can early," Sigel said. And that he did, eagling the second hole and taking much of the drama of the day away from fans. Gil Morgan made a charge with a 69, but Sigel's smooth 70 made 205 the right number for the victory.

"So this isn't the Hale Irwin Tour after all," commented *Golf World* writer Jim Martin, aware that Irwin had won four of seven events. Certainly anyone who had witnessed Sigel's precise play had to agree. Especially the six-iron shot he hit to the par-five second, leaving him with the four-footer for eagle. "That was the crucial shot," Sigel commented. "That let Hale know I meant business."

11

JAY SIGEL ATTEMPTED TO WIN BACK-TO-BACK TITLES AT THE HOME
Depot Invitational Tournament played at the TPC at Piper Glen in
Charlotte, North Carolina. Rounds of 73 and 68 pulled him into contention, but even a final-round 68 couldn't dent the leaders, who included the most famous "Dent" of all, Jim.

The tall, lanky Georgian with the loping walk and a ready smile
had opened play with 68 and 70, which positioned him four shots behind an unlikely thirty-six-hole leader, DeWitt Weaver. The big hitter
in the Panama hat shot 68 and 66 and appeared headed for his second
Senior Tour title. Two Morgans, Walter and John D., shared second
at −7, three behind Weaver.

Neither Weaver nor the Morgans contended on Sunday. Weaver
made triple bogey midway through the round and finished eighth,
leaving it to Jim Dent, Larry Gilbert—the Fort Knox, Kentucky,
native—and Lee Trevino to provide the fireworks.

While Gilbert shot a final-round 70, it was Dent and the Merry
Mex who carried the day. Their journey to the Senior PGA Tour
and approach to the game in general differed 360 degrees from each
other.

For Jim, the Senior Tour was indeed a second chance to show his
wares, the so-called mulligan at fifty. But his ascent to the professional
ranks of golf in the first place seemed like pure fiction.

"Big Boy," as he was known on the Senior Tour, first learned
about golf at Augusta National, home of the Masters. The product
of a broken home, Dent ventured to the shrine of golf looking
for work.

"The first time I caddied there, all I got was a whipping," Dent
remembered. "Mom died when I was eight, and my aunt took care of
me. She said if I hung around with caddies, I'd learn how to gamble
and drink. But you know, if they tell you not to do something, well,
you do it, and I went over to Augusta National whenever I could. My
aunt gave me a good whipping when she found out."

The young Dent's ambitions as a caddie came just as a monumental, long-overdue event was occurring in golf. In 1952, blacks were finally permitted to play in PGA-sponsored events if the participating club agreed. The Phoenix Open was the trailblazer, but former heavyweight boxing champion Joe Louis failed to make the cut.

That didn't mean blacks were allowed to play at Augusta, only caddie. Since club rules prohibited PGA professionals from bringing their own, there was plenty of work for young boys like Jim Dent.

"I caddied for Bob Rosburg in 1956," Dent recalled. "We were in contention, but he shot forty-one on the back side on Sunday. In 1958, Bob Goalby, who won ten years later, was my man."

Goalby remembered Dent. "He was a lazy bum, and I never would have rehired him," Goalby kidded. "No, he was great, knew all the breaks on the greens, and I sure needed that help."

Despite his experience at Augusta ("I got to see all the greats, Snead, Player, Palmer," he recalled), Dent had little love for the game. "I wanted to be a football star. Played offensive and defensive end in high school. I loved the hitting. It was the greatest part of football."

Dent's football days came at Lucy Laney High School in Augusta. A teammate was Emerson Boozer, who became a star running back with the New York Jets.

Dent's athletic ability in a sport other than golf made him part of a group that was the rule rather than the exception on the Senior PGA Tour. "You could field a pretty good team in just about any sport," remarked J. C. Snead, who played three and a half years of professional baseball in the Western Carolina League, the New York–Pennsylvania League, and the Florida Instructional League. "I played a little bit of everything, and so did many others out here." Ironically, Snead was a left-handed hitter who batted .318 one season, even though he played golf right-handed.

Among others on the Senior Tour, DeWitt Weaver had been a high school All-American quarterback and then a teammate of Dandy Don Meredith at SMU. Jim Colbert and Hale Irwin played Big Eight football, while Bunky Henry was a record-setting placekicker at Georgia Tech.

Bob Murphy pitched at the University of Florida, Rick Acton for Washington, and Jack Kiefer was the property of the Detroit Tigers for two days. Jim Albus boxed at Bucknell, John Morgan became a top cross-country runner in England, and Tom Wargo bowled well enough to consider a professional career.

South African John Bland and Aussie Graham Marsh were competent cricket players in their countries. Frank Conner played professional tennis, and Charles Coody was an All-State basketball player in Texas.

Though Jim Dent, the most well-rounded athlete of all of those on the Senior Tour, craved football, golf was his destiny. After being given his first set of clubs at fifteen, he'd throw them over his shoulder and head over to the Augusta Golf Course, a public layout known as "The Cabbage Patch." Jim and a buddy often snuck onto the sixteenth hole at Augusta National and banged balls around, all the while on the lookout for club officials.

After a brief stint at Paine, a local college, Dent packed his clubs and headed for Atlantic City. "I waited tables there," he remembered, "and played golf until I had to work. But I hated to be inside, and I wanted to play more."

From the get-go, Dent had always been able to smash the ball. At 6'2" and 225 pounds, he could hit the ball farther than anyone around. He just didn't know where it was going.

Dent's first thoughts of taking his game to new heights came in Los Angeles in the mid-1960s. "I was drifting around, working in a bar owned by a pal named Mo Stephenson. The only tournament wins I had were in the Queen Mary Open, a local event in Long Beach. Mo picked me up early in the morning, and we'd head to the football and track practice fields at Compton District Junior College. He'd stand at one end and I'd stand at the other, hitting balls back and forth. Mo finally got me thinking about the PGA Tour. Basically, I was headed nowhere, my life was dead-endsville. That's when I decided to give the Tour a shot."

It took three tries before Dent became eligible. He joined an elite list of African-Americans trying their hand at what had been basically a white man's sport. Especially in view of the "Caucasian Clause" in the PGA of America's bylaws that prevented blacks from competing.

The Tour Jim Dent joined in 1971 was filled with stars; Arnold Palmer, Jack Nicklaus, and Gary Player dominated play. Big Boy learned that while he could hit the ball as far or farther than they could, the rest of his game was inferior.

"I was way out of my league," Dent recalled. "Those guys all had great short games, and I didn't. And I was too stubborn to work on it. I just thought I could get by with a good long game. I was sorely mistaken."

Eighteen years on and off the regular PGA Tour produced no victories.

Worse, Dent only made the Top 60 money list one time. That was in 1974, when he finished fifty-ninth with just over $48,000.

What had seemed like a promising career for Dent bottomed out in 1987, when he entered only six tournaments and thirty-sixth was his best effort. Even wife Willye, a stand-up gal with a light-up-the-room smile, was discouraged, wondering where the money would come from to feed Radiah and James, Jr., who would go on to play golf for Talladega College and lead his team to the NCAA Division II Championship in 1997.

The answer for Dent turned out to be the J. C. Goosie Space Coast Mini-Tour in Florida. "It was hard for me to believe," Dent remembered, "but I finally realized I needed to work on my short game if I was ever going to have a chance to play well and earn a living. My thought process had been, 'Hey, you ever see the big hitters Mays and Mantle working on their bunting?' No way, so I thought I didn't need to work on the short stuff either. I was dead wrong."

At age forty-eight, Dent decided to chase his dream on the mini-tour. Most of the tournaments were close to home, and Dent followed the path former steelworker Walt Zembriski had used to wend his way to the Senior Tour. "Us old guys stood out," Dent said. "There weren't many forty-eight-year-olds playing out of the trunks of their cars. I'd put up $300 for a $25,000 purse. The flatbellies were tough, and to win the $25,000 you had to play like hell. I shot 131 one time and didn't come close."

As Dent approached his fiftieth birthday, the Senior Tour beckoned. And he was ready, entering the Bell Atlantic Classic the day after his birthday party. When Sunday evening came, he collected $21,800 and he and Willye had something to celebrate.

Dent's breakthrough first win came at Syracuse a few weeks later. A final-round 64 lapped the field, and the former caddie at Augusta won $45,000, more money than he had won in any year since 1984.

Gary Player saw the potential. "I have never believed there was such a thing in golf as a natural player, but there is. It's Jim Dent." Player said. "He has such natural talent, and with his new short game, he'll be a contender every week."

Player was right. Since that first victory in 1989, Dent garnered nine more. Four of those came in 1990, when he finished sixth on the money list.

As the sport of golf headed toward the twenty-first century, Dent remained one of the few of his race to play the game on a professional tour. In the thirty-five years since the Caucasian Clause was removed from the PGA of America (forerunner of the PGA Tour) regulations, only seventeen African-Americans have competed on the regular Tour, and only two, Tiger Woods and Jim Thorpe, fast approaching Senior Tour status at age forty-seven, compete today. The last black graduate of the Tour school qualifying event was Adrian Stills—twelve years ago.

At the Home Depot Invitational in May, Lee Trevino catapulted into contention with a final-round 67, and he and Larry Gilbert stood even at eight under par. But Jim Dent had the tournament in hand, especially when his ball lay less than three feet from the cup on the eighteenth hole. If he canned the putt, he finished at nine under par and could start counting the $135,000 first prize.

Maybe that's where his mind was since he took little time before sauntering up to his putting position. Hunching over the ball, he rushed his stroke. The result was a pull that left the crowd gasping. A tap-in meant he and Gilbert and Trevino were square. Dent's eyebrows drooped, and his facial expression indicated shock.

Trevino, Dent, and Gilbert headed for the first play-off hole, the par-five eighteenth. Along the way, Trevino provided Dent with some advice, in essence saying, *That was too important a putt for you to hit that quick.* Dent smiled, nodded, and thanked Lee, his stomach still in turmoil over the missed near gimme.

If anyone could rebound from such adversity, it was Dent. Though known to let little things, crowd noise, other players' distractions, bother him, Dent had the perfect casual demeanor to say, "Okay, I screwed up. Let's get on with it."

When Larry Gilbert bogeyed the first play-off hole, he was history. Trevino then left Dent the opening he needed by missing the green at the par-three seventeenth. Calmly, the father of four ripped a nine iron to within three feet. He took his time and didn't miss, causing Trevino to say, "I should have kept my mouth shut about how to putt three-footers."

While the win was a surprise to many who believed Dent's days in victory lane were over, he had predicted victory while competing at the PGA Seniors' Championship. "I'm playing well," he said, his huge muscular arms wrapped around two-year-old daughter Victoria. "Now, it's time to win." Three weeks later, he had.

If not for Jack Nicklaus, Australian Bruce Crampton would be a certain member of the Golf Hall of Fame. Though Bruce had much to be proud of during his forty-four years as a professional, the Golden Bear stood between Bruce and a record that positioned him among golf's greatest champions.

That's because Crampton finished second behind Nicklaus in three Major championships: the 1963 PGA Championship, 1972 Masters, and the 1972 U.S. Open, when Jack hit a one-iron stiff to the pin on seventeen. Those narrow defeats caused the rawboned Crampton to say, "I'm working on my slam, runner-up in all four Major events in one year." Jack also prevented Crampton from winning a Senior Major when he bested Bruce in the 1991 PGA Seniors' Championship.

Despite those near misses, Crampton's record was enviable. He won fourteen times on the PGA Tour, including the Bing Crosby Pro-Am, the Western Open, and the American Golf Classic. Coupled with nineteen wins on the Senior Tour, Crampton was one of the fine players to whom nobody gave much credit.

That was unfortunate, especially since Crampton completely dominated the Senior Tour when he won seven times in 1986. He was the leading money winner and Player of the Year.

Crampton's inability to gain his due and find a place in the hearts of fans and fellow competitors stems from an unfortunate propensity to be a grump. He was even nicknamed "Crabby." As a tournament volunteer at the Legends of Golf Tournament put it, "Why can't Crampton smile once in a while? Why be rude to those who work the events and enjoy watching him play?"

To be sure, there was a pleasant side to Crampton. One had to look no further than his wife, Marlene, a sensitive, caring woman who stood by Bruce through the good moods and bad. An incident at the 1989 Ameritech Seniors' Open held at the Canterbury Golf Club in Cleveland, where Crampton emerged victorious, illustrated the point well.

After holing a putt on the eighteenth green to win that championship, Crampton's son broke through the ropes and jumped into his arms. Standing nearby was USGA official Joe Luigs's daughter, Lisa, a budding photographer, who snapped a picture and sent it to Crampton. "He didn't have to, but he sent me the most endearing letter back," Lisa recalled. "Told me it was such a special thing that I had done."

Entering 1997, Crampton had not tasted victory for five years. At sixty-one, he was a weekly contender in the Super Seniors, having won that division at the Southwestern Bell when Bob Charles took a mini vacation. Six weeks later, his play in the Cadillac NFL Golf Classic at the Upper Montclair Country Club in Clifton, New Jersey, was superb. Not expected to be a front-runner, he won the tournament in a play-off with Hugh Baiocchi.

"When you get to be sixty-one, it's nice to win anything," he remarked. "Even if it's an argument with your wife." Crampton's win placed him third on the "oldest player to win on the Senior Tour" list behind Jimmy Powell and Mike Fetchick, who won in 1985 at the age of sixty-three. It even brought a smile to his face.

BOOK III

CHICAGO SWAMPLAND

12

ON A DAY WHEN MICHAEL JORDAN ELECTRIFIED THE SPORTING WORLD
with a buzzer-beater shot to defeat the Utah Jazz in the first game of
the NBA Finals, Gil Morgan and Hale Irwin were expected to provide
a classic confrontation at Kemper Lakes Golf Course in the Ameritech Senior Open. Unfortunately, the fight wasn't even. Irwin was suffering back spasms that hadn't disappeared despite three weeks off the
Tour. On the other hand, Dr. Gil was physically fit and ready to secure
Senior Tour victory number three. And to avenge the early-season
loss to Irwin in the Tournament of Champions when his putter had
acted like an unfriendly relative.

Morgan's lead was one when the final round began. Irwin couldn't
find the birdie range, and by the time the two players had reached the
thirteenth tee, Morgan led Irwin by three and fellow playing partner
Jerry McGee, headed for one of the best finishes of his Senior Tour
professional career, by two.

The final three diabolical holes would be pivotal. Even when
Morgan bogeyed the sixteenth, he still led by two over Irwin.

The two-hundred-yard, par-three seventeenth proved disastrous
for McGee, who dumped his tee shot in a greenside bunker. He came
up short with the bunker shot, the ball staying in the sand. McGee
then committed a mistake that would lead to the loss of several thousand dollars in prize money.

Upset with his flubbed shot, McGee waved his wedge in disgust.
Inadvertently, the flange brushed the sand. Neither of his playing
partners saw the error, punishable by a two-shot penalty due to the
rule that prevents a player from touching the sand with a club while
his ball is positioned in a bunker.

Though he blasted out of the bunker and holed the putt,
McGee, known for a hair-trigger temper that went from ignition to
burn in two seconds flat, had made a triple-bogey six. Informed of the
ruling on the eighteenth tee by a Tour official, he promptly butchered
the hole and made his second consecutive triple bogey.

Meanwhile, Morgan couldn't salvage par at seventeen, but he
still held a three-shot lead with one hole to play. Unfortunately, that

hole, a lengthy par-four with a half-moon-shaped, dogleg-left fairway, featured water nearly equal to that of nearby Lake Michigan. When he dumped his second shot in the lake to the front right of the green, Irwin suddenly had a chance. Would Morgan blow the tournament after having it wrapped up with three holes to play?

Despite the sudden emergence of a thirty-mile-per-hour gale, Irwin managed to rifle an iron to the back fringe, thirty feet from the hole. Though CBS commentator Gary McCord told his viewing audience, "Nothing bothers Doc," it appeared Morgan's nerves were shot since his approach shot barely cleared the water. "That was a much better shot than it was meant to be," extolled McCord's broadcast partner David Feherty. It rolled fifteen feet from the hole. If Irwin made his putt and Morgan missed, one of the great chokes might head for the record books.

Unfortunately, Irwin couldn't muster his first birdie of the day, hitting a lackluster putt that never had a chance. Morgan two-putted to win by one. "Thank you, Lord," Doc seemed to say, as he limped off the eighteenth green.

"I told my caddie the only way we have a chance is if Gil knocked the ball in the water," Irwin lamented later. "And then he did. I'm going to have nightmares tonight about no birdies."

On a day when the scores included 90 by Gene Littler, 84 by Gibby Gilbert, and 81 by Bob Murphy, Gil Morgan had prevailed despite a shaky bogey, bogey, double-bogey finish. The true winner was Kemper Lakes, home of the 1989 PGA Championship and one of the finest public courses in the country, but Morgan's win proved he could best a three-time U.S. Open champion in head-to-head competition.

To make certain Hale Irwin knew he had competition for the top spot on the Senior PGA Tour, Morgan contended the following week at the BellSouth Senior Classic at Opryland. Played over the rolling hills of the Springhouse Golf Club in Nashville, Tennessee—designed by Senior Tour player-to-be Larry Nelson—Morgan fought his way to a final-day confrontation with fellow professionals John Bland, Brian Barnes, and Dave Stockton, trying to find his game after a disappointing first half of the season. Irwin lurked in the background, four shots behind as the final round began, but he faltered early and never was a true factor despite holing out a five-iron for an eagle two.

The gallery favorite of the contenders was the ubiquitous Barnsey, who bounded onto the Senior Tour full-time in 1996 like a whirlwind gale off the British coast. That was just four years removed from a bout with depression, one that caused Barnes to consider suicide by driving his car off a cliff near his hometown of Sussex.

The cause of Barnes's woes in 1992 was alcohol. "I could drink anyone under the table," the stout, muscular Englishman admitted. "Way under."

The drinking began when he was thirteen. "I was big, six-feet-two, even then," Barnes, 6'2" and 240 pounds, said. "So when I went out with my buddies, I was the one who ordered the beer. No one questioned my age. The problem was that I never got a hangover, my legs were hollow, I could soak up the booze like a sponge."

A student at the Millfield School in England, which spawned sportsmen, Barnes gained notoriety by winning the 1964 British Youths Championship. That put him on schedule to bring home the Open crown, the hope of a British program designed to tutor future champions.

It was then that Barnes—who originally learned the game from his father, the secretary at Burnham and Berrow in England—met Max Faulkner, the 1951 Open champion at Royal Portrush, the only time the Open was contested in Ireland. Not only did Faulkner hone the young Barnes's game, he provided him a wife, daughter Hilary. And a spirit for the game Barnes never forgot. "Max was a gregarious guy, a colorful character, and I learned from him that golfers were entertainers as well as players. It was important to mix with the spectators, the press, everyone, to give them a chance to know what you were all about."

The mixing Barnes did turned out to be a mixed blessing. His game progressed to where he became a fan favorite, and his stories became the talk of the day. Clever quips made him the darling of the media. Couldn't find a quote? Go see Brian.

Barnes's storytelling ability was simple: "I was half crocked all the time. But nobody knew it." The secret was safe because he played the game so well that it shadowed everything else about him. By 1970, he was proficient enough that players like Nicklaus, Weiskopf, and Trevino were telling him he could make it on the American professional tour. "They were all saying I could play in the States," Barnes recalled. "I hit it long, I hit it straight. I hit it high. That was enough."

Despite the opportunity, Barnes shunned the PGA Tour life. "I had a young family, and my wife didn't want to travel around the States all year long." Instead, Barnes became one of the best players in Europe, winning eleven tournaments in twelve years, though he never won the British Open. His most famous image came in 1975, as a member of the Ryder Cup team, when he nailed Nicklaus twice in one day. The second win came after Nicklaus asked captain Arnold Palmer for another shot at Barnes. "Jack looked at me with those icy-blue eyes on the first tee in the afternoon as if to say, 'It ain't gonna happen again.' " But it did, Barnes winning two and one.

"I don't have recollection of those matches," Jack professed later. "Nor do I care to."

Other than the one-day miracle against Nicklaus, the freckle-faced, redheaded Barnes played spottily, though he was a six-time Ryder Cup player and captained Scotland's World Cup teams for ten years.

The records were most amazing in spite of the fact that Barnes played nearly every tournament under the influence. "In my early forties, I downed eight brandy-coffees before it was time to practice. I'd hit balls a few hours, then come in and drink for a few more. Sometimes that meant as much as fifteen pints of beer. Then I'd go home and drink until I hit the bed. In tournaments, my water bottle looked like it had orange juice, but there was more vodka in there than juice. What can I say, I had become a pisshead. I was a drunken bum."

Most of his competitors weren't aware of Barnes's alcoholic tendencies, though his appearance in a kilt at a European event gave them cause for concern. "I couldn't swing very well," Barnes admitted. "The damn thing kept getting caught up on my backswing."

Barnes made headlines at the 1968 French Open at Saint Cloud when he *twelve-putted* the eighth green. "I was only one shot out of the lead," he explained. "I put my tee shot in the bunker on the par-three and blasted to within four feet. I left the putt short, and then I was so bloody mad that I kind of blacked out. I just started tapping the ball like in hockey and then headed for the clubhouse." At Gleneagles in another tournament, Barnes took a bet from his caddie that he couldn't make par from the seventeenth fairway playing *one-handed*. He did, but lost more than he won by virtue of a heavy fine.

One of Barnes's pet peeves was slow play. "I'd carry a shooting stick, or maybe a chair, a newspaper, or a book," the golfer known for wearing shorts and long socks during hot weather admitted. "And then sit there waiting on those blasted players to get going." At Wentworth one year, he was late for a starting time and played in street shoes. At the fourth, Barnes was informed of a two-stroke penalty. A wee bit upset, he threw the tee box markers over a twenty-foot hedge as the official scampered for safety.

Barnes's legend grew when he marked his ball with a beer bottle at Dalmahoy. "The rules say the ball must be marked with a round object and a beer bottle is certainly round, isn't it?" Barnes explained. No way, said the officials, but the tabloids loved it, labeling him BIG BOISTEROUS BACK-SLAPPING BARNSEY.

While Barnes loved the attention, privately he was a mental mess. Whether it was because he had never lived up to expectations and won the British Open and other Majors or due to disappointment in his private life, depression set in as he entered his late forties. Suicidal thoughts continued, but it wasn't until a bizarre incident in 1993 that Barnes decided it was time to seek help.

"Looking back, it's a blessing that it happened, but it didn't seem that way at the time," Barnes said. "Hilary and I were sitting in the car in our driveway waiting for the traffic to clear. We were headed to the Roundabout Hotel to meet Peter Oosterhuis. Hilary asked me if I was okay to drive, and I lost it. I slammed down the gas pedal and headed full speed down the roadway."

Moments later, the two Barneses nearly met their Maker. "There's a hard left blind bend before you get to the hotel, and I took it at seventy miles an hour on the wrong side of the road. Thank God, there was nothing coming or we'd have been wiped out."

When they reached the pub parking lot, Hilary jerked open her door and walked home, never uttering a word. "I just sat there," Barnes said, "disbelieving what I had done."

When he finally left the car, Barnes stood on a cliff edge at Beachy Head on England's south coast overlooking the English Channel. "I thought about ending it all," Barnes admitted.

Inside the pub, Oosterhuis waited. Later, when he asked what Barnes wanted to order, the snap answer was "a pint." "But I only had one drink of it, the last I've taken," Barnes recalled. "The next night I was in London at the Priory Hospital. I stayed for five weeks."

Sober for the first time in nearly three decades, Barnes began getting his life back together. He practiced his game and discovered he could play well without the booze. The climb back was tough, but in 1995 Barnes was back on top, winning the British Seniors' Championship in a chilling play-off with Bob Murphy when Barnes, with a dark chocolate-colored pipe tucked in his lips, holed a fifty-foot eagle putt on the third play-off hole at Royal Portrush, where his father-in-law had won.

Barnes also led the PGA European Seniors Order of Merit. He played four tournaments in the United States and readied himself to qualify for the Senior Tour so he could test his skill against players he'd missed competing against in the 1970s. Asked if his vices were now part of the past, Barnes proclaimed, "Yes, and I'm going to go out and buy a cassock next week."

Once again, the barrel-chested Barnes found an obstacle in his way. This time it wasn't alcohol but an angry spider that bit him after he'd flown to Florida to practice. The toxic bite caused phlebitis, which became deep-vein thrombosis. His left leg ballooned up to five inches greater in diameter than his right after he'd returned to England.

Doctors treating the bite in Europe told him he couldn't fly, and Barnes was forced to travel by the *QE II* and Amtrak to Florida, where he practiced again, and went then to California for the Q-School. Exhausted from the trek, Barnes tied for sixteenth, losing a partial qualifying (the top eight are automatic, the next eight "conditional") spot in a play-off.

Though there was an outcry for Barnes to receive a special exemption for the 1996 season (Gary Player and Tony Jacklin wrote letters on his behalf arguing that the British Senior Open champion deserved an exemption), he was forced to do things the old-fashioned way. Earn his spot.

The opportunity came when several tournament sponsors welcomed Barnsey to the fold. And he took advantage of the chance to play, winning more than $500,000 to finish an exempt twenty-first on the money list. He also became a crowd favorite, unmistakable on the fairway with his trademark rolled-up sleeves on a golf shirt that looked two sizes too small. "That started in 1995," Barnes explained. "The long sleeves drag the arm, and I hate that. Because of the heat, I began rolling the bloody things up. It's been that way ever since."

Though he had the remarkable season in 1996, Barnes and his exposed biceps had suffered putting woes during the first part of the 1997 Senior Tour season. When he missed a close putt at the Bell-South Classic, NBC's Gary Koch remarked that "Barnes's ball seems to be afraid of the dark," an apropos remark based on Brian's inability to hole any significant putts. A few did drop, however, and Barnes eventually finished in a tie for sixth.

At the top of the heap was Gil Morgan, who bested John Bland with superb play over the final few holes.

Bland was a perfect gentleman in defeat. "Doc was just too good today," he said. "But I'll get the bloody bloke next time."

While Jack Kiefer, the Columbia, Pennsylvania, native, was winning his second Senior Tour crown at the du Maurier Champions Tournament at St. George's Golf and Country Club in Etobicoke, Ontario, Canada, by a one-stroke victory over Jim Colbert, four senior players were competing in the U.S. Open at Congressional Country Club outside Washington, D.C.

In the field were defending Senior Open champion Dave Stockton and former U.S. Open champions Hale Irwin, Larry Nelson, who would turn fifty in September, and Jack Nicklaus, playing in his 150th consecutive Major championship. Jack's trip was enhanced when his twenty-eight-year-old son, Gary, also made the field. That produced a memorable practice round that included the Nicklauses, Greg Norman, and John Daly. Nicklaus said later he and Gary held their own in a better-ball competition with the two long hitters, neither of whom contended once the tournament began on Thursday. "Let's just say we didn't have to pay," Jack announced.

The advance publicity surrounding the Open became Tigermania as the world focused on the twenty-one-year-old Woods's potential to win the second leg of the PGA Tour's grand slam. In a jam-packed press conference, questions ranged from what he ate for breakfast to how far he hit his three-wood (an astounding 260 to 280 yards). Exhibiting the bravado about his chances at Congressional normally reserved for professional competitors with years of experience, Woods said, "My game is ready, and I expect to win."

That contrasted with the mind-set of Jack Nicklaus. Did he expect to win? "No, but I'm competitive," he announced. Did the Open mean more to him since son Gary was alongside? "Of course," he retorted. "And Jackie will be caddying for me. It will be a real family affair."

While thirty-six years' difference in age separated Woods and Nicklaus, there was one characteristic that bound them together: a love for the game. An inner spirit, one thriving on competition, had brought them to Congressional, and each longed for the chance to test his game with the best of the best.

The first round of the Open featured a dream pairing. On the tee at 7:40 A.M. were Jack Nicklaus, Hale Irwin, and Ben Crenshaw, five years removed from the Senior Tour at age forty-five. Together they had appeared in the championship *ninety-three* times.

While all hoped to be a challenger for the championship on Sunday, goal number one was to make the cut against all the flat-bellies twenty years or more their junior. In round one, Irwin led the group with an even-par 70. Nicklaus fired 73, Crenshaw the same.

The thirty-six-hole cut was projected at +6 or +7. The middle-agers fell back in the early holes on Friday, but coming to the eighteenth hole, all had managed to stay within striking distance of the cut mark. Crenshaw, though, was teetering at +8 as he encountered the 190-yard, par-three finishing hole.

On the final hole, Nicklaus faced a tricky putt for par and Irwin a makable birdie putt. Crenshaw eyed a testy ten-footer he knew meant either teeing it up on the weekend or taking an airplane back to Texas.

In just over two minutes, the three great warriors electrified fans bunched solidly around the eighteenth green. Nicklaus and Irwin holed their putts, and then Crenshaw, the master putter, in the mold of Bobby Locke and Billy Casper, rifled home his putt for a birdie to get to +7. When the scores were totaled, Ben was safe to play the weekend.

NBC commentator Dick Enberg later said of the performance on the eighteenth green, "Isn't that what golf is all about?" Certainly, it was.

Though Ernie Els won his second U.S. Open championship, Nicklaus had a hand in the victory. Els acknowledged that as a youngster in South Africa he was given *Nicklaus's Guide to Golf* as a present on his eighth birthday.

Irwin and Nicklaus finished far down the leader board at +13, but it didn't matter. "It's a long walk around here," Irwin lamented. "I'm a beaten man with a beaten body." Still, he and Jack finished tied with Fred Couples and ahead of such established PGA Tour stars as defending Open champion Steve Jones; Vijay Singh; forty-eight-year-old Tom Kite, the 1997 Ryder Cup captain; Tom Watson; and Ben Crenshaw.

And the love for the game that Nicklaus possessed had not diminished. "I've enjoyed the years and the memories," Jack said. "The way I feel now, I'd like to enjoy some more."

13

ONE HUNDRED AND THIRTY MILES DUE EAST OF AUGUSTA NATIONAL Golf Club was the Golf Club of Georgia, site of the Nationwide Championship. Previous winners included Mike Hill, Isao Aoki, Lee Trevino, Dave Stockton, Bob Murphy, and 1996 champion Jim Colbert. It was Colbert's electrifying three-stroke victory that year which catapulted him toward a season-ending battle with Hale Irwin for the coveted money title.

Colbert began playing golf as a kid in Kansas City, Kansas. His first love was football, but his competitive spirit led him to all sports. After high school, he matriculated to Kansas State with a scholarship to play on the gridiron, but golf was his destiny.

Colbert's personality was set at an early age. "I've got my mom's tenacity, my dad's even disposition," he recalled. "It took a lot to upset him. And that's a key to being a good player. Professionals lose a great deal more than they win, and you have to deal with that. The pressure comes from within, and I learned to use that as a motivator. Each time I play I try to remember, 'The game starts right here, right now, with the lie of the golf ball,' and then I go from there."

Colbert's inconsistent play on the PGA Tour prevented double-digit visits to the winner's circle, but he kept his card by finishing in the top sixty on the money earnings' list from 1969 to 1976. He won four times while working on his game with Lionel Hebert, Bob Toski, and Jack Grout (Jack Nicklaus's mentor). Then a chance lesson with golf guru Jimmy Ballard gave Colbert the feeling that better days were ahead.

"I told Jimmy, 'I came here to learn what happens in the golf swing,'" Colbert said. "'I am very athletic, and if you can explain what happens, I can do it today, not six months or a year from now, but today.' He looked at me like I was nuts, but we spent four days together, and when I left him I felt that for the first time I knew what the swing was all about."

And what were the pearls of wisdom Ballard imparted? "Basically, Jimmy broke down the three myths about the golf swing: keeping the head down, the left arm straight, and the idea of turning in a barrel. He showed me how swinging a golf club is like throwing a baseball or a football, the backhand in tennis, or bowling. All are triggered with movement of the shoulders and the chest, not the hands and arms."

Utilizing Ballard's thought process, Colbert's game improved dramatically. The breakthrough win in a major championship never came, mainly because Gentleman Jim continued to experience pain from an old childhood injury. "I was always playing with pain in the shoulder and back area," Colbert explained. "Sometimes it would get so bad I just couldn't play. Never being injury free held me back, and finally in 1987, when I was a fifteen-aspirin-a-day guy, I decided enough was enough."

In 1989, the Las Vegas gambler edged his way back into the game he loved. He joined ESPN's television coverage of the Senior PGA Tour alongside another broken-down future senior citizen, Bob Murphy. Colbert's flavorful comments notwithstanding, the experience with ESPN provided four factors that propelled him toward his date with destiny on the Senior PGA Tour.

"Being with ESPN allowed me to rest my back since I wasn't playing much," Colbert pointed out. "By watching all the good players, I picked up some positive thoughts. My competitive juices started to boil again, but, more than anything, the time away from competition permitted me to forget most of my bad old swing habits. All the little idiosyncrasies went away. I felt like a new man."

When Colbert joined the Senior Tour in 1991, he came charging out of the gate like a thoroughbred. Three victories and five runner-up finishes propelled him close to the million-dollar mark in prize money. Even so, the bad back still haunted him. "I was now a fifteen-a-day Advil man," Colbert recalled. "What a nice little short career I'll have, I thought." But his play was stellar and continued into the 1992, 1993, and 1994 seasons, when he recorded six more victories, including his first Major, the 1993 Ford Senior Players Championship.

Colbert wanted more, and the first step to the top of the mountain came in 1995, when a meeting with Mickey Gallagher, an assistant professional at the PGA National Golf Club, introduced Jim to the miracle of magnets. He was dubious at first, but soon Colbert was wearing a belt full of the positive ions, two magnets the width of half dollars on both sides of his spine.

"All those aches and pains were suddenly gone, and I could swing pain free," Colbert reported. "I just had to watch myself when I walked near the refrigerator."

Colbert thought so much of the magnets that he purchased part of Magnetherapy, the company that makes tectonic magnets. He also took wearing magnets to another level. "I have a mattress pad filled with three hundred and fifty magnets that I sleep on every night," Jim admitted.

Close friend Bob Murphy became a believer, along with more than thirty other professionals on the Senior Tour. "Magnets certainly can't hurt you," Murphy offered. "And they've been great for me."

Being healthy increased Colbert's confidence, but his outlook on the game had improved as well. "I had decided when I joined the Senior Tour that I was going to have more fun this time," he said. "I was going to play a little faster, be a little friendlier."

The miracle of the magnets and a less intense attitude spearheaded Colbert's play in 1995. Wearing his familiar bucket hat and golf shirt with the collar turned up, both designed to keep the sun off his sensitive skin, Colbert won four times, capturing the money title with just under $1.5 million. He was named Player of the Year.

Then came the 1996 season when Colbert secured a spot in the annals of golf with a breathtaking putt at the season-ending Energizer Senior Tour Championship. If one moment could provide an image that would forever mark the career of a golfer, it came for Jim Colbert on the eighteenth green at the Dunes Golf Club in Myrtle Beach, South Carolina, on November 10, 1996. The moment-of-truth putt to win the money title added another link to Colbert's reputation as a player with the ability to win under pressure.

"In the clutch, he's as good a putter as I ever saw," said J. C. Snead.

Colbert's chief asset was his dogged determination to be the best. When he was concentrating, his eyes the merest of slits, Jim could tough it out with anyone. "I'm a hard trier," Colbert admitted. "I wake up that way every day."

To those who panned him for the turned-up collar, the swagger (Colbert's right shoulder was six inches lower than his left, causing him to swivel his hips), and the propensity to waggle his index finger like a Texas gunfighter after a holed putt (Colbert picked the habit up having fun with an ESPN cameraman), the Kansas native pointed to his record on the Senior PGA Tour as proof of what he might have accomplished on the regular Tour free of pain and injury. To those who said he was arrogant, beyond just being cocky, Colbert replied, "I'm not arrogant, I care about people. I just have my own style."

Longtime jovial caddie Willie Miller, a staple on the Tour for what seemed a lifetime, said, "Jim's just misunderstood. He's simply the most competitive person I've ever been around. And he'd do anything for you. He's been more of a friend than a boss. I love the man."

More than anything else, Jim Colbert never forgot that the PGA Tour had been good to him. Commissioner Tim Finchem knew he could always count on Colbert. When absence of the "big names" at the American Express Invitational in February threatened the tournament's chances for success, he called Colbert and asked him to compete. Colbert was on the first tee Friday morning after canceling other plans.

Lee Trevino applauded Colbert's accomplishments, explaining, "He's one tough dog to shake off." Bob Murphy added, "Jim grew up scrambling and scrapping and putting up his own money to play. A lot of his success is down to pure fight."

Midway through the 1997 season, Colbert's ability to fight back when the times were toughest was tested once again. Prior to Ontario's du Maurier Champions Tournament in June, Jim had undergone a routine physical. To his shock, a test for prostate cancer was positive.

In a year when the fifty-six-year-old golfer had endured his father's bouts with illness, wife Marcia's facial skin cancer, her brother's bout with prostate cancer, Willie Miller's difficulty of dealing with the death of his sister, and a variety of injuries that had nagged him, Colbert screamed, "What now, Lord?"

"I was shocked beyond belief," Jim explained. "Not so much in the daytime, 'cause I was active and could play golf, but at night I'd lie awake and think, 'I have cancer.' Even on the golf course, sometimes I'd miss a putt and say, 'I have cancer. No, not me, I'm Jim Colbert. That's not supposed to happen.'"

True to his private nature, Colbert told few people about the disease. Not even buddy Bob Murphy. Instead he played at the du Maurier Champions, where he nearly won, and then in the Nationwide Championship. At the final hole there, Colbert drilled a fifteen-footer for birdie. He strutted around as if he had just won the U.S. Open, bobbing and weaving to the gallery with characteristic, charming form. Only he knew that unless the prostate cancer surgery was successful, it might be the final putt he ever hit in professional competition.

Fortunately, the surgery was a success, and Colbert was back on his feet within a few days, albeit his plans to return to competition unclear.

Though Colbert wasn't a factor in the Nationwide Championship, Hale Irwin, Bob Murphy, and Graham Marsh were. From day one, the three men positioned themselves for a Sunday shoot-out for the top prize.

The contrast among the three players was notable. Murph, a fisherman with the patience to match, relied on his calculated hesitation swing that required precision timing. And he still had as fine a putting stroke as anyone in the game.

Irwin, ever the meticulous one, was still searching for the perfect golf swing. When a shot veered even a millimeter to the left or right, it was as if Hale wanted to escape the course for a laboratory where he could research exactly what went wrong before proceeding.

Marsh acted as if the Sunday round was just a match with the boys. He relished the challenge and hoped that his hard work on the practice tee was finally going to pay off with a victory.

The Aussie's reliable one-piece flowing swing with a bit of a flurry to it continued to produce efficient shots through the eleventh hole, though it was his putting stroke that curled in a die-at-the-hole five-footer to keep the lead at two over Murphy. Irwin's balky putter was driving him crazy, and he stood another shot back.

For Murphy, the 183-yard par-three thirteenth became a nightmare worse than any shark attack he'd thought of while trying to land a fish. He hit his seven-iron heavy, came up shy, and watched in disbelief as the ball kerplunked unceremoniously into the pond in front of the green. Caddie Mark Huber's face turned ashen as he picked up Murph's heavy bag and trailed after him.

Shoulders slumped, Murphy bounded off the tee toward the drop area. His ball found a cuppy lie and instead of playing safe and merely lofting the ball onto the green with a half wedge, he tried to get cute and knocked his third shot into the same pond. Huber, realizing his percentage of his boss's winnings was dwindling with every shot, reluctantly retrieved another Titleist from the bag and tossed it to Murphy.

The crowd breathed a sigh of relief when the red-faced Murphy barely cleared the water with his fifth shot. Two putts totaled quadruple-bogey seven. His head bowed, he ambled off the green, his cherub face looking as if a fish had caught *him* and deeply embedded a hook in *his* heart. Though he rebounded for a much-needed birdie on the fifteenth hole, Murphy stumbled home to a top ten finish that had him shaking his head in disbelief.

The competition was decided at the sixteenth. Marsh and Irwin faced mid-iron shots to the green, which favored Irwin, regarded as one of the finest iron players of all time.

This time, though, it was Marsh who was better, and his shot stopped five feet from the hole. Irwin's effort was lackluster, and when he two-putted for par and Marsh eked his ball into the hole after it hesitated on the edge, the Australian's lead had stretched to three with two holes to play. Not even Irwin could make up that much ground, and Marsh was the champion.

"Beating Hale down the stretch was very special," Marsh reported while counting his winnings. "You want to play your best against the best, and to do that is what golf is all about."

One week later, South African John Bland stood in the middle of the eighteenth fairway at Olympia Fields Golf Club outside Chicago, his arms folded, his left hand wiping sweat from a furrowed brow. Eighteen yards to his left, Graham Marsh readied himself for an eight-iron shot to the green on the final hole of the 1997 U.S. Senior Open Championship.

Moments before, Bland had lofted a mid-iron toward the putting surface from the intermediate rough. To his dismay, his weight never pulled through, causing a blocked shot. The open face of his Taylor Made iron imparted a left-to-right spin on his Titleist, and it tumbled into the bunker guarding the right side of the green. With the pin tucked to the right side, Bland faced a bunker shot he knew meant the difference between a win or a loss in the third Major on the 1997 Senior PGA Tour.

Marsh and Bland had entertained golf fans and television viewers alike with their memorable duel for the championship throughout the day. "Swampy" had begun with a two-shot lead, but a three-bogey start opened the door for Bland and the rest of the field.

The eighteenth U.S. Senior Open, the most prestigious tournament on the Senior Tour, had taken form when 2,918 golfers, an increase from the 631 who entered the first Senior Open in 1980, sent in their entries in order to qualify. From that list, 156 had found their way into the championship.

Once the field was set, attention was focused on the venue for the tournament, the fabled Olympia Fields, designed by two-time British Open legend Willie Parks, Jr. In 1928, the course had played host to the U.S. Open. Johnny Farrell beat Bobby Jones by a shot.

Tree-lined and full of pep, with undulating greens that resembled linoleum, Olympia Fields was ready for the challenge of the world's finest senior players. High-as-shoetop rough and demonic pin placements dreamed up by Tom Meeks of the USGA meant the players needed their A game to break par 70.

The difficulty of the course and its 6,800-yard length guaranteed that only a handful of players had a chance to win the coveted title. Before round one, the talk was of the rivalry triggered by the superb play of Hale Irwin and Gil Morgan, one-two on the money list and considered to be the elite players on the Tour.

While tournament officials and NBC television hoped for a down-the-stretch confrontation between the two, their personal duel never played out, though both challenged as the tournament wound down. Irwin began with rocky rounds of 73 and 74, and though he threw together 70 and 67, the best round on the final day, he was left to wonder if he would ever join Nicklaus, Player, Trevino, and Casper as the only golfers ever to win the U.S. Open and the Senior Open.

Morgan opened with 69, but then dealt out a mediocre 74, blaming a balky putter. He stayed in contention during the final thirty-six holes, but even a superb final round of 68 couldn't propel him to the top spot on the leader board.

In the first two rounds, the story was the "Moon Man," Kermit Zarley, the tall, stately Texan with the devout Christian views and the wide-brimmed straw cowboy hat. Kermit strutted out two bulletlike 69s to lead the pack. But the Big Z blew to a third-round 80 that dropped him out of the limelight like a has-been politician.

For the sentimentalists in the crowd, Palmer, Nicklaus, Player, Rodriguez, and Trevino all played well enough to make the weekend cut, set at an amazing eleven strokes over par. Palmer barely made it with 75 and 76, but nobody cared as the sixty-seven-year-old legend strode the fairways looking for birdies and some semblance of his old form. The Army, still outnumbering any other band of admirers, walked with Arnie and cheered his every shot.

Player's 76-72, Trevino's 75-69, and Nicklaus's 73-72 made the cut easily, but it was Rodriguez with 71-72 who beat them all. The Cheech performed his Zorro antics at every chance, and the galleries whooped and hollered.

As round three began, it had been Zarley by one over a trio of contenders: Dave "Ike" Eichelberger, the Waco, Texas, veteran with four PGA Tour victories to his credit; Tom Wargo, the local favorite from downstate Centralia; and the two foreign contenders, John Bland and Graham Marsh.

Round three saw the deep rough of Olympia Fields blast back

opponents left and right. When the sun set, Marsh, at four under par after a superb 67, had taken the lead by two over Bland, his partner in victory at the Legends Tournament in Palm Springs in March.

The final-round pairing would be a study in contrasts, though both players were grinders who had honed their games in international competition for thirty years. Bland had found his foes on the European circuit, and Marsh had cut his teeth mostly in Asia, though he had briefly competed in the United States during the 1977 season when he won the Heritage Classic at Harbour Town.

"Coming back to America to play is like walking down memory lane," Marsh said upon his arrival at the Senior Tour in 1994. "It was great to see old friends and compete against the best there was."

Those old friends knew one thing: Swampy was a force to reckon with. He hadn't won fifty-nine international tournaments, including twenty-four on the Japan circuit, sixteen on the Australian Tour, and fifteen PGA European events without a first-class golf game. And besides a Western Australian accent, Marsh had a bit of royalty to him. The Queen of England had dubbed him MBE, a Member of the British Empire.

Marsh was born in Armidale, New South Wales. His dad, Ken, was a brick manufacturer, Mom worked as a hairdresser. Brother Rodney grew up to be one of the finest cricket players in the history of the game. Graham intended to follow his brother and become a wicket keeper, but a broken arm at age fifteen (his left arm is one half inch shorter than his right) doused those hopes.

The alternative was golf, though the courses available to him had sand greens, or "scrapes," as they were labeled. Ken Marsh was a four handicap, and Graham toted his bag and listened to his dad tell golf stories in the pubs. Then Graham started practicing. "My game got to the point where I could hold my own with the good players, especially my dad," Graham recalled. "I started thinking about turning professional, but my parents thought that made no sense."

Once Marsh began competing internationally, the travel was never-ending. "Home was the front end of a 747," he admitted. "Being away from the family was tough, but that's the way I made a living. Looking back now, I wish I'd spent more time at home, but it was impossible."

Marsh the gypsy did what he did best, win golf tournaments around the globe. "Graham may be the best golfer of his generation who never won a Major championship," Tony Jacklin said. Gary Player, who faced Marsh many times in far-off places, agreed, saying, "Graham was a top player for a long time. But nobody over here really knew much about him."

When the gray hairs started to appear, Marsh decided the Senior PGA Tour made sense. The tournaments were televised in the Far East, and the exposure was good for his budding golf course architectural company. "Besides," he admitted, "I was still a very competitive person, and I wanted to see what I missed by not competing on a regular basis against Jack, Lee, Gary, and the boys."

Though he didn't win in 1994 (his first year on the Senior circuit), nearly half a million dollars came Marsh's way. The second year brought victory number one, and he added two more in 1996 while totaling more than a million dollars in prize money.

Marsh's success was due to a great work ethic and an intricate knowledge of his golf swing. "That's what separates everyone," he said. "You've got to work hard. And the guys who don't know their swings are lost. If you don't have a game, it's a waste of time out here."

But Marsh did have a game. And a reputation for being a gritty player who was cool and calm under pressure. "Like a former teacher of mathematics," one opponent explained, "Marsh dissects each golf course with a protractor and slide rule. And he never rattles." Five-time British Open winner Peter Thomson, who won nine times on the Senior Tour during his record-breaking year of 1985, called Marsh, "probably the most intelligent professional golfer I have ever met."

John Bland, Marsh's friend and chief competitor for the crown at the 1997 U.S. Senior Open, agreed as they began the final round. "Graham is a fierce competitor, one of the game's great players," Bland said. "Our game should be a beauty."

With eighteen holes to play, the two buddies readied themselves for combat. Typically, Bland traded quips with reporters and fellow players alike, laughing as if he were having a beer with the boys back home. Marsh, the reticent one, went about his practice regimen, butterflies filling his stomach.

Both hoped that by the close of play on Sunday, they could carry home the Francis D. Ouimet Memorial Senior Open Championship trophy. A win for Bland would help compensate for a few bucks he'd had to pay Marsh on a cricket bet when his South African team came up short against the Australians.

* * *

When Marsh and Bland ascended the tee on hole number one in the final round, both sought a lifelong goal. Marsh explained that winning a Major "is the third goal I set for myself when I began play as a professional. The first was to win fifteen international events, the second a million dollars. Winning a Major would tie it all together."

For Bland, the Senior Open win would provide a triumphal note to a stellar career. He still relished his good fortune on the Senior Tour and his days in the limelight brought a fresh personality to the competition. Everyone loved Bland, and a victory would be most popular with those who knew the chain-smoking gent who walked with a bit of a waltz from tee to green.

Graham Marsh's game plan for round four was simple: "I know fairways and greens are the key. And keeping my composure. When you're close to the lead, that's what is required. Keeping the wits, trying to play smart."

Bland was his usual unflappable self. "I need a bit of good fortune," he relayed. "And to hit it in the short stuff."

Twenty-eight years of experience as a golf professional had done Marsh little good when he stood on the fourth tee, having bogeyed the first three holes. Olympia Fields, which would be awarded the 2003 U.S. Open, was playing tough, but Marsh knew that unless he pulled his game together, breaking 80 might be his only goal on the back nine.

Having recorded five bogeys in ten holes—"I've got too many 'boxes' [bogeys] on my card," Marsh said—he attempted to steady himself. The eleventh proved pivotal when he spun a mid-iron to within five feet of the cup and holed the putt for birdie. He led by one, but a bogey at twelve leveled him with Bland, who had won four of his five Senior Tour victories coming from behind.

Marsh eased out a par, while Bland's dicey pitching wedge propelled the ball over the green and into the high rough. A sixty-degree wedge flop shot flopped too much, and Bland made bogey. Advantage: Marsh by one.

The match-play environment was reminiscent of a previous dogfight they had encountered in the 1976 Benson and Hedges tournament, where they rammed against each other in the final holes. Marsh had pleasant memories of the event since he'd holed out a wedge to beat Bland.

The twosome shared another important characteristic. By honing their games in international play, Bland and Marsh had become true shot makers, able to compete under any condition. Their ability to play the pitch-and-run permitted them an advantage with the hard Senior Open putting surfaces. While their American counterparts were trying to stick the ball on the greens with high wedge shots, Bland, Marsh, and the other foreigners were playing low, piercing shots that bounded onto the greens like Texas jackrabbits. "We've sort of learned to manufacture shots," Bland noted. "It really helps when you get hard, fast greens. We keep the ball down on the ground all the time. It's more target golf here."

Through sixteen holes, the two veterans battled back and forth. With the galleries packed ten deep along the seventeenth, Marsh and Bland needed to play their best golf of the back nine. They stood at +1 as the hole began. One more bogey without a birdie would permit Gil Morgan and Tom Wargo, at +2, a chance to back into a play-off.

That wouldn't happen since Marsh and Bland played like champions on the seventeenth. Despite Marsh's ball being encased in a covered-over divot, he hit it a low trajectory shot to within five feet. "It was my best shot of the day," Marsh said, "just when I needed it."

Not to be outdone, Bland planted his approach just outside of Marsh's ball. Now it would be man-to-man with the putter with the U.S. Senior Open title in the balance.

Bland was the first to play. His straw hat pulled down over his glistening face, he ambled around the green spying the putt. A brief word with brother Roy, a like personality with a friendly smile, and Bland was ready. His stroke, a choppy one reminiscent of fellow countryman Bobby Locke, one of the greatest putters ever to play the game, was tried and true, and for the moment Bland stood alone atop the leader board at even-par for the championship. Barring a double-bogey at eighteen, that meant neither Wargo nor Morgan could win the Open.

Marsh's workmanlike demeanor took over after Bland's birdie putt tumbled into the hole. His Maxfli visor soaked with perspiration, he stalked the five-footer that now looked as if it were ten. He peered from behind the ball, from the side, and then from behind the hole, which had shrunk in size. What he saw was unattractive, for he read no break in the putt. "A straight putt," he thought to himself, "the professional's worst enemy. Give me a curler anytime, but a straight putt, no."

Marsh finally set to his position and hovered over the ball, concentrating on a smooth stroke. His hands were steady, but he knew a slight jerk would take the ball off line. Back and through, the result was commendable. His ball disappeared, and he was once again tied with Bland.

The key to the par-four eighteenth hole at Olympia Fields was to position the tee shot either short of the twin bunkers guarding the fairway or scoot a bouncing ball through the twenty-four-yard spread between the bunkers. Bland was first to play, and in characteristic, rather nonchalant form, he braced himself beside the ball, took a couple of practice efforts, swung the club outside-in with a dip of his right shoulder, and watched as the ball flew through the air toward the right side of the hole. As he eased his head back and observed its flight, John knew he hadn't come through the ball as usual and the blocked shot flew toward the right bunker. His brain froze because he knew he had hit an errant shot at crunch time, but he relaxed just a bit when the ball uncharacteristically stopped after a little roll just short of the sand.

When Marsh teed up his ball, he tried to block out the demons that had haunted him since the 1994 Senior Open at Pinehurst. He had bogeyed the eighteenth hole to lose by one to Simon Hobday. He vowed this time would be different.

With an air of confidence, Marsh envisioned the flight pattern of his ball down the fairway. A balky driver had caused him to use a two-wood for most of the round, but his swing with the driver was fluid, catapulting the ball dead center toward the short grass.

Once Marsh picked up the tee, the two warriors, the only ones to play Olympia Fields to a draw, marched toward the humongous crowd surrounding the eighteenth green, Marsh, head down and arms waving in the air, and Bland, with a cigarette dangling from his lips. This was it, the gunfight at the OK Corral, one hole for the championship they might very well trade for every single trophy won over their professional careers.

When Bland found his ball, he knew the shot to the green would severely test his skill. The tiny sphere had nestled deeply in the intermediate rough, and any chance of spinning the ball was lost. With the hole location to the far right of the putting surface, the smart shot was a high, lofted ball to the left side of the green. That meant little chance for birdie, but a safe par, and, unless Marsh pulled Jack Nicklaus eighteenth-hole-like heroics, at least a tie.

Since Bland hit the ball right to left, the safe shot was his intention, but his weight didn't transfer through the ball as usual, and the ball whipped into the air toward the right side of the green. Bland's heart sank, though he realized the lofted shot still could stuff itself on the right edge of the green, which would be fortunate in view of the less-than-perfect swing he had just taken. Up, up the ball went, but then it suddenly disappeared from view. Bland knew the inevitable, the ball was in the right greenside bunker.

While brother Roy's head dipped in disappointment, John Bland now watched Graham Marsh prepare to hit his shot. Realizing his opponent's fate, Marsh elected to play toward the center of the green. If the shot strayed just slightly, it could end up by the flagstick. Over the ball, the cagey veteran told himself not to block the shot but to let his mechanics work. The result was a good pass through the shot that propelled the ball toward the intended center of the green.

Just as Marsh's face began to relax, the ball started to veer a bit right. Graham watched with anticipation, anxiety a part of the equation. Only when the white dot plunked down just inside the fringe bordering the right side of the green did the muscles in Marsh's neck relax.

Bland's sand shot was one he'd tucked in close a million times. The ball was slightly above his feet, but he knew he could get it close, maybe even hole it. After giving the shot the proper thought, he stepped lightly into the bunker and carved down at the ball with an uplifting swing.

On the green, less than thirty feet away, Marsh watched the explosive shot. The results of Bland's effort would dictate his next move. If Bland got close, Marsh might try to hole the tricky, sidehill, fast-as-hell breaking putt. If Bland was less than successful, he could two-putt for the win, as he'd just done at the Nationwide Tournament a week earlier.

What Marsh saw was a golf ball that came out heavy. Bland had excavated too much sand, and the ball stopped twenty-five feet short of the hole. That was outside Marsh's marker, meaning Bland would play first.

Tension cloaked the eighteenth green as the clock rounded toward dinnertime. Bland now was the stalker, scrutinizing the crucial putt from every angle. Commentator Johnny Miller called it "a straight putt" with the "chance to drift off to the right." Bland later agreed, but a solid stroke with his Ping Answer Two putter couldn't keep the ball on line. The ball rolled left of the hole, and a subsequent bogey tap-in meant Bland had finished at +1. He was now at the mercy of the "cool customer."

Though four over par for the round, Marsh knew he could now

salvage an acceptable score and win his first Major. He tried to keep focused, addressing the task at hand, and to concentrate as never before. He knew that many times it was harder to two-putt than to hole one for victory. Fortunately, the previous week's experience had given him confidence. As he hovered over the ball, he called on his vast experience in the clutch in hopes of coddling his ball to within gimme range.

With Bland looking on, Marsh positioned his hands softly on the grip of his putter and readied himself for one of the most important putts of his life. One, two practice swings, and then the Odyssey 662 putter was positioned behind the ball. He had read the putt to break several feet right to left, and when he took club to ball the dimpled sphere rolled its way across the speedy green and toward the hole.

When he needed it most, Marsh's touch was superb. The ball had perfect speed. Though a bit off line, it gently rolled to within a foot of the hole. Rising from his crouched position, Marsh took great care to tap in the short putt. His even-par 72, 67, 67, and 74 total meant a win in the most prestigious tournament on the Senior PGA Tour.

While the hug of Tiger Woods and his father at Augusta topped the top ten "hug list" for the year, the one Marsh enjoyed with Bland was a close second. Two men, superb at the game they play, congratulating each other. Affection, love, and respect, all quadrants of the great game of golf.

After the ceremony, Bland was gracious in defeat, though he couldn't help needling Marsh, his adversary in betting matches over world play in cricket. "He's a good friend and a worthy champion," the South African said. "You've got an Australian as your champion . . . I don't know how you're going to cope with that. But he's a wonderful guy, and you'll get him right by the end of the year."

At the victory ceremony, Marsh, though eyeing the Francis Ouimet Trophy, named after the amateur who won the 1913 U.S. Open, the golf medal, and the $232,500 first-place check, remembered to send along get-well wishes to his buddy Jim Colbert, on the sidelines with prostate cancer. "Jim," he said, "if you're watching, get well quickly . . . we're all pulling for you . . . you're a fighter and you're a champion, and we're looking forward to you coming back next year."

Using the words "fighter" and "champion" was appropriate. Marsh was not only talking about Colbert but about himself, the 1997 U.S. Senior Open champion, a fighter to the finish.

As for John Bland, he nearly bowled over Marsh when he entered the press tent after the trophy presentation. "I'll buy the first drink," Bland blurted out.

Aware of Bland's reputation for being a frugal sort, Marsh retorted, "That would be the first time." Then he turned to reporters standing nearby and said, "And he'd probably charge it to my account."

BOOK IV

ONE FOR THE CLUB PROS

14

"I never played better. Made everything I looked at. That cup looked like a big bucket."

So spoke Arnold Palmer after winning the 1985 Ford Senior Players Championship at Canterbury Country Club outside Cleveland. The Pennsylvania strongboy had defended his title with a ten-under-par-round total that smoked the field by eleven strokes.

The Players Championship, the fourth Major on the Senior PGA Tour, was born in 1983, when Miller Barber won at Canterbury, beating another legend of the game, Gene Littler, by a shot. Through the years, the winner's circle was filled with the greatest names in golf: Gary Player, Billy Casper, Jack Nicklaus, Dave Stockton, Jim Colbert, and the 1996 champion, Raymond Floyd. In the 1990 Players Championship, the Golden Bear gobbled up the Dearborn, Michigan, Country Club with a twenty-seven-under-par total, the lowest in the history of the Senior PGA Tour.

Floyd's win in 1996 was his thirteenth on the Senior Tour, added to twenty-two on the regular Tour, including a PGA Championship, a U.S. Open, and a Masters Championship. He hoped to repeat in 1997, but his golf game had been subpar since the beginning of the season. Heading into the Players Championship, he stood a mediocre twenty-third on the money list. Worse, he had not won a golf tournament in a year. Five top finishes meant he had contended on occasion, but those numbers weren't acceptable for a player of Floyd's caliber.

Floyd admitted that while lower back problems haunted him, it was his mental game that had gone south. His career as a golf course architect demanded much of his time, but it was dedication to his family, more specifically his sons, that had soaked up much of his brain power.

Like many of the Senior Tour players who had boys ready to become men, Ray Floyd had one main hope: like father, like sons. Though he hadn't forced Raymond, Jr. or Robert toward a career as a professional golfer, it was Floyd's dream ever since he squeezed his sons' tiny hands around a golf club at an early age.

Floyd had plenty of company on the Senior Tour for father-son relationships. Jack Nicklaus, Bruce Summerhays, and Dave Stockton, among others, had multiple sons. Nicklaus had four (Jack II, Steve, Gary, and Michael), Summerhays four (Bryan, Joe, William, and Bruce, Jr.), and Stockton two (Dave, Jr., and Ron). Summerhays also had a daughter, Carrie, who could beat him on occasion.

Dave Stockton's son, Dave, Jr., was still chugging away on the PGA Tour, his first victory still eluding him. "Sure I check the tournament where Dave's playing," Dad said. "It's the first thing I do after my round is done."

By far the most successful of the sons of late had been Brent Geiberger, Al's twenty-nine-year-old son. His play during the year, including a runner-up finish, would exempt him for the 1998 season.

Brent was a tall, lanky player with a fluid swing and an even-par demeanor. He was one of those kids who had his head on straight. At the Legends tournament in March, Brent committed to caddying for his father when he wasn't eligible to compete on the PGA Tour at Doral. The day before the first round of that tournament, he received a call saying he had moved up the list and could play. Nevertheless, Brent declined the invitation and caddied for Dad. Nothing could have made Al more proud, even another 59.

While Al Geiberger was pleased with his son's progress, Raymond Floyd could have strangled his boys. Both were college golfers, Raymond, Jr., at Wake Forest and Robert at the University of Florida (though he would turn professional later in the year). Talent wasn't Floyd's concern since both boys had been champions at an early age and now exhibited golf games with PGA Tour potential.

What disturbed Floyd was the boys' inattention to the other details of their lives. In May, it appeared all three Floyds would assault the Chicago area, Raymond to play in the Ameritech Senior Open, Raymond, Jr., and Robert in the NCAA Championships at Northwestern University.

Just prior to the tournaments, however, Raymond, Jr., was demoted from the team for an infraction of team rules. If that wasn't disconcerting to Floyd, Robert hadn't taken enough credit hours and was also declared ineligible.

"Seeing the kids run into trouble is awful," Floyd admitted. "But they'll learn from this. Just like I did when I was their age."

By the first week of July, prior to the 1997 Ford Players Championship, all the calamity with his sons and Floyd's attempts to juggle outside business interests and his golf game had left him badly in need of a vacation. And that's just what wife Maria ordered. So Raymond,

Raymond, Jr., Robert, daughter Christina, and Mom packed their bags and clubs and flew to Scotland, where they toured the great courses of golf's birthplace.

It was at the revered St. Andrews where Floyd found the magic of old in his golf game. "I shot sixty-five there," he exulted. "Really played well. And it's the only place I beat my kids."

Fresh from that trip, Floyd believed his revamped golf game would permit him to defend his title at the Players Championship. Golf experts disagreed and looked to Hale Irwin, Gil Morgan, Graham Marsh, and David Graham as the favorites.

They should have included cigar-chomping Larry Gilbert, the former club professional who had been "just this close," as he put it, to some sensational golf. At fifty-four, Gilbert was on a mission, unsatisfied with his performance even though he had won nearly $500,000, placing him eleventh on the money list in 1997.

For Gilbert and others on the Senior Tour who didn't possess marquee names, the challenge was to keep from being intimidated by the game's elite. "Sure, I'm in awe of them, Jack, Lee, Hale, and so forth," Gilbert admitted. "But come Sunday, if I'm a winner, I'll just say this poor ol' country boy from Vine Grove, Kentucky, beat the best in the world."

A five-under-par 67 helps do that. Followed by a four-under-par 68. Those scores launched Gilbert to the top of the thirty-six-hole leader board, after he had shared the first-round lead with another former club professional, fifty-year-old Dana Quigley, who was quietly making his presence known on the Senior Tour after what he called "a thousand years at the country club."

Quigley's game had been enhanced after several sessions with Bob Rotella, the psychologist/guru for both Tours. "There isn't one thing different from me today than there was last year, other than what's up in the squash," Quigley pointed out.

Dave Stockton, who opened with a 68, had received a helping hand from another source, son Ron. "He's been rough on ol' Dad," Stockton lamented. "His parting shot was that my mental attitude had gone downhill for a year and a half."

Stockton wanted to disagree, but he couldn't. Outside interests and what he called "just too much golf" had worn down his mantra. To unwind, he and his family traveled to Canada on a fishing trip. Though wife Cathy caught the biggest fish, Dave was able to forget the errant tee shots, the slicing mid-irons, and a putting stroke that was at best mediocre for the first time in a decade.

Stockton's 68 tied him with Jack Nicklaus and John Bland, in search of the Major that eluded him at the U.S. Senior Open. Bland could do no better than par 72 in the second round, but Nicklaus plucked another 68 out of his golf bag to assume second position behind Gilbert's nine-under-par total.

Heading into Saturday's round, other pretournament favorites had fallen by the wayside. Hale Irwin had opened with a lackluster 73 and followed with 70. Dr. Gil Morgan fired a first-round 70 and then added a mediocre 71. David Graham was the worst of the lot, shooting 76 and 70. Arnold Palmer, despite being one of the saviors of the game, was absent, having not made the top seventy-eight money list.

With two rounds to play, would-be-star Larry Gilbert would be paired with the greatest golfer of all time, Jack Nicklaus. "This is what I've been waiting for," Gilbert explained. "What I've worked for all my life."

When the final round began most contenders (seventeen golfers within three shots of the lead) were thinking about winning the tournament. Jack Nicklaus's mind-set was a bit different. He was not only hoping to add the Players Championship to his eight other Senior PGA Tour Major titles but to win the British Open the following week.

Such had been the life of Jack Nicklaus, the great champion and still a contender in Major championships thirty-seven years after his memorable U.S. Open appearance in 1960. Tiger Woods, at the midpoint of the 1997 season, was still *sixteen* Major titles short of Jack's record.

Jack William Nicklaus deserved immense respect for the outstanding record. A champion at fourteen, and still one *forty-three* years later, Jack changed the face of golf. Nicklaus's main ingredient for success was pure and simple: He could motivate himself better than anyone before or since. Through four decades of play as a professional, he had beaten the best the game had to offer, including those with last names like Snead, Hogan, Palmer, Player, Trevino, Watson, Miller, Ballesteros, and Norman.

Jack's ability to motivate himself and to record championship after championship was made possible by a cunning mind that strategized the game better than anyone. His concentration level permitted him to follow a game plan, thinly sliced between conservative and aggressiveness play. Armed with those tools and a confidence level off the chart, the Golden Bear, a nickname given him by an Australian journalist, literally destroyed the opposition, especially in Major events on Sunday.

Throughout his career, the opposition watched Nicklaus in awe. "Jack would look at you with those icy-blue eyes and you knew he knew you knew he was going to beat the shit out of you," related Tom Weiskopf. Nicklaus's longtime caddie Angelo Argea said, "Jack Nicklaus approached a round of golf as if he were F. Lee Bailey entering a court room. He had it down to a science."

Attention to detail and dedication to continually improving his golf game separated Jack from the rest, but a tip he picked up from his idol, Bobby Jones, at an early age may have been the true key to his success, especially in Major competition. Jones told young Jack he needed to learn how to adjust his swing and correct flaws during a round when the bogeys start piling up. Nicklaus was a superb listener, and he took Jones's words to heart. Nobody ever knew the mechanics of his golf swing better than the Bear, and he could cure even minor defects when a Major championship was wilting away.

Though he was a great champion, Nicklaus's idiosyncrasies were endless. He was the consummate hypochondriac, at one point telling business associate Tom Peterson, "My big toe is dead." When Peterson shook his head and replied "Well, Jack, I've never heard of that," the Bear said, "Oh, Tom, it's quite common."

"It's either his ass or his elbow," Jack's dad, Charlie, lamented.

Nicklaus was highly superstitious and a constant worrywart about his health. No Nicklaus male had ever made it past the age of sixty, and Jack feared that number as if it meant certain doom. He was also a control freak and believed he was an expert on everything.

To his credit, Nicklaus balanced his life like few before him. A modern Renaissance man, Jack was the champion golfer, both as an amateur and a professional, a successful businessman despite a land-development debacle that brought him close to bankruptcy in the mid-1980s, a well-respected golf course architect, though his first courses were only playable by golfers who could hit the ball long, hard, and with a fade, and the consummate family man, who was always there for his wife Barbara, dubbed the "classiest woman in golf," and five children.

In many ways, Jack Nicklaus was the ultimate paradox. "Jack Nicklaus hit the ball so far one would have thought he was Paul Bunyan," one author wrote. "His precise play reminded observers of an Olympic champion firearms marksman. Jack putted as if he had the composure enjoyed by a seasoned librarian. And he was as meticulous as Felix Unger of *Odd Couple* television program fame. No wonder future generations will wonder if Jack Nicklaus was really a human being or simply a sophisticated robot."

At the Ford Players Championship, played at Jack's TPC Course at Michigan outside Dearborn, Nicklaus challenged for the title with birdies at three and six in the third round. Nicklaus's caddie toted a Golden Bear golf bag splattered with miniature golden bears, whose unusual shape caused one spectator to say, "There's Jack Nicklaus over there. He's the one with the little gold pigs on his bag." Using the small-headed George Lowe putter, first acquired in 1962, that had been his friend for fifteen of his eighteen professional Major championships, Jack was darting ten- and fifteen-footers into the cup like the Nicklaus of old.

Jack's mediocre play earned him nothing to shout about on the final holes, though he did leak his intention to play in the British Open. At the fifteenth, Nicklaus had a delicate pitch shot and remarked to his caddie, "Well, I might as well practice these shots this week for use next week."

The Golden Bear's lackadaisical play positioned him at eight under par for the championship. Ascending to the top rung of the ladder at nine under were John Bland, passionate about winning his first Major; Dave Stockton, armed with the new attitude one of his sons had instilled in him; Bob Dickson, whose holing out of mid-iron at the seventeenth hole propelled him to a round of 69 and a share of the lead; and Larry Gilbert, the former club professional with the slumped shoulders and a new short stick that had turned him into one of the best putters on the Senior Tour.

After eleven holes, in the final round, Larry Gilbert's four birdies propelled him to thirteen under for the tournament. He sported a bucket hat with the brim turned down and a steely demeanor that said, "Watch out, boys, this is *my* golf tournament."

In fact, it had been Larry Gilbert's since day one, when he fired a 67 in the first round. A second-round 68 was followed by a grinding 72. Now Gilbert was making a stab at the championship, one he could have only wished for when he'd decided to try his luck at battling the best senior players in the world back in 1992.

Like other former club professionals such as Jim Albus, head professional at Long Island's Piping Rock Golf Club for fourteen years, and Larry Laoretti, who worked as a club pro for twenty-eight years, Larry Gilbert earned his way to the Senior Tour. With wife

Brenda and two children—Allen and Chris—to support, he ran the pro shop, serviced the carts, provided the lessons to duffers who would never break a hundred, and put up with the nonsense from the membership that went with the job. All for minimal money that would barely put the two children through college and at the expense of a golf game that would never get better playing twice a week, if that.

Not that Larry Gilbert didn't have talent. Once a year, he polished his golf game and went to the PGA Club Professionals Championship. He won that title in 1981, 1982, and 1991, the year he and Brenda decided to take the financial risk of their lives.

"As I approached fifty, I knew I had to do something," Gilbert recalled. "I wasn't going anywhere with my club job, and the money was awful. Brenda and I decided to take a risk, and it was a big risk, because the kids were in college. We didn't have to sell the house, but we did have to dig deep into our savings account."

The Gilberts's decision was for Larry to quit his club job, leave the steady paycheck, and attack the Senior Tour with the same fervor that had proven successful in the PGA Club Professionals Championship. First stop was the Q-School, and Larry's game was on target. He overwhelmed the field by six shots. He had earned his card, and now it was time to find out if he had the skills to compete with the big names on the Senior Tour.

Compete he did, and in 1993 Larry Gilbert became a player to be reckoned with. Two second-place finishes and more than $500,000 in prize money meant he and Brenda could relax.

Gilbert's second year on the Senior Tour brought his first two victories and nearly $900,000 in earnings. Two solid years of play kept his Senior Tour card, but as Gilbert approached 1997, he was yearning for more. "It's time to make my mark," Gilbert professed. "Time to move up."

The year began with a new club—a short putter that felt right the moment Gilbert gripped it. The results were immediate, and, with a more seasoned look toward the game, Gilbert's game continued to improve from week to week. On the eve of the Players Championship, he felt a cool, calm resolve that caused him to believe his turn in the winner's circle was imminent.

"Great golf comes in stages," Gilbert said. "Coming into the Players I felt like I was on the verge of really playing well. You need to get hot out here at the right time, and I hoped my time had come."

Perhaps it had, but the hot golfer on the back nine in the final round was Isao Aoki. His tipped-off-the-ground putter started working its magic, and he birdied five consecutive holes to climb to minus twelve with the eighteenth to play. That was just one shot off Gilbert's lead, but then Aoki made an adventure out of the last hole. He blocked his drive to the right, leaving a tall cottonwood tree between him and the green. He attempted to defy physics and hit the ball through the tree. The ball ticked a limb and darted toward the green like a road runner.

Second or third six times in 1997, Aoki knew he had to chip the ball in from behind the green to have any chance to win, but his effort was too bold. When his eight-foot putt slid to the right, his −11 total was low for the finishers but definitely not good enough to catch Larry Gilbert, unless he fell into one of the wetlands areas that dotted the course.

And Gilbert wasn't about to do that in the Senior Players Championship. With Brenda holding her breath on every shot and Gilbert puffing on stogies as if he had to quit smoking by day's end, the club pro was on a mission. One that years of tournament play as a club professional had prepared him for.

When Gilbert holed out the final putt for the victory, a mere two-footer, he kicked up his right leg and pranced off the green with a smile a mile wide. The champion knew that it would have taken many years of teaching golfers on the practice range to earn him the $270,000 he'd just won in four days.

Standing by the green as Larry Gilbert made his way to the scorer's tent was Jack Nicklaus. Even though he had finished half an hour earlier and his shirt was soaked with perspiration from his long day on the links, he wanted to shake the new Senior Players champion's hand. "Nice going, Larry," Nicklaus said, realizing how special it was that a man from the club professional ranks had broken through once again.

Larry Gilbert stared at Jack with reverence as they shook hands, the ever-present stogie clenched between his teeth. More than the trophy and even more than the money, Nicklaus's congratulatory handshake would live forever in Gilbert's mind.

The week before the Players Championship, the over-fifty crowd visited the Kings Island Golf Center in Mason, Ohio, for the Kroger Senior Classic. Defending champion Isao Aoki was expected to be pressed by Graham Marsh, Bob Murphy, and Dave Stockton.

The playing of the Kroger had marked the halfway point on the

1997 circuit. Nineteen full-fold tournaments were now in the record book, with nineteen full-field events, including the Kroger, to follow.

Competing on the Senior Tour was a coveted privilege for those who had passed the half-century mark. The circuit provided a second visit to the promised land. For most, the chance to play made their hearts sing. Others had good days and bad, sometimes permitting the sour side of their personality to appear, offsetting benevolent acts that underscored their love for the game. Though they could be as sweet as sweet potato pie on occasion, players such as Walter Zembriski, Bruce Crampton, Terry Dill, J. C. Snead, Jerry McGee, Rocky Thompson, Dave Hill, and Tom Weiskopf appeared to be unapprecia- tive of their second chance on the Tour, forgetting that they otherwise might be toiling as club professionals or be out of the game altogether.

From time to time, they griped or were rude to fans, to sports- writers only trying to do their job, or to volunteers—the saving grace of the Senior Tour, who catered to the professionals and patrolled the golf course for long hours with no pay. Such sourpusses needed, as one fellow professional stated, "for someone to kick the you know what out of them. Maybe that would make them realize how lucky they are."

A good case in point was Rocky Thompson, the colorful player and mayor of Toco, Texas, population 164. Resplendent in his knick- ers and plus fours of every imaginable color and armed with the Bumblebee driver and black golf bag with bumblebees all over it, Thompson could be a delight at times, especially when telling stories. But fans, fellow players, and the media never knew which Rocky had shown up—the grump who tilted his head toward the ground and never flashed a hint of a smile or the effervescent Rocky who was everyone's best pal. Later in the year, the Texan seemed so preoccu- pied at the Comfort Brickyard Classic that no one dared approach him. Minutes later, he was reaching deep into his golf bag, drawing out a bevy of hats and distributing them to swarms of needy kids who witnessed his ready smile.

While Bruce Crampton had earned his reputation as a grump, the worst of the lot was Tom Weiskopf, who'd worn out his welcome years ago. His pompous "me" attitude offended nearly everyone, es- pecially Tour officials who were shocked when he decided not to de- fend his title at Pittsburgh. No one was sorry to see him cut back his tournament schedule to the bare minimum. "The only thing better," one professional exulted, "is if he didn't play at all."

Every tournament director and official was aware of the chosen

few. At the U.S. Senior Open, "the asshole pairing" was an annual
event, coupling three players whom no one else wanted to play with.
They were accompanied, appropriately, by an "asshole rules official,"
a gentleman whom no group wanted with them.

Fortunately, the "assholes" on Tour were the exception, not the
rule. The great majority of the competitors knew they were the most
fortunate men on earth, playing the game they loved for million-
dollar purses when they could win as much in a month as they had
won in a lifetime on the regular Tour.

To play on the Tour was a privilege, not a right. And a privilege
that only extended if competitors continued to exhibit skills that
qualified them to compete from week to week.

Though criticized by many of the players as a "closed shop,"
especially the ones on the outside looking in, the qualifying system
set up by the Senior PGA Tour seemed fair. The goal was to reward
players who had performed with excellence and longevity that earned
them the right to play the circuit. The system was set up to permit
those fifty and older who had not played the regular Tour or had competed internationally with a chance to qualify.

Each week, in official Senior PGA Tour events, the formula was set
and seventy-eight players competed.

There were exceptions to the rules that complicated the formula,
so each week those fringe players seeking entry would pencil down the
spots open and then analyze their chances to compete in the various
tournaments. That was especially true of players who were positioned
on the second rung of the Q-School list in spots nine through sixteen.

With several of the exempt players taking the week off, the
Kroger Senior Classic was one tournament where nonexempt players
had a real opportunity at being able to tee it up with their counterparts. To fill the openings, competitors such as Tony Jacklin, who had
finished twenty-fourth at the Q-School, John Paul Cain, Dan Wood,
Hugh Baiocchi, Bunky Henry, and David Ojala, the former pharma-
cist and bond broker, were chosen from the various lists for inclusion
in the tournament.

Sponsor's exemptions at the Kroger were subject to controversy.
Well before the July date, players wrote letters to tournament officials
stating reasons why they should be considered for a spot in the field.
Based on the specifics of the tale of woe, four players were chosen. At
the Kroger, the exemptions were given to Ed Sneed, the former star at
nearby Ohio State University in Columbus; Bob Duval, father of Tour
player David, who had won more than $50,000 in competition in

1997; Seymour Rose, a Jamaican who impressed tournament officials when he chose to miss the 1997 Q-School so he could represent his country in international competition; and former PGA Tour commissioner Deane Beman.

Whenever Beman was selected, it pained the players like a toothache. Despite his wondrous accomplishments as commissioner in elevating the Tour to a different level by extending the number of tournaments and escalating purses into the stratospheric multi-million-dollar range, Beman was arguably the most unpopular player on the Senior Tour.

The surprising reaction was based on three factors. First, Beman had not endeared himself to the old guard by bad-mouthing his predecessor, former executive director of the USGA, Joe Dey. Dey had provided instant credibility when the PGA Tour was saved from destruction during the wars in the late 1960s when the players revolted and wanted their own Tour. Former PGA champion Dave Marr was especially critical of remarks Beman made regarding the unstable nature of the Tour when he took over. "Joe Dey saved the Tour," Marr recalled. "And Beman tried to take all the credit. Hey, if there hadn't been a Joe Dey, there never would have been a Deane Beman."

Marr may have been right, but Beman was a visionary who forecast the great potential of golf around the world. He was a risk taker, hiring controversial course designer Pete Dye to create the TPC Stadium Course at Ponte Vedra, Florida, when others urged him to select a more well-known architect. The result was a one-of-a-kind gem that became the cornerstone for all of the TPC courses to follow. "Deane Beman was the first one who could grasp the concept of stadium golf," Pete Dye said. "And how it could make the game more fun for the spectator."

Despite his achievements, many Senior Tour players felt Beman took far too many monetary benefits from the kitty when he resigned as commissioner. More important, they were stern in the belief that Beman, an outstanding amateur player with two United States Amateurs and a British Amateur to his credit before winning four times on the PGA Tour, was not worthy of competing on the Senior Tour. Put simply, he hadn't met the standard for play: that a golfer earned his right to compete and then earned the right to continue through his performance.

The displeasure with Beman was especially strong with those who were knocking on the door hoping for a chance to play in any of the tournaments. Early in the year, unknown culprits had Super Glued shoe trees into Beman's golf shoes in Hawaii. Other players were openly rude to Beman, refusing to play with him.

"They don't remember what Deane did for professional golf," one competitor related.

Deane Beman was disliked by no one more than the Monday qualifiers, nomads who roamed the country facing insurmountable odds simply to gain entry into a single tournament. They saw Beman as the ultimate affront to what being on the Senior Tour was all about, a guy who took a precious tournament spot away from them. As one put it, "Deane Beman needs to go home and stay home."

Kroger Classic tournament director Burch Riber saw it differently. "As long as I'm tournament director, Deane Beman has a spot in our event," he explained. "Hell, he's the one who started the damn thing. All these guys need to realize that."

While Beman readied himself for the competition, eighty-four contestants battled Shaker Run Golf Club near Kings Island outside Cincinnati for four spots. They had a one-in-sixteen chance of succeeding, having paid $350 (less if they were members of the PGA Tour or PGA of America) for a chance to play with the big boys Friday, Saturday, and Sunday.

The crowd that hovered around the scoreboard at Shaker Run in midafternoon on a sweltering-hot day were not the fancy Dans of the Senior Tour, those with lucrative endorsements, agents, and secretaries back at the home office juggling appointments. Many played out of the trunks of their cars, their wives or girlfriends their only supporters. They all sat in golf carts, eyes glued to the scoreboard waiting to see if their eighteen-hole effort would make the field.

Each had ground it out trying to save every stroke in the do-or-die qualifying round. "On Mondays there can be no mistakes," Tom Wargo, once a Monday qualifying hopeful, said. "When you're in the show, there can be some, but if you make a mistake on Monday, you can put it in your trunk and get out of town." One contestant who failed at the Royal Caribbean Classic in late January lamented, "Only two things make me cry: the dentist and missing on Monday qualifying day."

Among those at the Kroger was Bill Hall, who'd hit the Monday qualifier seven times in 1997. He'd played four times on the weekend and knew he'd made the fifth by carding a round of 38-30-68. Several fellow players dubbed him "Chipsie," having heard that he'd chipped in twice on the back side.

Hall, former club professional at Glen Echo Golf Club in Saint

Louis, the home in 1904 to the only Olympic competition in golf ever held in this country, had tasted play on the Senior Tour in 1994, when he was low qualifier. He played sporadically that year, finishing sixty-first on the money list. That meant another trip back to the Q-School in 1995, but he couldn't crack the top eight. Mediocre play in 1995 sent him back in 1996, but he was unsuccessful. Monday qualifiers were now the only means of entry.

"Being on the Senior Tour was something I'll never forget," he recalled. "It was truly a dream come true. And to lose that privilege, well, I'm still not over it. I look back and wish to hell I'd played better to keep that card."

Another who had made the show but then lost his exemption was Chicago club professional Terry Carlson. "Having the card and then losing it, that was awful," he remembered. "To play with Arnie and Jack and all of them was really something. I'll never forget it. It was the highlight of my life."

Hall's belongings were packed in the car he used to travel the circuit whenever possible, paying his own expenses, living the lonely life on the road. There were no million-dollar contracts with Callaway or Taylor Made, no cases of golf balls sent to him by Titleist. He merely made his way from site to site, unloading his clubs, playing the qualifier, and then hoping his score would be good enough for entry. If not, he drove home or tried to play in a Senior Series tournament nearby.

And why did he continue trying to make the big show? "Because I still think I can compete out here," Hall said, sweat pouring down his brow. "It's just me, myself, and my expenses, but if I can become a better striker of the ball, I can beat these guys. And I'll never quit trying."

That Monday, the last day of June, was a good day for Hall, whose best finish on the Tour had been a fourteenth at Nashville in 1994, and another with the same last name, Walter. Their 68s guaranteed a spot, as did the 69 recorded by Randy Wood. Four players carded 70s and would play off for the last qualifier in what the competitors called the "Monday four-spotter."

On the sidelines would be such fine players as José Canizares of Spain, an eleventh-place finisher in the U.S. Senior Open at Olympia Fields; Labron Harris, the 1962 United States Amateur champion; Rick Massengale; and Tony Perla, a club professional from the East Coast who kept chasing the dream. Scores ranged from the two 68s to a 95 carded by a golfer named J. Diaz. Sprinkled in between were a 93, a 90, two 86s, and several scores in the mid-eighties. That from competitors whose only credentials had been that they were professional golfers and had the money to enter. Even the golfer who shot 104 in 1994 (a record) could come back for more.

To the first tee walked Ted Hayes, sixteenth at the Q-School, who was still struggling to make the Tour in his eighth year of trying; Fritz Gambetta, a Scottsdale, Arizona, professional who had carded 294 at Olympia Fields in the Senior Open the week before to tie David Graham for fortieth; David Lundstrom, hoping to play his first tournament of the year; and local Cincinnati club professional Bob Hauer, given a sponsor's exemption in 1996 but bumped in 1997 when Deane Beman was allotted his spot.

A bogey on the first hole eliminated Lundstrom. At the par-three second, Gambetta darted a mid-iron to within fifteen feet, but Bob Hauer, after pats-on-the-back support from his wife/caddie, provided all the fireworks when he holed a cross-country sixty-five-foot putt to grab the fourth qualifying spot. It was certainly poetic justice for the club pro. He had earned a spot in the field.

When Bill Hall ascended the practice tee at the tournament site the next morning, he was still known as "Chipsie." But those who came by to congratulate him were not only his fellow rabbits, but the elite of the Senior Tour. "We've got immense respect for guys like that," newly crowned U.S. Senior Open champion Graham Marsh said. "They work hard to play here. Talk about pressure, the Monday qualifiers have just one shot at it."

When Friday's first round came, Bill Hall was in the starting lineup, square with Marsh, Murphy, and Jim Dent, and all the rest. And he could win, as Larry Mowry, John Paul Cain, Rives McBee, John Bland, and Vicente Fernandez had done in the past, rising from qualifier to champion. But he didn't, finishing with 75, 73, and 73 to earn seventy-first spot in the tournament. The $940 he won barely covered expenses, but Hall set out for the next tournament site with a full tank of gas and a dream that would never die.

Working hard to keep his precious Senior PGA Tour card was what New York native David Oakley had in mind. The former furniture company executive was one of the fortunate ones, having gained a full year's exemption when he finished among the elite eight at the January 1997 Q-School. The challenge was to keep his card, and never to return to that awful Q-School, where four days of pressure were comparable to that of a U.S. Open championship. Bob Dickson and company had been the survivors, eight winners out of 108 finalists (the total entry was 487) from forty-one states and twelve countries. "Talk about days and nights with the Grim Reaper next to you," one competitor professed. "I was so nervous during the last round, I nearly shit my pants."

With half the 1997 season behind them, Oakley and his Q-School graduates knew it was either make the magic top thirty-one or face extinction, for none of them had career winnings or the big names necessary for sponsors' exemptions. They knew that if they were unsuccessful at the Q-School, they would become Monday rabbits like the Bill Halls of the world. Or play the minor-league Senior Series, the Nike Tour version of the Senior Tour.

During the first nineteen tournaments in 1997, the lucky eight had mixed results. Dickson had been the most successful, earning more than $250,000. The bespectacled Oklahoman with the ready smile, easygoing style, and the Snake Eyes apparel stood twenty-eighth on the money list, just ahead of Jerry McGee and just behind Tom Wargo. John Morgan was thirty-ninth with nearly $200,000, Mike McCullough forty-fifth, Buddy Whitten sixty-second, Dick Hendrickson sixty-fourth, Will Sowles sixty-eighth, and Dennis Coscina seventy-second.

Oakley's winnings coming into the Kroger were $86,516, which left him a step above Whitten in sixty-second place. Each week the pressure was mounting to climb up the list.

As Oakley stood on the first tee at the Kroger Classic, he was more than $150,000 behind newcomer Hugh Baiocchi, lodged in magic position number thirty-one. Scrambled between them were other Tour notables who would have to scamper over the final half of the year to gain exempt status, including John Schroeder, Frank Conner, and Brian Barnes.

Oakley's first year on the Tour had been full of surprises. "The biggest pitfall is listening to too many people," he surmised. "Everybody wants to give you something, clubs, balls, and, most often, advice. I had heard that, but I couldn't avoid it, especially the advice. It got me into trying shots that I can only maybe hit one out of five times. Trying to emulate others doesn't work. Three weeks ago, I started playing David Oakley's game and I'm playing better. My manager Vinny Giles [low amateur in the recent U.S. Senior Open] told me, 'Be yourself,' and that's what I've got to do. Play more within myself."

The competition level on the Senior Tour impressed Oakley. "At the top, these guys are awfully good. But they're good all the way through. There's not that much difference between a seventy-three or seventy-four and seventy-one, but if you shoot seventy-three or seventy-four everybody passes you big time. The field is so compact, there's forty to fifty guys who can win. And on Sunday, these guys never back up. In Canada, I was in twelfth going to Sunday. I shot one under and finished thirteenth. In my amateur days, guys went backwards in the final round. Out here they zip past you."

Two other factors hit Oakley, who had shown promise as a senior by finishing second to Brian Barnes at the 1996 British Open, when he toured the country. "The golf courses are a lot harder than I expected," he said. "And the travel is murder. Play on Sunday, drive or fly to the next tournament, week after week, and I've got to play 'cause this is my shot. It's very physically demanding. I know I need to play better, get better starting rounds, to make the top thirty-one. But I'm having fun, having a ball. This is what I always wanted to do. It's my dream come true."

─────

15

─────

WHILE DAVID OAKLEY TEED IT UP AT THE KROGER LOOKING FOR better days and heftier paychecks, the remainder of the field had their eyes on a victory.

The leading money winner halfway through the 1997 season was Hale Irwin, with $1,115,769 in his bank account. Less than $84,000 behind lurked Dr. Gil. Graham Marsh was third, with a little more than $800,000. The Tour results had been mostly as expected. Irwin and Morgan had been the front-runners. Jay Sigel, John Bland, David Graham, Isao Aoki, and Bob Murphy had been the major challengers. Dave Stockton, Ray Floyd, Lee Trevino, Gary Player, and Chi Chi Rodriguez hadn't contended. Jim Colbert's play had been sporadic (no wins, five top tens) before he was sidelined with prostate cancer.

Arnie and Jack had sparkled at the tournaments they had played. Arnie's scores made no difference; tournaments such as the Kroger were tickled that he played. For the most part, Jack had been the effervescent Bear instead of the grizzly one, and fans delighted in watching the two greats compete in the twilight of their careers. U.S. Senior Open galleries had yelled "Long live the King" at Arnold and "We love you, Jack" as Nicklaus passed by.

The competitors felt the same way, too. Just playing with Palmer and Nicklaus was a thrill. Joe McDermott, the King's playing partner in the final round of the Senior Open, said, "I could have shot a hundred and still enjoyed playing with him. It was a very special experience. I'll always cherish it." Nicklaus was melancholy about his appearance at the Senior Open. "The people were very nice," he said in a hushed tone. "I guess they don't think I'm going to play much anymore and they were saying good-bye."

At the Kroger, Arnold was in attendance; Jack wasn't, even though he had designed the Kings Island Golf Center. Palmer's presence made the tournament worthwhile, even though Chi Chi, Lee, Gary, and other name players were absent.

Arnie was never in contention with rounds of 76, 76, and 73. He beat only two players in the field, a far departure from his good play at the Senior Open. "I still get too tired toward the end of the round," the King said as he left the golf course. "The stamina just isn't there."

It was for Jay Sigel, who lapped the field by firing 66, 63, and 66. Sigel dominated with workmanlike play that featured pinpoint iron play and a superb putting stroke. The former insurance executive and two-time U.S. Amateur champion played bogeyless golf during Money Sunday, leaving defending champion Isao Aoki seven strokes behind.

David Oakley's attempt to climb the money list would have to wait another week, but there was a bright spot that brought confidence for the future. Rounds of 72 and 73 had placed him near the bottom of the pack, but a Sunday 67 (his best score on Tour) pushed him past several competitors. His 211 score tied for thirty-eighth place, earning $4,800 in official prize money.

Another qualifier, Dave Ojala, the Duluth, Minnesota, native whose hero was Detroit Red Wings legend Gordie Howe, made the biggest move on the money list, shooting 65, 68, and 71. He won $60,000 by tying for third, a stroke in front of Mike McCullough, who earned $32,400. Both players improved their chances toward competing for the pot of gold on the Senior Tour in 1998.

By tournament's end, golfers on the bubble near the thirty-first spot included Frank Conner, John Morgan, John Schroeder, Brian Barnes, Mike McCullough, Bob Duval, and Tony Jacklin. They'd have eighteen more tries to advance into the elite group and continue their sojourn along golf's second-chance highway.

One golfer who'd never make the top thirty-one was Deane Beman. Using his sponsor's exemption, as he had at the PGA Tour Kemper event earlier in the year where he'd fired an embarrassing 81 and then withdrew, the former commissioner shot a first-round 79, complained of a shoulder injury, and withdrew once again. He'd taken the spot that otherwise would have gone to Ted Hayes, who would have given his left arm to compete in the Kroger.

Deane Beman's status with his fellow professionals was 360 degrees opposite that of Lee Trevino. Ever since he'd made his debut on the Senior Tour in 1989, the Texan who never, ever quit talking had been welcomed with loving arms by competitors who still marveled at his rags-to-riches, could-only-happen-in-America story.

When Lee Trevino teed up his Strata Tour 100 at the Burnet Senior Classic in Coon Rapids, Minnesota, just outside Minneapolis, in mid-July, he was attempting to break the *$7 million* mark in earnings on the Senior circuit. Bob Charles and Jim Colbert lurked a few hundred thousand behind.

Added to the $3.5 million Trevino had won on the PGA Tour, where he totaled twenty-seven victories (including two U.S. Opens, two British Opens, and two PGA Championships), the Dallas, Texas, native had pocketed over $10 million in career winnings. But 1996 had seen only one victory, the late-season Emerald Coast Classic. And through the first half of the 1997 season, Trevino had seldom been a factor, triggering thoughts of banishing his golf clubs to the attic.

"If I play in 1997 like I did in 1996, I'll start playing less," he explained. "Put a fork in me 'cause I'll be done. And Claudia needs me at home. Daniel, four, will be in school and Olivia, seven, is already involved in things I need to help with."

Few took Trevino seriously, though they realized that if anything could retire him to the sidelines, love of his family was it. When he entered the Burnet Senior Classic, Lee's frame of mind was to play out the season and then confer with wife Claudia to decide what lay ahead. No victories and a nineteenth-place position on the money list weren't up to Trevino standards. Maybe it was time to retire from competition.

Then the swing that had propelled Trevino to golf stardom started producing precise shots reminiscent of old. In the first round at Burnet, Trevino carded a 66, his finest round in months. When he added 68 to the total on Saturday, Trevino found himself one shot off the lead held by Hale Irwin. Sunday's final round would be an old-fashioned shoot-out, and Trevino relished the idea of being back where the action was, not just finishing the final round hoping for a respectable finish.

Despite the presence of Larry Gilbert, Bob Murphy, and John Bland near the top of the leader board, Trevino was certain the battle would be between him and Irwin, six years his junior. The excitement caused Lee to rip his good-luck charm, a red golf shirt, out of the drawer to prepare for a one-on-one confrontation reminiscent of so many that had dotted his career.

Paying tribute to Trevino, Tom Weiskopf once said, "He had Jack's number." The Jack he was talking about was Nicklaus, and Weiskopf was right. While the Golden Bear paraded past opponents in the 1970s, Trevino more than held his own when the two faced each other.

Lee's legacy began near Dallas, where he was forced to climb out of the shadows of poverty. His family was very poor, and Trevino was raised by his grandfather, a local grave digger. Lee's father had long since departed; the home Lee grew up in had no electricity or indoor plumbing.

Trevino never made it past the eighth grade, believing education was a waste of time. Instead, he picked up a golf club at an early age, realizing it might be the key to his future. He began playing well, beating the bigger kids, and soon he was hustling every unsuspecting gent who wanted to bet a dollar or a dime.

At seventeen, he was headed nowhere, a self-proclaimed "hell-raiser." Four years in the Marines straightened out his attitude, and when he returned to Dallas, the golf course summoned.

"You don't know what pressure really is until you play for five bucks with two in your pocket," he exclaimed. Tenison Park in Dallas and later Horizon Hills outside El Paso provided the proving ground, and Lee Trevino took on all comers, beating them out of every piece of change they would bet.

One golfer passing through town was Raymond Floyd. A group of gamblers around Dallas set up a high-stakes game, but Floyd wasn't concerned with his opponent. When asked if he wanted to play a practice round, Ray replied, "Hell, no, I'm playing the locker-room guy. I don't need to look at the golf course." Five hours later, Floyd left shaking his head. "I still can't believe I lost to Lee," Floyd said. "He played like nobody *I* ever saw."

The Lee Trevino of those days woke up at the crack of dawn hitting balls, as many as two thousand a day. His arms covered with mud to shoo away the mosquitoes, Trevino patented the famous fade that served him well against big-name competition. "You can talk to a fade," he once quipped. "A hook won't listen."

Trevino's swing, a looping saga that took the club outside and back in with pinpoint timing, never would make the instructional books, but it worked for him. Of that swing, Jim Ferree once said, "Guys learn to play with a swing, and that's what they're stuck with. With a couple of lessons, I could turn Lee Trevino into a high seventies shooter."

The games Trevino played were difficult to imagine. Sometimes the opponent competed from the women's tees while Trevino played from far back. Other times he was required to intentionally miss the greens with his approach shot, setting up a chipping opportunity. And, of course, Lee became famous around Texas for being the kid who could play with a thick thirty-two-ounce Dr Pepper bottle as a club and beat an opponent's brains out.

Regardless of his talent, few believed Trevino could make it on the big-time circuit. His mentor, Hardy Greenwood, owner of Hardy's Driving Range, wouldn't sign a Class A PGA card application for Trevino when he wanted to try the Tour. "What, *you* out there?" he said. "They don't play with pop bottles."

But Trevino was undaunted. "I had fifty bucks in my pocket when me, my wife, and kids moved to El Paso. I played cotton farmers and whoever for some money. My dream was to play the Tour, and nobody could stop me."

Though he was a legend in Texas and qualified for the U.S. Open in 1966, it was one year later when the world learned about the squatty Mexican (Trevino once said that if he won some money people would call him a Spaniard) who could hit a golf ball with precision and putt as if the hole were bushel-basket size.

Trevino's astounding fifth-place finish in the 1967 U.S. Open at Baltusrol was simply a preview of the future. At Oak Hill Country Club the next year, Trevino shocked the golf world by winning, becoming the first player in history to shoot scores under 70 in all four rounds. "Who is this guy?" golf fans wanted to know.

"That still ranks as one of the great achievements in golf," Jack Nicklaus later said. "Lee's play was unbelievable."

Three years later, Trevino established a never-to-be-forgotten image that remains vivid to this day. Four days of play at revered Merion saw Lee and Jack Nicklaus tie for the Open Championship. On the first tee in the play-off the following day, Trevino reached into his golf bag, toted by longtime caddie Herman Mitchell, and withdrew a rubber snake he'd picked up for his daughter. Without hesitation, he flipped it over toward the unsuspecting Nicklaus, and Jack's heart nearly exploded as he jumped away.

"It was just a spur-of-the-moment thing," Trevino remembered. "I just lightened up things a bit." And showed the stone-faced Nicklaus, all business to that point, that his opponent for the day was as loose as a golfer playing for the fifth-flight championship at his local club.

Their titanic match turned on Nicklaus's spotty play on holes two and three. He had won the first with par, and Trevino was on the ropes when the Golden Bear let it be known he was human. Trevino explained, "On [two and three] Jack hooked his ball into the left bunkers and hit some poor shots, trying to get out. I parred both holes, and took a one-shot lead. But more important, I realized he was nervous too."

Showing weakness to Trevino was a mistake, but the golfer

from nowhere learned something else that day. "The play-off taught me something else. The Good Lord doesn't give you everything. He kept one thing from Jack Nicklaus: his sand wedge. He's a poor wedge player . . . he left his ball in two bunkers and chili-dipped two wedges."

Trevino's second U.S. Open title launched him on one of the most remarkable months in the game's history. He won the Canadian Open two weeks later and the British Open six days after that. "That's the best I ever played," Trevino admitted. "It was an amazing streak."

In 1972, Trevino added a second British Open to the equation. Only the Masters at Augusta, which Trevino grumbled about every chance he got, eluded him.

Just as Arnold Palmer had upped the ante when he competed in 1980, Trevino's appearance ten years later was the boost needed to provide more credibility for the Senior Tour. Lee still played like a magician, and the fans who yearned for a hero, a crowd pleaser, greeted Trevino's play with boisterous applause. The graybeard division of "Lee's Fleas" was reborn. "I was like a 1967 Cadillac," he said. "I've changed the engine twice, rolled back the odometer, and replaced my transmission. If all the tires don't go flat and they don't put me in the junkyard, I can still play well."

And he did, winning seven times in 1990. Another Major, the U.S. Senior Open, was added to his collection. Three more Majors were earned in the coming years.

By the time the 1997 season rolled around, Trevino was the all-time leading Senior Tour money winner. His twenty-seven victories were also a record. One year, Chi Chi Rodriguez quipped, "We have three tours, the Senior Tour, Super Senior Tour, and the Lee Trevino Tour."

While the inside-out swing that faded the ball with uncanny accuracy and the crouched, open style with a blade putter that rolled so many big putts into the hole served to remind golf fans of Trevino's great skill as a player, it was his chameleon-like personality that baffled those who knew him.

On the golf course, Lee chattered away, and most competitors enjoyed the banter. He was gregarious to a fault with spectators, never one to refuse a fan's request for an autograph. Yet when the sun went down and he left what he called "the office," Trevino became the ultimate loner, guarding his private life as if a *National Enquirer* reporter were tailing him.

Trevino's personality perplexed the competition. "Lee's much more high-strung than most people realize," observed Tony Jacklin. "He just wants to be left alone," said another. "Lee's very insecure. Like Jack, he doesn't want anyone to get to know him."

Tom Boswell of *The Washington Post* had another opinion: "Lee's the funniest man in golf and perhaps the most bitter. His humor— usually about class, race, sex, or physical appearance—is a sword with which he entertains the world while also keeping it at bay."

Trevino's quips were as legendary as Chi Chi's: "The two things that don't last long are pros putting for bogeys and dogs who chase cars," he said, later adding, "If my IQ were two points lower, I'd be a plant." To those who questioned him at an event deep in Dixie as to what he fed his rather rotund caddie, Herman Mitchell, he replied, "Rednecks, and he's hungry."

Though Trevino had enjoyed success in the early 1990s playing his brethren over fifty, he won just twice in 1995 and once in 1996. The new year had brought putting problems. "I'm putting so bad it's taken my heart away," he exclaimed. Coupled with family illness and the desire to be home with wife Claudia and the kids, Trevino was frustrated with his golf game to the point of considering retirement.

"I spend all my time with my family," Trevino said. "Each time it gets harder to leave. My little boy . . . we have such a great relation- ship. I never spent much time with my other children [four from a previous marriage], but this time I want to do that. Used to be when I left Daniel, he didn't really notice it. Now, he grabs me around the neck and starts crying and begs me not to leave. Then I cry, and ask myself, 'Where am I going, why am I doing this?' "

Few thought Lee would quit, but they cringed at the thought. "If we lose Lee or Cheech or Arnold, I'm telling you that would be a sin," a Senior Tour official observed. "There are no more like them out there. Jack, Raymond, Gary, Jim Colbert, Hale, Gil Morgan, even Johnny Miller, they're important, but without Super Mex, the Cheech, or Arnie, the Tour would never be the same again."

That official found hope in Trevino's performance in the Burnet Classic. He battled Hale Irwin to the final hole before succumbing by two strokes.

Though he was denied victory despite a final-round 67, Trevino's leap into the fray was a delight to all. His attitude toward the game and ability to cheer up anyone with a sour note to their life with just one Trevino quip epitomized why it will indeed be a sad day when the Merry Mex no longer strides the fairways in competition. Even after losing the Burnet tournament at the seventeenth hole with lackadaisical play, there was Trevino joking and laughing with John Bland and Irwin, who captured his fifth win of the year, in the middle of the eighteenth fairway. That zest for life, to live for the moment and tell all the world that, despite setbacks, everything really wasn't so bad, would be Trevino's legacy. As Lee put it, "I didn't win today, but I had a ton of fun out there. And that's what it's all about."

Gil Morgan hits his drive on the ninth hole during the second round of The Tradition in frigid Scottsdale, Arizona, in early April 1997. He won going away. *Courtesy of AP/Wide World*

Isao Aoki has a prickly lie during The Tradition. *Courtesy of Andrew Redington/Allsport*

Hale Irwin cozies up to a huge trophy for winning the 1997 PGA Seniors Championship at Palm Beach Gardens, Florida, in late April, en route to being named the Senior Tour Player of the Year. *Courtesy of Andy Lyons/Allsport*

The legendary Sam Snead is presented with an 85th birthday cake on May 27, 1997, by Bob Goalby. *Courtesy of the author*

Jack Nicklaus signs autographs on his way to the first tee for his practice round at the 1997 U.S. Senior Open on June 24th. *Courtesy of AP/Wide World*

Arnold Palmer, happy to be back on the golf course after undergoing prostate cancer surgery in January, fields questions from the media at the 1997 U.S. Senior Open at Olympia Fields, Illinois. *Courtesy of Agence France Presse/Corbis-Bettmann*

Graham Marsh embraces John Bland at the 18th hole of the 1997 U.S. Senior Open. Marsh won by one stroke. *Courtesy of Agence France Presse/Corbis-Bettmann*

Gary Player holds the silver claret jug aloft after winning the 1997 Senior British Open at Royal Portrush in County Antrim, Northern Ireland, on July 27th. *Courtesy of AP/Wide World*

An intense Lee Trevino wills his par-saving putt into the hole during first-round action at the Northville Long Island Classic in Jericho, New York, during early August. *Courtesy of AP/Wide World*

Journeyman golfer Dana Quigley sinks a birdie putt at the 1997 Comfort Classic at the Brickyard in Indianapolis. He'd won his first Senior PGA Tour event on the same day his father died, back in August. *Courtesy of AP/Wide World*

Chi Chi Rodriguez, attempting to conquer his putting woes, tries out his new putter, 27"-long "Little Bertha." *Courtesy of the author*

It's lonely at the top. Hale Irwin and his caddy head for the Hollywood Hills during the Ralphs Senior Classic at the Wilshire Country Club in November 1997. *Courtesy of Jon Ferrey/Allsport*

START	LEADERS	PAR	1	2	3	4	5	6	7	8	9	10	11	12	13	14	15	16	17	18
		HOLE																		
			4	4	4	5	3	4	4	5	3	4	4	3	5	4	5	4	3	4
9	G. MORGAN		9	10	10	10	10	10	10	11	12	13	14	14	14	14	14	15		
9	IRWIN		9	10	10	10	10	10	9	10	10	11	11	11	11	10	11	12		
3	SIGEL		3	3	3	3	3	4	4	5	5	5	6	7	7	7	7	7	7	
6	BAIOCCHI		6	5	6	6	6	6	6	6	6	7	8	8	8	7	8	8		
6	MURPHY		6	6	6	6	7	7	7	7	7	7	7	7	7	7	7			
5	HILL		5	5	5	6	6	7	6	7	7	7	7	8	8	8	8	8		
	MASTERCARD CHAMPIONS																			
6	COODY		6	5	4	5	6	5	5	5	5	5	5	5	6	5	5	6	6	6
E	HENNING		E	E	1	2	2	1	1	1	E	2	2	2	2	2	2	2	2	2
3	HENDRICKSON		3	2	2	2	2	2	2	1	1	1	1	1	1	1	E	1	1	1

The scoreboard tells it all. Gil Morgan leads by three strokes with two holes to play in November's Energizer Senior Tour Championship at Myrtle Beach. *Courtesy of the author*

Jim Colbert's bid for a three-peat as Senior Tour Player of the Year was thwarted by his battle with prostate cancer. *Courtesy of the author*

16

JULY 25, 1997, MARKED THE PASSING OF A LEGEND AND THE EMERGENCE of another. On that day, Ben Hogan, nicknamed "The Hawk," the "Wee Ice Mon," and "Bantam Ben," died at the age of eighty-four in his hometown of Forth Worth, Texas. Cancer and Alzheimer's disease had stolen one of golf's great champions.

A few states to the north and west, former golden boy Johnny Miller made his Senior Tour debut at the Franklin Quest Championship, the twenty-fourth stop on the 1997 Senior PGA Tour. His 9:40 tee-time playing partners were Don January and another legend, Arnold Palmer.

Golf had no two players who were more complete opposites than Johnny Miller and Ben Hogan. Johnny had the ready smile, a chatty nature, and Hollywood looks, and Hogan a dour manner that rarely produced the hint of a grin, let alone a word or two.

The golf world mourned the passing of Ben Hogan, though it never knew quite what to make of him. During his playing days, his stoic demeanor chilled friends and opponents alike, and while they applauded Hogan's play and respected his achievements, privately many crucified him with their harsh comments.

Hogan toyed with every opponent's emotions. And then beat them soundly.

Playing on the Senior Tour was never a consideration for him. Hogan considered it a step down, an embarrassment to those who competed. Instead, he became a recluse, playing little and devoting himself to operating the Ben Hogan Golf Company.

Perhaps the finest tribute to Hogan came in the late 1980s when he shocked the golf world by attending a dinner in New York, set up by *Golf Magazine* to honor the greatest golfer of the century. The program featured a silhouette of the fabled amateur Francis Ouimet swinging a golf club. One hundred heroes of the game were present, including Palmer, Nicklaus, Player, Sam Snead, Tom Watson, and Nancy Lopez.

When it was Hogan's turn to speak, the crowd was mesmerized.

He began by remarking that Ouimet's elbow position as characterized on the program cover was quite correct. Per usual, his words were few, but Hogan brought a tear to everyone's eyes when he said, "I love this game. I really love this game."

Shortly thereafter, Nicklaus took the podium. He looked over at Hogan and then said, "Arnold and I have our speeches ready, but we've both been sitting here checking out the position of Ouimet's elbow."

Nicklaus's obvious tribute to Hogan brought a smile to Hogan's face. Later Jack was named the greatest player of the century, but everyone in that room knew that William Benjamin Hogan, who labored throughout his life in the pursuit of golf perfection, epitomized what the great game was all about.

On the day Ben Hogan died, Johnny Miller was as nervous as a child entering first grade. Not only was he going to play his first round as a Senior PGA Tour professional, but there were those who said his appearance would be the saving grace for the Tour itself.

For at least eighteen months, golf experts had been sounding the death knell of the Senior Tour. They pointed to the absence of the marquee names, Nicklaus, Palmer, Player, Trevino, and Rodriguez, from the winner's circle. And the fact that all of those players were edging toward the sunset of their respective careers, destined to play more exhibition golf than competitive golf.

"Who wants to watch Tom Wargo and Jim Albus play every week?" one sportswriter asked. "Fans don't give a damn about those guys."

While PGA Tour Commissioner Tim Finchem and officials of the Senior Tour scoffed at the remarks, they admitted that new and exciting faces were needed. Though Hale Irwin and Gil Morgan were excellent players, and Hubert Green a personality to be sure, none of the three was a "must-see" player to rank with the great characters of old.

The time was ripe for a bright and shining face to inflict some excitement into the Senior Tour, to cover the ground between the Trevinos and Palmers of the world to the 1999 season when Lanny Wadkins, Tom Kite, and, most important, Tom Watson were eligible to join the Tour. Fuzzy Zoeller would be two years later, and it was but four more when Greg Norman might make things interesting once again. Norman playing the Senior Tour? Would it really happen?

But the 1997 and 1998 seasons needed a lift. With Nicklaus fading due to health and his usual lack of interest in the Tour (Jack discontinued play after the Ford Players Championship every year with half the season to go), Palmer near retirement after the bout with prostate cancer and frustration with too many 76s and 77s, Trevino intent on spending more time with his wife and children, Player rarely a contender despite his youthful appearance, and Rodriguez slowing down at age sixty-two despite his injections of lamb hormone shots, the Senior Tour beckoned for a new hero.

The chosen candidate was Johnny Miller, the perfect fix. Still razor-thin and boyish-looking at fifty, "The Desert Fox," known for his propensity to carve up the Tour with championship play in California and Arizona (thirteen wins in all), was ready to assume the role of new kid on the block and save the Senior Tour.

Best of all, Miller had not gone into hiding as Ben Hogan had after his days on the PGA Tour were completed. Instead, in 1990, he had created a new career as a television broadcaster, and a bratty one at that. Known for his sharp wit and tell-it-like-it-was style, Miller was as controversial as he was popular. Many players on both Tours resented his remarks, but Miller was quick to defend them, saying, "I may pull their pants down, but I leave on the underwear."

Miller's brashness made him a sportswriter's delight, his candid behavior a welcome relief from commentators who coddled their favorite players. When he announced that, yes, he would play the Senior Tour, the PGA Tour headquarters in Ponte Vedra, Florida, went into party mode.

As usual, Miller would do things according to his own style. First, he would honor a commitment to make his Senior Tour debut at the Franklin Quest Championship in Park City, Utah, just a few tee shots down from BYU, where he had been a championship college player. He also announced that every dollar he earned in the Senior Tour would be forwarded to Junior Golf. He hoped other Senior Tour players would do the same.

The golf game that Miller brought to compete with the over-fifty bunch was just three years removed from the one that had shocked the golf world when sweet-swinging Johnny won the AT&T Championship at Pebble Beach in 1994. Some called it a miracle, pointing out that Miller had crawled out of his NBC broadcasting booth and beaten the devil out of the best the PGA Tour had to offer. "Get your butt back up in that booth," Tom Watson bellowed, "and leave us alone."

The championship had been Miller's twenty-fourth during a

career that seemed to race across history. Miller joined the PGA Tour in 1969, won the better part of his championships in the next ten years, and then faded as fast as denim jeans.

The short span of his playing days didn't diminish his accomplishments. In 1971, he won the Southern Open, then elevated his play with victories at the 1973 U.S. Open, and the 1976 British Open. During that span, when Jack Nicklaus was at his peak, Miller was the dominant player, winning sixteen tournaments between the years 1972 and 1976. Eight of the victories came in 1974.

If any one event characterized the Miller persona for slashing play that produced birdies in bunches, it was the 1973 U.S. Open. That year Miller dented the record books forever when he forged a final-round 63, making a mockery of fabled Oakmont. He had started six shots off the lead, behind Palmer, Boros, Weiskopf, Trevino, and Nicklaus. Birdies at the first four holes jump-started the round. A bogey at number eight set him back, but his rhythmic swing and a wunderkind putting stroke propelled him to five birdies in the next seven holes. History was in the making for what many called the finest final round in a Major tournament in golf history.

Although Miller won six times in the 1980s, the magic disappeared. Like Greg Norman, only two Major championships came his way. Miller was the ultimate paradox, fading from view as time wore on, the zest he had for the game but a glimmer of that possessed by the lad who tore up the Tour in the 1970s.

Nicklaus was puzzled by Miller. "I can understand a fellow like Miller with his talent getting a little bit off his game at times," he observed in the mid-seventies, "but frankly, getting as far off as he appears to have been in the past couple of years is beyond my comprehension. My guess is that he hasn't been able to work out a formula that allows him to balance the various compartments of his life—most notably his keen desire for privacy and a full family life—to his emotional satisfaction."

Jack was right. While Miller enjoyed the excitement of the competition, his heart yearned to be home. A devout Mormon, he was dedicated to his family, and, with his children growing up, it became more and more difficult to stray from wife Linda and the gang.

Finally, realizing the magic days were at an end, Miller played less and less on the Tour. Coupled with nagging injuries and a severe case of the yips (Miller said they got so bad that at the 1986 British Open he painted a red dot below the thumb on the grip because he couldn't look at the putter head), the California Golden Boy with the shaggy blond hair put his clubs in the closet and looked for new challenges.

Those included corporate outings as a spokesman for Callaway, and golf course design work, but it was his commentary for NBC that brought him new fame. Partnered with Dick Enberg, he quickly became an insightful broadcaster who wasn't afraid to broadside Tour professionals. Along the way, he chastised Phil Knight at Nike for charging $120 a pop for sneakers ("Isn't fifty bucks enough, Phil?" he barked), Earl Woods for anointing son Tiger as the next coming of the Lord ("Earl has this crazy idea that Tiger is the chosen one. C'mon, Earl"), and hotel magnate Bill Marriot, a Mormon, for selling liquor and showing slutty movies in his hotel rooms. But Miller saved most of his hard-hitting remarks for golfers, especially those he called the "prima donnas on the PGA Tour."

"I know more about the golf swing than ninety percent of the people out there," Miller proclaimed. "Most don't know anything. I see the U.S. players like thoroughbred sheep. They are tremendously bred and trained and they run correctly, but the problem is they are still sheep, and sheep want to be part of the flock instead of breaking out and being their own man."

When Miller, whose comments made him unpopular with many of the touring professionals, turned fifty, he wasn't certain he had enough zip to play the Senior Tour. "I'm gonna try five tournaments or so," he explained, "and see where I am, whether I've got the will to play with passion. Guys like Trevino love the game, can't wait to wake up in the morning and get to the first tee. I love the game and all, but not necessarily me playing it. Thus far, my heart isn't saying I've got to do this."

While many took Miller at his word, others maintained Johnny's reluctance to play was for another reason: He wasn't good enough to contend anymore. He still putted, especially the medium to short ones, like a bricklayer, and his shot making, though adequate, would not get better without constant competition. "Miller's making a big deal out of this," one opponent commented. "But he just doesn't have it anymore. Same reason he quit before."

Before Miller teed it up on the Senior Tour, his quick tongue angered many of his potential opponents. Johnny bragged, "It isn't like I haven't beaten all of these guys before." He followed that up with "If I'm on for a week, I can still win just walking out the door."

With NBC covering several of the Senior PGA Tour events over the year, Miller was a targeted man, his caustic remarks fresh in many players' minds. Miller defended his work, saying, "What am I supposed to report when a guy duck-hooks his drive thirty yards out of bounds?"

Miller's debut in the Franklin Quest Championship came in the five-hundredth Senior Tour event, a far cry from what Don January anticipated when the Tour was the germ of an idea in 1978. "I remember Julie [Boros] saying that he didn't care how little or how much we played, just as long as he could get out of the house ten or twelve times a year," January recalled. "And look what we have now."

At 9:42, after January and Palmer hit their tee shots, the announcer bellowed out for all to hear, "From Napa, California, Johnny Miller." To great applause, Miller, dressed in an aqua-blue shirt with the collar turned up, teed up his ball, strode up beside it, and then with his characteristic dip of the club three times, ripped the ball down the center of the fairway. The era of Johnny Miller on the Senior Tour had begun, a moment marked in time just like when Palmer had debuted in 1980, Trevino in 1989, and Jack Nicklaus in 1990.

Predictions regarding Miller's chances on the Senior Tour abounded. "He's a thoroughbred. He's got what it takes inside. He'll do real well, but he'll have to play more than four or five times to get going," said Jim Colbert. "He won't go bam-bam right away and have impact. It'll take time," added Raymond Floyd. "Nobody is good enough to make an impact in five events. Well, maybe Tiger, but Johnny ain't Tiger," observed Gary McCord.

Miller's debut at the Park Meadows Golf Club, surrounded by the Wasatch Mountains, was a stumbling one, but he kept his score around par most of the day. His first birdie didn't appear until the eighth hole, and Miller appeared shaky in the seven-thousand-foot elevation, where the ball could be socked another ten yards farther than at sea level.

Miller had been a bit nonplussed before the round. "I know there are guys out here who want to get their mitts on me. Say 'Hey, Johnny, nice seventy-four,' but I'm not intimidated," he explained. "If I putt okay, and get some luck, I should be able to finish in the top fifteen."

While his putting was sporadic (Miller even joked about trying left-handed), good fortune did follow him at the twelfth, where an errant iron shot bounced off the head of a spectator and onto the front part of the green. "An Arnie bounce," Miller yelled before adding, "No, if that had been an Arnie bounce, I would have been closer to the pin."

Over the last six holes, Miller was less than dashing with his long putter, but the swing that brought him so many birdie attempts in the 1970s seemed in sync. ESPN's Andy North pointed out that Miller's leg movement was as brisk as ever and that "the faster Johnny's legs move, the better he plays."

The duel between Miller and Palmer was a classic. It was as if Arnie had his own private tournament, one being played for pride. Calling on the magic of old, Palmer kept pace with Miller, seventeen years his junior, as they faced the final three holes. At the par-five seventeenth, Palmer hit a second shot that barely became airborne. He followed it with a flubbed wedge that was embarrassing, with the ball still short of the green. It seemed likely he would drop a shot to par, as would Miller, who had hit his tee shot out of bounds. But angels were perched on Palmer's shoulders, and he holed the sixty-footer from off the green for a birdie four. Arnie pumped his arm in the air as if to say, "Take that, Johnny. The King ain't dead yet. Long live the King."

When the round was completed, Palmer had shot 70, Miller 72. The leader board had several other names atop it, including Tom Shaw, who had recorded ten birdies in the Pro-Am the day before, but most of the attention was paid to Miller and Palmer. At PGA headquarters in Florida, Tim Finchem had a big smile on his face.

Miller improved on his 72 at the Franklin Quest by two the next day, still fighting an erratic putter. He finished the tournament with an average 73 that placed him far down the pack, in a tie for forty-seventh place. The effort earned Miller $3,700. "No big deal," he said. "About what I expected. Except with the putter."

Meanwhile, another golfer with a passion for the mountains and nature in general assumed command of the tournament. Dave Stockton assaulted the Park Meadows Course with an eight-under-par 64 and assumed a three-shot lead over six players, including Bud Allin and Bobby Stroble. Defending champion Graham Marsh was three more back.

Mother Nature turned Sunday's final round into an electrical show. The sky darkened in the afternoon, and bolts of lightning were dancing over the Wasatch Mountains. Play was suspended twice, postponing the battle between Stockton and fifty-eight-year-old Larry Ziegler.

Ziegler's poor first half of the season meant one of the Tour's true cornballs hadn't been around much. Many of his fellow players and their wives had been victims of Ziegler's practical jokes. His best prank was to sneak up behind the unsuspecting and bark like a rabid dog at ankle level, scaring the wits out of his prey. Helen Bland, John's wife, explained, "Larry sounds more like a dog than a dog does. Scared the hell out of me. I fell off my seat."

Ziegler enjoyed watching golfers playing the hole adjacent to his home—the fifteenth hole at Arnold Palmer's Bay Hill Club—make fools of themselves. Realizing that they tramped across his property line to retrieve balls hit out of bounds, he affixed a ball to a PVC pipe and buried the pipe in the ground. Golfers tugged at the ball until sweat dripped down their brow while Ziegler sat in his lawn chair, howling.

Ziegler was quite a hunter of golf balls himself. "Seventy-five to a hundred balls is a bad week," he proclaimed. "Best place is down at Disney. Snakes, alligators by the water. Nobody goes after their ball. It's like picking candy."

One of fourteen children, Ziegler vied with Chi Chi Rodriguez and Simon Hobday as the Senior Tour's greatest funnyman. "When one of these guys asks me why I have so much fun," Ziegler proclaimed, "I tell them that when I grow up I'm not going to be a grouch like you."

Midway through the back nine in Utah, Ziegler had caught Stockton, just before the skies opened all over Park Meadows. Players and caddies took cover. True to his eccentric form, Ziegler had Mark Eaton, the 7'4" former center for the Utah Jazz, as his caddie. Eaton, scrunched in a cart, made it look like a toy.

When play finally resumed, Stockton proved he was the best player in the field. Taking heed of fifteen tips to improve his long game and five to polish his putting stroke offered by offspring Ron at the Kroger Tournament, the stern-faced veteran also improved his attitude, which Ron had earlier termed "terrible."

Stockton also took a cue from son Dave, Jr. over the phone during the delay after learning that he'd birdied four holes during the last round of the Hartford Open being played on the same day as the Franklin Quest. "Dave, Jr., told me he'd been four under and I had a birdie and an eagle, and so I needed another birdie to tie and two to beat him," Dave, Sr. explained.

Armed with the challenge, Stockton pulverized Park Meadows, birdieing holes fifteen through seventeen. The ensuing victory meant Stockton had won every year he'd been on the Senior Tour.

David Knapp Stockton banked $150,000 for his win. The late hour prevented too much celebrating with his wife, Cathy, longtime caddie Todd Newcombe, and Newcombe's girlfriend, Toni Billie, all part of the "Stockton team." They barely had time to savor Stockton's first 1997 win before Dave fired up the jet and headed for his buffalo ranch and a two-week vacation.

Johnny Miller wondered if he should have played at all. "I still have a classic case of the yips," he admitted. "I have a physical problem. Sometimes when I sign my name, the pen jumps, and there's nothing I can do. There's a wire loose back there or something."

Maybe he needed to spend some time with Dave Stockton.

17

WHILE DAVE STOCKTON WAS BATTLING FOR VICTORY AT THE FRANK-lin Quest, several members of the Senior Tour had journeyed to Northern Ireland for the British Senior Open. Played at Royal Port-rush on the Irish coast north of Belfast, a course designed by H. S. Colt, the tournament attracted such players as John Bland, Tom Wargo, Gary Player, and Dave Eichelberger—lured to the venue by his sons, residents of London.

Bland was still in search of Major victory number one, and he stayed at or near the lead from the first hole on Thursday. Playing superbly and putting like a savant, Bland fired an opening-round 66, a 72 on Friday, and a 70 on Saturday. Entering the final round, he held a two-shot lead over Player, winless on the Senior Tour in 1997, and Australian Noel Ratcliffe, "The Rat."

The final round featured a scintillating match among the three. Ratcliffe challenged to the end, but an errant second shot at eighteen ended his bid for the title.

It was left for the two South Africans, fast friends for nearly forty years, to square off as the sun set on the Irish coast. Player was attempting to prove he could still win a big one, and Bland trying to shake off the heart-wrenching defeat he'd suffered from another close buddy, Graham Marsh, at the U.S. Senior Open.

Both men played to their potential. At the par-five seventeenth, tied at nine under and one back of Ratcliffe, Bland blasted two shots on the green to set up a makable eagle putt. Player, described by commentator Peter Allis as bearing a resemblance to a hunting dog, tumbled his ball into the greenside bunker. But a superb shot by Player, who had once boasted, "Yes, I am the finest sand player ever to play the game," resulted in a near-gimme birdie. When Bland's eagle try slid ever so slightly left of the hole, the two countrymen were tied.

At the eighteenth, both managed par, though Bland had to hole a knee-knocking five-footer to tie Player. The South Africans then tied the first play-off hole, the eighteenth, and they marched back to seventeen for the next test in the shoot-out.

Gary Player was attempting to add victory number 161 to his

résumé, but the past few years had been lean ones. Even though the physical fitness buff was just as robust as ever, he couldn't string enough good rounds together to pull out a championship on the Senior Tour. Entering the British Senior Open, he stood fifty-first on the money list with winnings of just over $140,000.

Player's first PGA Tour win had come in 1958 at the Kentucky Derby Open. Like a Wayne Lukas–trained racehorse, the whirling dervish who made black clothing his trademark leaped onto the golf scene and never looked back.

At first, Player wore white to reflect the sun's heat, but then he decided black was better. At the 1959 British Open (which he won), Player seemed confused. He wore trousers, one leg black and the other white.

"The idea for the black outfit came from old western movies I used to watch," Player admitted. "I loved to watch the cowboy dressed in a black hat with big silver guns, boots, and spurs. He was the big man in town."

Regardless of what Gary Player wore, over the next twenty years, he captured nine Major victories. That meant he, Jack Nicklaus, Gene Sarazen, and Ben Hogan were the only ones to have won all four Major tournaments.

Player never let his size (5'6") bother him. "He's one of the greatest competitors who ever lived," extolled Vinny Giles, a former U.S. and British Amateur champion. The late golf writer Dick Taylor said, "Player is the true bulldog. A champion in every sense of the word."

Player was full of gamesmanship. At the 1974 Piccadilly Match Play Championship, he faced Hale Irwin in the finals. The night before, Irwin, holed up in his hotel room awaiting the match, received a peculiar phone call. "It was Gary," Irwin recalled. "Wanted to know what time we teed off. That was my first time in the finals, and he had won the tournament so many times, I figured he was playing with me, using a bit of psychology." It didn't work. In one of the most memorable finals, Irwin defeated Player one up, the turning point being a two-footer the South African missed on the fourteenth hole. "It was a ding-dong match," Player remembered. "A great one."

A true visionary in the 1960s with regard to physical fitness, Player kept himself in fighting shape through the years. But it was his love for the game and his ability to globe-trot, playing in obscure countries for championships nobody ever heard of, that set him apart. "Two or three weeks somewhere," Dick Taylor said of the man who was approaching *nine* million miles of travel in his life, "a week home,

then about again. I don't know how he did it. All he told me was that
there was one time a stewardess came along during a transatlantic
flight and couldn't wake him. She thought he was dead."

Along the way, Player captured the Australian Open and PGA,
the South African Open twelve times (five in succession), as well as titles in Japan, Chile, Egypt, Ireland, and Brazil. Nobody in the history
of the game had more wins in more countries.

Player had a never-quit, grind-it-out quality that made up for
what many experts believed was a mediocre golf swing. Nicklaus analyzed it, saying, "Player's swing is sound, but to compensate for his
lack of size and to produce bigger and more powerful swings, Gary
thrusts himself into many artificial positions. But he's such an excep-
tional athlete and has such great concentration that he can get away
with it." Senior U.S. Amateur champion Bill Hyndman explained,
"Gary looks like he's jumping off the ball, but he stays in back of it.
That's the key."

Player professed to be amazed at the diverse ways there were to
strike a golf ball. "Some golfers play a shut face, Palmer, Trevino,
Claude Harmon, and Weiskopf to name a few," he explained. "Then
there's those open at the top. Doug Sanders could swing inside a telephone booth. Compare that to the beauty of Snead's swing. And Nelson, he had no wrist break on the backswing. Bobby Jones, he dragged
his hands back first, the club following. Ben Hogan used his hips,
Palmer said he just used his hands. I guess I'm a hip player. For every
great golfer that you tell me did this, I can tell you a great player who
did that."

Player's match-play record was incredible. "For years, every
golfer dreaded going up against Gary Player," Lee Trevino said. "He
was the bulldog, never let you relax for a minute." That mental toughness permitted Player to win the Piccadilly Match Play Tournament
five times, defeating, among others, Tony Lema, Johnny Miller,
Arnold Palmer, and Jack Nicklaus. In 1966, he iced Jack 6 and 4 in the
finals. "Jack hit the ball a hundred yards farther than I did," Player
said, "but I got him with my wedge game. That was my only weapon,
and I practiced until I became the best at it."

Player's introduction to golf came through his future father-in-
law, Jack Verwey. Gary's early goal was to beat his teacher's daughter,
Vivienne, who once shot 71 and bested her new love. "Right then I
decided to have six kids and keep her from practicing," Player exclaimed. Later, he joked, "If I had to choose between my wife and my
putter, I'd miss her."

Player's travels to the ends of the earth started in his early years as a golf professional in South Africa. "I went to the driving range and gave lessons for a dollar," he recalled. "I had to give my boss fifty cents and I kept fifty cents. On weekends, I used to give eighteen lessons a day. A young man who turns pro today has no idea what it was like to give eighteen lessons a day for fifty cents a lesson. That's how I earned the money to go overseas."

And overseas he went. Player's frequent flyer miles were astronomical, and he had no thoughts of slowing down. "My body is sound, my mind is quick, and my game, though it comes and goes, still is competitive," he explained. "I can still win, no doubt about it."

Competitors agreed, realizing that mental toughness, long a Player trademark, was still part of the great golfer's mental makeup. "You can't shake Gary," Nicklaus observed. "You can make a big putt on a pivotal hole and he'll just knock it in on top of you." Trevino added, "He'll line up a six-inch putt four ways even if it's for twelve."

Nicklaus admired Player's grittiness. "More than any other player I have seen," Jack said, "Gary has that thing, whatever it is, that champions have."

Player tried to define it in his autobiography, *To Be the Best*, writing "I am an animal when it comes to achievement and wanting success. There is never enough success for me."

Player's son Wayne explained, "Dad is full of positives, never negatives. He always has the proper frame of mind to win."

That characteristic enabled Player to come from seven holes down with seventeen to play and beat Tony Lema in the 1965 World Match Play Championship. And make up five shots at the 1978 Masters, where he birdied six of the last eight holes to win.

In addition to his dogged attitude, Player had superior eyesight. "You need to have what I call street-smart eyes," Player explained. "You have to see a ball and see it quickly. I was blessed with great eyes. I could see everything far away. I'd hit a shot, and people would think it went in a bunker. But I knew better. And my eyesight helped with distances and where to place the shot. To chip over a bunker or see breaks in the greens, you have to see well. Look at Tom Watson when he went bad; I saw him hitting balls and squinting to see them."

Player believed the line between the very best golfers and the next best was a thin one. "You take the twenty best players in the world and the next twenty," he proclaimed. "The only difference is that some hit the right shot at the right time and the others didn't. That's why Jack Nicklaus was so good. He had incredible patience, and he could play well even when he was playing poorly. He was able to gather himself and hit the shot he needed at the critical time."

That could only occur if the golfer was in good shape, something Player had made sure of in the 1950s. "Frank Stranahan and I used to visit the YMCA and work out," Player stated. "Everyone thought we were crazy. Now golfers are worried about their bodies and work out all the time."

Player baffled those who tried to emulate him. "Guys would suck in their bellies around me," he remembered. "I weighed one hundred and fifty when I was in my early twenties and had a waistline of thirty. Forty years or so later, I weigh one hundred and fifty-two and my waistline is up to thirty-two."

Player's regimen off the golf course paralleled his fighting spirit on it. "Three hundred sit-ups, a stationary bike for thirty minutes or so, a few curls to strengthen my forearms, some stretching, and swinging of a weighted club, that's all part of it," he admitted.

Player's ability to keep his body in superb shape, coupled with an unbelievable zest to compete at the highest level possible, to squeeze every possible stroke out of a round, had brought him to the brink of victory at the 1997 Senior British Open. He had bested the field—save Bland—and knew that another championship was possible, even at age sixty-one.

At the second play-off hole, the par-five seventeenth, Bland curled a short-iron third shot to within twenty feet. Player had nudged his ball down the fairway just short of the green in two. He elected to putt the ball, but the effort bounced from the get-go and came up ten feet short of the cup. "Gary's miscued it," Peter Allis announced.

After Bland and his caddie, brother Roy, sized up the putt, John rolled it toward the hole. His effort was unsuccessful, and the stage was set for Player.

From every angle, Player surveyed the putt, making certain no spectators were in his direct line. Despite the ever-present smile and a kindly demeanor with fans, Player was fidgety, one of those golfers bothered by the slightest disturbance while competing. At the Ralphs Classic, Player noticed two marshals behind the green who had unintentionally moved into his line. He stood stern-faced, flapping his arms at them, but it took a PGA official to get their attention before they moved. In contrast, Player once putted out on a green while a frightened squirrel scampered around the putting surface. Gary barely noticed the intrusion.

With no officials or animals to worry about at Royal Portrush, Player wasn't about to let the 161st championship of his long and glorious career get away, and he knocked the putt into the middle of the hole. He pumped his fist in celebration, removed his hat like the true gentleman he was and put his arm around Bland, the genial loser. Two fellow countrymen stood there for all the world to see, arm in arm, winner and loser, friends to the end.

Coupled with the death of Ben Hogan, the emergence of Johnny Miller on the Senior Tour, and the victory by Dave Stockton at the Franklin Quest, Gary Player's march to victory in the Senior British Open made the last weekend of July 1997 an unforgettable one.

Player had a link to Hogan in a famous story that will live through the ages. It occurred after Player was in the midst of a heated debate with a friend over the proper position at the top of the backswing. "I called up Hogan from Brazil," Player quipped in his Down Under accent. "It was about eight o'clock in the evening Texas time. He answered and I said, 'Mr. Hogan, I'd like to ask you a question about the swing.' Dead silence. 'Hello,' I said. 'I'm here,' he said. 'We would like to ask you a question about the top of the backswing.' 'Well, who do you represent on the Tour?' Hogan asked. 'Dunlop,' I replied. 'Then call Mr. Dunlop,' Hogan said."

Despite Hogan's put-down, Player became a champion. Of the final-round 68 in the Senior British Open, which placed him in the winner's circle for the first time since 1995, he exclaimed, "It's one of the two best ones I've ever played, the other being when I beat Bob Charles in the 1988 U.S. Senior Open at Medinah. And it's especially sweet since the win gives me nine Senior Tour Major titles to go with the nine I won on the regular Tour."

And Player wasn't through yet. "I want to carry on playing through the 2000 British Open," he predicted. "I've played in forty-two consecutive, and that will mean forty-six. I might even win it." How could anyone doubt the great champion?

When Tony Jacklin's name appeared on the leader board after the second round of the BankBoston Classic the first week of August, a trip down memory lane continued for many fans.

Jacklin's appearance reminded those who covered the Senior PGA Tour that making the grade wasn't a given. No one knew that better than Jacklin, holder of both the U.S. and British Open championships.

When Jacklin, described by a fellow professional as "looking a bit like a stuffed toad," decided to try his luck on the Senior Tour in 1992, he was accorded no special treatment despite his playing credentials and marquee name value. Without sufficient qualifications to be exempt under any of the Tour regulations, the Brit faced an uphill battle with a golf game that had been dormant for the better part of a decade.

The decline had come well before that, in 1972 to be exact. That summer he faced a final-round duel with Lee Trevino at Muirfield with the British Open Championship at stake. Jack Nicklaus was attempting to add a third leg to his quest for the Grand Slam, but conservative play made him a third wheel to the Jacklin-Trevino confrontation.

By that time, Jacklin had made his mark in golf. He bounded into the headlines as the hero of Britain when he won the 1969 British Open. The "can't-miss" label was added the following year when he wrapped up a U.S. Open title at Hazeltine in Minnesota.

When Jacklin stood on the seventeenth green at Muirfield alongside Trevino in 1972, the golf gods seemed ready to crown him with further glory. He had a makable birdie putt, while Trevino, the defending champion, attempting to win his fourth Major championship, was shoe-top high in gnarly rough behind the green on the par-five. Jacklin was securely in control, ready to assume either a one- or two-shot lead with one hole to play.

In the next few moments, one career advanced while the other hit a dead end. Trevino, a master of the invented shot, chipped the ball into the hole. Jacklin, his heart in his stomach, missed his putt and, worse than that, never resumed the top-level play that was expected to bring more Major championships into his fold.

As Jacklin faced the prospect of turning fifty, he recognized that lack of competition would be his biggest obstacle in attempting to play at a high level on the Senior PGA Tour.

To prepare for the Q-School in 1996, Jacklin practiced his short game and played the Gold Coast Pro Tour, a mini-tour where he won twice. But too many lagers had provided an undesirable tire around the midsection, and Jacklin's twenty-fourth-place finish left him without an exemption.

"I'm just not prepared to stare at a dish of lettuce at every meal," Jacklin joked. "I enjoy a bottle of beer or wine; I enjoy eating. I may be fifty percent deaf in each ear, but otherwise my mind is clear and I'm in good physical shape. Sure I could use to lose ten pounds, but that's not going to make my short game any better."

When Jacklin realized he would have to rely on sponsors' exemptions or the Monday qualifiers, he began a crusade to plead his cause. An article he wrote for *Golf World* professed his belief that two Major championships should be enough to warrant play, and sponsors did come through, providing him the chance.

Entering the BankBoston Classic, Jacklin had failed to take advantage of his good fortune. He had seldom been a contender, and earnings of $132,860 placed him fifty-seventh on the money list, a far cry from the top thirty-one number needed to be exempt on the 1998 Senior Tour.

In Boston, Jacklin showed some spark. Putting cross-handed with the thumbs straight down on the shaft resulted in a score of five under, just three shots off the lead shared by Hale Irwin, who said he had conquered what he called a "miss pattern" (flare shots to the right) by compensating with directional factors, and Bob Betley, the former motorcycle policeman plagued by injuries throughout his career. John Jacobs, sporting a new gray beard reminiscent of Burl Ives, was tied with Jacklin, and Tom Wargo and Jerry McGee were sandwiched in between them.

Kermit Zarley was at 141, shooting a second-round 75 after blistering the course with a 66 on opening day. And that was despite a painful left knee, injured while, as Zarley put it, "jiving on the dance floor" with his daughter/caddie Monica at a pretournament party. "Monica wants me to withdraw," Zarley said after a trip to the Senior PGA Tour fitness trailer, "but I want to give it a try." Eighteen holes later, the 66 was posted, in spite of the wounded knee and use of only thirteen clubs after Monica added to the calamity by breaking Kermit's three-wood after catching its head on a gallery rope. When a fellow competitor heard of Zarley's day at the links, he simply shook his head. "And you wonder why we call him 'The Moon Man'?" he asked.

The MasterCard Super Senior Series was won by sixty-five-year-old Gay Brewer, the 1967 Masters champion. He pocketed $18,000 for his victory, amazing those who still couldn't bear to watch a herky-jerky swing that looked as if he'd break an arm or wrist at any moment.

For every Tony Jacklin or Hale Irwin, there was a Bob Betley competing on the Senior PGA Tour. Such players' names might appear on television or in the press for just one week, or after just one round, but they chased the dream nevertheless.

Through the years, the list of golfers like Betley—a gifted artist whose poignant painting of Tiger Woods's first win in Las Vegas was to be presented to the young superstar when he defended his championship—was a long one. In addition to Rives McBee, famous for a magical second-round 64 at the 1966 U.S. Open at Olympic, there were Moon Mullins, Mason Rudolph, Johnny Pott, Babe Hiskey,

Joe Campbell, and Cesar Sanudo. Each had taken a shot at the Senior Tour with mixed results.

Challengers also included Bruce Summerhays, the former club professional from the Rocky Mountains who ground it out every week, hoping that victory number one might be just around the corner. After qualifying in 1994, Summerhays had played in a remarkable ninety-six consecutive tournaments, a tribute to a gutsy disposition and a never-ending desire to compete. At the BankBoston, that streak would end, back problems finally forcing him to the sidelines.

While Summerhays was safely ensconced in the top thirty-one at number nineteen, several other golfers knew time was running out on their attempts to make the magic list. Frank Conner, Tony Jacklin, Brian Barnes, John Schroeder, Terry Dill, Larry Laoretti, and Bobby Stroble, among others, fought every week to improve their standing.

When round three of the BankBoston began, Hale Irwin was the prohibitive favorite. "When Hale plays well, we play for second place," lamented John Jacobs.

While Tony Jacklin faded to 73 and finished far down the leader board, Irwin broke fast on the Sunday front nine, combining superb iron play with a hot putter. By the time the golfers reached the twelfth hole at the Nashawtuck Country Club in Concord, Massachusetts, Irwin led by two over Bob Wynn and Jerry McGee. Wynn, a crossword puzzle aficionado, had joined the hunt when he holed a mid-iron for an eagle two on the front side, earning a peck on the lips from caddie Helen.

Irwin was trying to win his sixth tournament of the year. His margin stayed steady through fourteen, and then he faced a five-footer on fifteen that could shut the door on the competition.

But Irwin missed badly. McGee, battling neck and back pain, arthritis in his hands, and a blood pressure level that even shocked his physician; Wynn, the streetfighter in the Foster Grants; and Tom Wargo, making a late charge, kept close, hoping Irwin would make a mistake.

And he did. One of those flared tee shots Irwin had spoken of dropped his ball at sixteen into a bunker. The stance was awkward, and Irwin's slashing swing zipped the ball like a line drive toward the water that guarded the front portion of the green. Double-bogey loomed large, but the ball carried a foot past the water, and leaped onto the green. A messy lie produced a bogey, but Irwin's chances of winning were still in place.

Since both McGee and Wynn had birdied seventeen, the three were deadlocked as Irwin played the par-three. Wargo, still lurking a shot back, hit his tee shot into the drink. So long, Tom. Then Irwin hit a pulled mid-iron to the left portion of the green, forty feet from the cup.

ESPN commentators Andy North and Frank Beard analyzed the putt as being near impossible, what with the mogul-like humps and bumps between Irwin and the hole. But Irwin knew something they didn't—a year earlier he'd had the same putt and made it.

Recalling those positive thoughts, Irwin stepped up beside the ball and placed the putter head behind it. One of the few players who took no practice swings, he catapulted the ball up the ridge, across the hogback, and down toward the hole. As if it had eyes, the ball broke to the right at the precise time and hit the cup—kerplop.

Reminiscent of the enthusiasm Irwin showed at his miracle win in the 1990 U.S. Open at Baltusrol, he pumped first his right arm in the air and then, moments later after retrieving the ball, his left. North called it the "Tiger Double Pump."

By all accounts, the tournament was over. Wynn and McGee couldn't birdie the eighteenth and, after Irwin did, the margin of victory was two strokes after rounds of 69-67-67. With fourteen official Senior Tour events remaining, Irwin was closing in on Australian Peter Thomson's all-time record of nine wins in a season, set in 1985. He collected $150,000 for the win, taking him over the $1.4 million mark for the season. Only Tiger Woods had won more.

18

PUTTING IS THE NAME OF THE GAME IN PROFESSIONAL GOLF. ALWAYS has been. Always will be. Many great players have managed to post Major tournament wins despite an average stroke with the putter, but only because they possessed superior skills beyond what most mortals could manage.

Heading into the Northville Long Island Classic at the Meadow Brook Golf Club in Jericho, New York, Hale Irwin, Frank Conner, Graham Marsh, and Larry Gilbert led the Senior Tour in putting. While those golfers had found a winning stroke, others struggled. Jim Colbert admitted his putting had been off in 1997, a major reason for his inability to win before being sidelined with prostate cancer. "I even started to miss the four-footers," he admitted. "Those kill you more than not making a lot of long ones."

Another player doomed to wondering if he could ever find his old magic with the putter was Johnny Miller. Though his overall play at the Franklin Quest had been tolerable, his putting stunk. It worsened during an embarrassing match being taped for *Shell's Wonderful World of Golf* at the Olympic Club in San Francisco the week prior to the Northville Classic. Miller totaled 81 to Jack Nicklaus's 70, but the yips caused him to putt so badly some officials suggested not televising the match out of respect for the former U.S. Open champion. On several holes, it appeared Nicklaus couldn't bear to watch Miller putt, staring off into space while Johnny tried to coax his backswing through the ball without missing it entirely.

While Miller had the yips, other Senior Tour players simply had been mediocre or bad putters most of their lives. DeWitt Weaver, for one, could hit the ball a mile, but his putting stroke was atrocious, even after he went to the extra-long putter. Though Gil Morgan was a superb ball striker, his downfall had always been the putter. His inconsistency contrasted with that of such gifted putters as George Archer, Hubert Green, Bob Murphy, Bob Charles, and Billy Casper, who once labeled his putter "Sweet Charity" because "it covers such a multitude of sins from tee to green."

Those golfers always seemed to putt well, causing one Tour veteran to exclaim, "If I could putt like Murph or Hubert, I'd have a jet and three green jackets in my closet instead of riding coach and wearing eight shades of blue when I go to dinner."

Theories as to the best way to putt the ball were as varied as the personalities of the players on Tour. Bob Murphy felt touch was the key, and his slow, deliberate stroke fit that method. "Feel is the key," he said. "Feeling the ball in the hole. That's why the hands are so important."

Murphy, the second leading putter on the 1996 Senior Tour, added, "Putting is like the rest of golf. It's overtaught. We miss easily eighty percent of putts on the high side. We overread. We give too much consideration to break. When a caddie says, half-inch, right edge on a putt from twenty-five feet, that's crazy. I defy anyone to hit a putt to half an inch."

Murphy, owner of three putters in his long career, had a specific regimen for practice. "I work on the speed of the putts, on the long ones, trying to get them close," he explained. "You'll rarely ever see me work on the short ones. I swing the putter back and through. Don't mess with mechanics much. It's more of a hit than a swing or stroke. 'Stroke' is a paralyzing term."

George Archer believed the eyes made the difference: "You've got to see the ball into the hole, see the line and see it fall," he explained. "And be steady, be real steady. Murph's right though, you hit the ball, not stroke it. Look at Aoki, his way is real wristy, but he repeats it like a piston, and it works for him."

Putters ranged from the short one Larry Gilbert found to be successful during the 1997 season to the pool cue–sized weapons Rocky Thompson and Jim Ferree used. Former Senior Tour professional J. C. Goosie once used two putters during the same round, one for the short ones and another for long efforts. J. C. Snead tried that on the PGA Tour during the Tucson Open. "I started out using a long-handed putter," Sam's nephew said, "but after missing a short putt at the fourteenth hole, I tapped in with the short one, and then heaved the long one into the canyon. I'm sure it's still there."

Sam Snead laughed when he heard J.C.'s tale of woe, but the Slammer's putting had become so bad he had gone to the sidesaddle method thirty years earlier. Jimmy Demaret took one look at him and bellowed, "You look like you're basting a turkey."

Another golfer who struggled with the putter was Orville Moody, the storybook winner of the 1969 U.S. Open. "I tried everything," he admitted. "When my putting went bad, I tried closing my eyes, tried cross-handed, backhanded, left-handed, all of that. Nothing worked until I went to the long putter. Now I can at least hit the hole once in a while."

J. C. Snead's and Moody's pursuit of perfection with the putter was not unlike others on the Tour whose brains were fried with tales of woe regarding the most important club in the bag. "If you can't putt out here, stay home," Archer said. "Every single week it's the guy who gets the ball in the hole who ends up with the green."

Those words would prove more than true at the Northville Long Island Classic. While Hale Irwin took a week off to caddie for his son Steve on the Golden Bear Tour in Florida, former four-time Ryder Cup player José Maria Canizares of Spain, struggling to win enough money to bypass the impending Q-School in November, assumed the first-round lead with a record-setting 64.

That was five shots better than Walt Zembriski, the ex-steelworker whose unlikely trail to the Senior Tour circuit will one day undoubtedly be fodder for a Hollywood film. The same year Orville Moody won the U.S. Open, Zembriski was a four-hundred-dollar-a-week high-beam steelworker laboring in the clouds above Fort Lee, New Jersey. He'd seen five of his fellow skywalkers plunge to their deaths, including friend Red Dalton. "I'll never forget the day Red fell," the brisk Zembriski recalled. "At lunch, he's talking about the pony he was buying for his grandson. By two o'clock Red's dead."

Instead of boozing it up with his fellow workers after work, especially Mohawk Indian laborers, who, Zembriski said, had "no fear on the high iron and were crazy as hell otherwise," the pint-sized, barrel-chested New Jersey native with the scratchy voice found solace in hitting golf balls at a nearby public course. The course was crowded. "On Saturdays, you'd have to get in line on Friday to get a tee time. We'd take turns, staying up all night. I'd just get a six-pack of beer and a blanket and wait for the sun to come up."

A near-collision with a crane-load of lumber made Zembriski decide there had to be better things in life. "I'd sucked enough steel dust," he said after quitting.

Walter had taken up golf at an early age, hitting rocks at a local sand pit. He used twenty-five-dollar Golfcraft clubs that his dad, who once caddied for Babe Ruth at the Out of Bounds Golf Club in Mahwah, New Jersey, had brought home for Walt and his four brothers.

An early "caddie hook," as Zembriski recalled it, was cured, and he began to post scores in the 60s around Mahwah. At the Out of Bounds Club, Zembriski caddied, then was promoted to club cleaner.

After a stint in the army, Walter stunned area golfers with a 9 and 8 victory in the final of the 1966 New Jersey State Amateur.

Armed with confidence and an unbridled spirit for the game, the square-jawed Zembriski headed for the PGA Tour, earning his card in 1967. But his game went sour, and he exhausted the sponsor money provided by his father-in-law. "My wife said, 'It's time to get a job,' and that was it," Zembriski said. "I started working as a steelworker."

Zembriski savored an unusual experience at the 1978 U.S. Open at Cherry Hill in Denver. "In the locker room, my name was next to the big boys," he recalled. "Watson, Weiskopf, Zembriski, Zoeller. Since I didn't know if I'd be playing Saturday or Sunday, I dressed up for the second round. Had on a white golf shirt and red pants, the same colors the locker-room attendants wore. Tom Weiskopf came in and said, 'Hey, open my locker.' I looked at him, told him he'd made a mistake, that I was in the championship. Even said I had him by a shot."

Despite that fleeting moment of glory (he made the cut), a career as a steelworker appeared likely for Zembriski. He worked in a tack factory in New Jersey, feeding sheets of steel into the cutting machine, and then on the high beams. After eight years, Walt had had enough. Divorced from his wife, he drove to Florida to chase his dream of once again playing competitive golf. "I cleaned swimming pools, did maintenance, whatever I could," he remembered. "There was no Senior Tour then. I played the Space Coast Tour, against guys like Paul Azinger, Bob Tway, and Mark Calcavecchia. I held my own and waited for the day when I turned fifty in 1985."

That year, Zembriski played in the Senior Open at Lake Tahoe. "I led the field after two rounds," he recalled. "Everyone was in shock. 'Who was this guy?' they asked. All I was worried about was paying my caddie."

Zembriski, still packing his union card, finished fourth in that tournament and impressed fellow competitors with his razor-sharp iron shots and passion for the game. "He was a breath of fresh air," Peter Thomson recalled. "But it was hard to believe how this guy made it to the Tour."

Slowly, Zembriski climbed up the leader board until he won his first, the 1988 Newport Cup, in Rhode Island. "Walt is an example of what can happen out here," Arnold Palmer explained. "He played the mini-tour and did well. He's a scrapper. It's great to see a guy come right off the street and make it out here."

Steady earnings and two more victories followed for Zembriski in the next seven years, but 1996 and the first half of 1997 had been disappointments for one of the Tour's most unlikely contestants. Better things were ahead. His back-to-back 69s at the Northville Long Island Classic were good enough to win the MasterCard Grand Masters title. Zembriski, whose putter had picked up the pace for him, won $18,000 for his efforts, putting him over the $100,000 mark for the year.

In that second round, José Maria Canizares recorded a 70, but lost sole possession of the lead to a pair of upstarts, Walter Hall, a lean North Carolinian, and Dana Quigley, both of whom had conquered the "four-spotter" on Monday to gain entry to the tournament. Since the Spaniard was playing on a sponsor's exemption, reporters dubbed the threesome "the outsiders."

"Let's face it," Hall, a seasoned professional encouraged to try the Senior Tour by longtime amateur great Vinny Giles, admitted. "The money is important, but a win means we can forget the Q-school. Dana, José, and I all would love to do that. It would be like sidestepping a trip to the gas chamber."

Hall bowed out, but Quigley and Canizares continued to contend on the back nine on Sunday. Joining them were Jay Sigel and Hubert Green, sporting his trademark wide-brimmed Panama hat. Though he'd won a good chunk of money in the first two-thirds of the season, Green wanted a trophy. "Finishing second doesn't cut it," he bellowed. "I'd rather throw up."

The failure of Green and Canizares to make critical putts in the final few holes left the door open for Sigel and Quigley, two men in pursuit of far different goals. For Sigel, a win meant he passed the million-dollar mark in winnings for the second straight year. Perhaps a late-season push might even challenge Hale Irwin for Player of the Year honors.

For Quigley, a win certified that he had climbed the mountain, one that had seemed out of reach after his failure to be successful on th PGA Tour in the 1970s. "My attitude was as bad as my preparation back then," Quigley admitted. "I drank too much, didn't believe in myself. I didn't believe I was good enough to play that Tour. I was very intimidated."

ESPN's Frank Beard knew what Quigley had gone through. Though he had won the money earnings title and been Player of the Year in 1969, Beard's bout with the bottle nearly ate him up.

Admitting he was an alcoholic took time, but in recent years Quigley, like Beard, had gotten his life back together. "I decided to face the problem and deal with it," he said. "My wife, Angie, and other friends stayed with me. While I was the head pro at Crestwood Country Club in Rehoboth, Massachusetts, I played a lot of golf in the region. When I started approaching fifty, everybody kept telling me I had to take a shot at the Senior Tour."

At the BankBoston the week before Northville, Quigley's rounds of 68, 72, and 68 earned a top ten finish and $36,000, his biggest paycheck. But without an exemption to the Northville, Quigley was forced to do things the hard way and travel to Long Island for the Monday qualifier. "Having to make it on Monday is a very humbling experience," he lamented. "It's make-it-or-break-it time. You get one shot. If you can handle that pressure, you can handle anything."

Fortunately, Quigley's game was still in tune, and he made the field. Now he faced being in contention for the second time in two weeks, with the coveted exemption from Mondays and the November Tour Q-School hanging in the balance.

Through the first two rounds and nine holes, his putter had kept him in contention. "I'm not playing the best golf I can," he admitted. "But I'm making all the five- and six-footers. That's what counts." Enough to earn a tie with Sigel and force a play-off.

Winning the title came down to two short putts at the second play-off hole. Sigel had a four-footer for par, while Quigley, who ended up being the fourth best putter in the field, was just two and a half feet from the cup for the same score. Another play-off hole loomed on the horizon, but then the lords of the game decided Quigley had finally climbed his mountain and deserved a just reward. When Sigel blew his little one past the top of the hole, the crowd gasped. Moments later, Quigley nudged his into the cup and the drama was over.

The instant the ball snuck into the cup, the boyish-faced Quigley threw his hat in the air and jumped around the green like an adolescent. Angie, who had been through more downs than ups as Dana fought to find himself, suddenly appeared and Dana's hug nearly broke her in two. Frank Beard nearly suffocated when Quigley bear-hugged him as well.

"Tell my father I love him," Quigley, the sixth Monday qualifier to win a championship, roared. "And tell my kids I'll be home for their birthdays."

Later, the new champion acknowledged the real meaning of his win. "Monday, well, I don't know what I'll do on Mondays. It'll seem funny not to be out there, but I'm sure I'll get used to it."

Moments after he'd received the championship trophy, Quigley's victory became bittersweet. On the way to the clubhouse to meet the press, he was handed a cellular phone. His face tightened when he put it to his ear, for he suddenly realized he was hearing bad news. The caller was brother Paul, who informed Dana that their eighty-two-year-old father, Wallace, had died earlier that afternoon at the hospital in Providence, Rhode Island.

Quigley's knees buckled and he collapsed to the ground in tears. It took several minutes for him to regain his composure before he continued to the press tent. "This is supposed to be my happiest moment ever," he said emotionally to reporters. "And it probably is. But my dad's dying is going to make me remember this day forever. It's funny that God would work in this way, take his life and give me mine, all in one day."

Since his father's condition had worsened, Quigley had nearly given up his qualifying spot in the Northville Classic. His dad, a constant companion who had worked with Dana every day in their golf shop at Rehoboth's Crestwood Country Club before Quigley's decision to play on the Senior Tour, convinced him to play. So had mother Dot, but Dana had left his dad's bedside reluctantly to play the Northville event.

"Oh, man, I didn't do it soon enough," Quigley sobbed as he tried to answer questions from reporters. Under his breath, he eked out the words, "God, this one was for him."

Undoubtedly, Wallace Quigley heard his son's words. On that humid day in Jericho, when Dana Quigley won his first tournament on the Senior PGA Tour, he had also made Mr. Quigley one proud father.

19

As the Senior Tour players began preparing to compete in the First of America Classic in Ada, Michigan, defending champion Dave Stockton was one of several who recalled his early years as a touring professional. "Back then, we put seventy thousand miles on our car a year," he said. "Money was short, too. In 1965, I made five thousand dollars and spent ten. Next year I won ten and spent twelve."

Other members of the Senior Tour jet set identified with Stockton. Irwin recalled staying at the Temple Motel along the route from Boulder to Los Angeles. "The room cost ten bucks, but the bed touched the walls on three sides," he explained. "I had trouble closing the door." Don January recalled a hotel room in North Carolina that was "smaller than my hall closet at home."

Jim Colbert knew about those ten-dollar motels as well. "Marcia used to pack a hot plate, and we cooked food right in the hotel room. Dean Refram and his wife doubled up with us. One time, I returned early to my room and heard someone inside. I thought it was a maid, but when we got the door open I saw some guy running across the parking lot with a bag of potato chips in his hands."

Touring the country was a family affair. "We never knew where we'd be staying the next week," Marcia Colbert said. "We were always on the go." That hadn't changed until recently, when Jim had been sidelined with prostate cancer surgery.

At the First of America Classic, Gil Morgan jumped to the thirty-six-hole lead at eight under par, thanks to an eagle three at the third hole. He was two in front of Tour rookie Bob Duval, whose son David was competing at Winged Foot in the PGA Championship a few states to the east.

The elder Duval was hoping to repeat Dana Quigley's win at Northville, extinguishing his need to qualify for every Senior Tour tournament. With that goal in mind, he stayed close on Morgan's heels throughout the final round. With two holes to play, Duval, whose quick pace had been passed on to his son David, caught Morgan, but at the seventeenth Dr. Gil rolled in a sixteen-footer for a birdie four. When Duval couldn't match it and failed to birdie the eighteenth, the optometrist prevailed.

Morgan's win was his fourth on the 1997 Senior PGA Tour, and he and Hale Irwin had now won ten of the twenty-seven events they played. First prize of $150,000 moved Morgan to $1,489,561, just $213,399 behind his chief rival.

While Irwin and Morgan were on a collision course for the money title and Player of the Year, several players tried to improve their standing in order to make the magical top thirty-one list. With eleven events and the Energizer Senior Tour Championship remaining, Frank Conner stood thirty-fourth on the ladder, John Morgan thirty-seventh, and John Schroeder thirty-eighth. Nearly $75,000 away from the thirty-first spot was Brian Barnes, whose physical problems forced an MRI after the First of America Classic. Mike McCullough was just behind him in forty-third place, with Bob Duval in forty-eighth, encouraged by his second-place finish in Michigan.

Struggling to make the exemption list were Bobby Stroble in fifty-third position and Tony Jacklin in fifty-seventh place, nearly $200,000 behind J. C. Snead, who currently held the thirty-first spot.

For competitors like Buddy Whitten, Dick Hendrickson, David Oakley, David Ojala, and Will Sowles, who had battled their way through the Q-School, only a tournament victory would preserve their exemption. "To work that hard and now face the prospect of returning to the Q-School isn't something I want to think about," Oakley lamented. "But if that's what it takes to stay out here, I'll go back and try to qualify again."

One golfer, Harry Toscano, lodged in 130th place with earnings of less than $6,000, had other ideas. Believing the process by which exemptions were handed out to be discriminatory and illegal, he had filed suit to extinguish the present exemption system, especially the provision that permitted four sponsors' entries in a tournament. Most players on the Senior Tour considered Toscano a crybaby, suggesting he hone his game instead of spending his time whining about Tour regulations.

Of the legends of the game, only Lee Trevino had made much of a dent on the 1997 Senior PGA Tour. Though winless, the fifty-seven-year-old's play had garnered him nearly $600,000 in winnings, placing him eleventh on the money list. Chi Chi Rodriguez hadn't entered the winner's circle and stood forty-first with a shade over $250,000 in winnings.

Arnold Palmer held spot number one hundred with slightly over

$20,000 in earnings in eight events, but just having Arnie back with the boys had brightened everyone's year. And his golf game was rounding into shape. After besting Johnny Miller in the first round of the Franklin Quest Championship, he turned in a solid performance at the Northville Classic. Rounds of 73, 70, and 70 buoyed his spirits. "Slowly but surely my game is coming back," the King exclaimed with a smile and sparkle in his eyes. "I might even beat all these boys one day."

Whether he did or not didn't matter to Tour rookie Will Sowles, who summed up the feelings of all of his compatriots when he told of a chance meeting with Palmer at the Home Depot Invitational. "I was sitting in the clubhouse sipping a Diet Coke when Arnie walked in and sat at my table," the former potato salesman recalled. "I wanted to say something, but I didn't know what. I wasn't sure he even knew who I was. I mumbled something and then asked for his autograph on my visor. I felt like a fan, but he has always been my hero."

During the Saint Luke's Classic in Belton, Missouri, the twenty-eighth full-field event on the 1997 Senior PGA Tour, several good things happened for the lesser-known strugglers chasing dreams every week. Since Arnold, Jack, Lee, Raymond, caddying for son Robert in the U.S. Amateur Championship in Chicago (he lost in the third round), and Chi Chi had skipped the tournament, the grinders were in the spotlight. To their credit, they gave the exuberant fans their money's worth all week long.

Among those playing well was Bobby Stroble. Standing fifty-third on the money list meant he was more than $150,000 behind number thirty-one and only a spectacular finish in the remaining events could prevent a return to the Q-School. At the Saint Luke's, Stroble took a giant stride toward the magic list by finishing at −9, good enough to tie for fourth and $54,000 in prize money. Brian Barnes and DeWitt Weaver had good tournaments, finishing in the top twenty.

The tournament became a dogfight between fifty-three-year-old Bruce Summerhays, the former Stanford University golf coach and assistant professional at the Olympic Club in San Francisco, and Hugh Baiocchi, the South African ball striker with the cross-handed putting stroke.

The stakes were high for both golfers, though Baiocchi had more to gain. Summerhays had already proven himself a capable player in 1995 and 1996 by winning more than a million dollars and finishing comfortably in the top thirty-one. He was the Senior Tour's iron man, having played in ninety-six consecutive tournaments before lower back problems sidelined him in the BankBoston Classic. The Saint Luke's Classic was his ninety-eighth event, and he yearned for victory number one to seal his position as one of the top players on the Senior Tour.

Baiocchi's goal was a bit different, for although he had played well in the first three quarters of the 1997 Senior Tour, he still had to rely on sponsors' exemptions and Monday qualifiers to gain entry to tournaments. His earnings total of $406,068 positioned him in twenty-first place, but a victory meant automatic entry into all tournaments for the remainder of the year.

Baiocchi's appearance on the Senior Tour followed in the footsteps of one of his South African brethren, John Bland. Both had labored away on the European, Asian, and South African tours in the 1970s when they were all but barred from the American golf scene. The PGA Tour at that time had an unwritten rule that the American Tour and the bag full of money awarded to contestants was solely for Americans. Players like Baiocchi and Bland couldn't afford to come to the United States and hope to play since costs were prohibitive. Instead, they competed overseas, hoping that one day they might gain entry to events in the United States.

Their chance came with the dawning of the Senior Tour. Roberto De Vicenzo had been a competitor from the outset, followed by Peter Thomson and a host of others. Meanwhile, Hugh Baiocchi piled up his credentials, winning such titles as the Western Province Open, the Swaziland Holiday Inns Invitational, and Vaal Reefs Open. In 1977, Hugh finished second on the Royal Order of Merit list behind a Spaniard named Seve Ballesteros.

Like Bland before him, competitors on the Senior PGA Tour had heard about Baiocchi. "He's been a good player for a lot of years," Bob Charles explained. "People are going to see just how good."

When Baiocchi turned fifty, he fled South Africa for the promises of the Senior Tour, but an eleventh-place finish at the 1996 Q-School meant he only had a partial exemption into tournaments. Superb play through the early portion of the 1997 season sped him toward the $500,000 mark in earnings, but a victory at the Saint Luke's would complete the cycle begun when young Baiocchi learned the game as a youngster from his father and dreamed of winning a tournament in the United States.

Baiocchi's main adversary at the Saint Luke's was Bruce Summerhays, a deceptively good golfer, with an unusual method of addressing the ball before he swung. Instead of positioning the club directly behind the ball, he placed it a clubhead beyond. After several jerky motions bobbing the club up and down as if he were a beginner, Bruce launched into his backswing.

The regimen was painful to watch, but Summerhays's method was effective. "It's just my version of the forward press," he explained. "Something to get me started."

Over the final few holes on Sunday, the tournament was Baiocchi's to win or lose. But Summerhays made a miraculous birdie at the eighteenth after having his golf ball ricochet off a beer can and a spectator's elbow. Baiocchi needed a par to tie and a birdie to win at the fifty-fourth hole, but the pressure was unbearable. At the seventeenth, he told an ESPN cameraman, "I'm about to faint." He had described the final nine holes as "claustrophobic" the day before.

Nerves caused Baiocchi to push a tee shot that nearly went out of bounds. When he hit a mid-iron just left of the green and junked a chip shot seven feet past the cup, it looked like "Good-bye, Hugh," but he calmly stroked the right-to-left breaker square into the cup, necessitating a play-off.

At the eighteenth tee, the two men looked like brothers playing for the family championship. They congratulated each other like the close friends they were and then loped down the fairway chattering away, comrades in arms.

Final-round play gave an indication of the eventual victor. Baiocchi had struggled all day, while Summerhays was razor-sharp. After tying the first two play-off holes, Summerhays, with son William beside him as caddie (seven of the eight Summerhays children took turns caddying), finally prevailed by making par despite nearly dunking his second shot in the pond behind the green. The $150,000 first prize soared his earnings toward the $600,000 mark. Baiocchi received $88,000 and the memory of playing poorly despite recording his ninth top ten finish in fifteen events.

Though the victory was exciting for the effervescent Summerhays, who had paid his dues as a club professional for so many years, it was a downright adventure for wife, Carolyn, his lifelong cheerleader:

"I'd only missed two tournaments Bruce had played in," she explained. "The way we work it with the kids is that I go home every Sunday night and come back on Tour each Thursday. Bruce played every week because we thought everybody did. I missed the Saint

Luke's since I was with our daughter Carrie at the PGA Juniors in Florida. Going into Sunday, we knew he was in contention. We didn't know how he was doing when we left Palm Beach, but when we got to Atlanta, Carrie called our son Joseph and he said, 'Haven't you heard? Dad just made a long putt and has the lead.' "

Carolyn and Carrie had to board the plane from Atlanta to Salt Lake City before further updates. "I expected to use the phone on the plane to call Joseph, but there were none," Carolyn explained. "I couldn't believe it. They're always there when you don't need them. I told the flight attendant the problem, and she said write a note to the captain and maybe he can find out for you what happened. I felt silly, but I did and she took it to the cockpit."

The minutes seemed like hours to Carolyn. "I wrote that I was in seat 2E, and I just hoped the captain would let me know. Finally, he appeared and said, 'I'm sorry to tell you this,' and then he paused. 'But your husband won.' I started crying, and then I found Carrie and told her and we both started crying. What a special moment it was for us."

The day after Bruce Summerhays's win, Arnold Palmer held a garden golf party in his hometown of Latrobe, Pennsylvania. In a charity event labeled the Arnold Palmer Golf Gala, Arnie needed a partner to compete against Tom Lehman and newly crowned PGA champion Davis Love III. He asked Tiger Woods, and the two, separated in age by forty-six years, strode to the first tee ready for the challenge at the Latrobe Country Club, more famous as the backdrop for Arnie's Pennzoil television commercials than the championship golf played there.

Seeing Palmer and Woods together was a portrait in time, a special link between the wizard of the 1950s and '60s and the new savior of golf, one whose best asset was his boyish way, reminiscent of the youthful Palmer when he entered the professional golf world in 1955.

"Woods has some of that charisma that Arnie possesses," Ernie Vossler said. "But Arnold's personality is one of a kind. I used to sit beside him when he'd sign autographs. 'Just let me have the leftovers,' I'd say. But those fans didn't care about me, only Arnie."

In the history of the ancient game, three significant moments defined its evolution to becoming a major sport. The benchmarks were Francis Ouimet's startling victory over British champions Harry Vardon and Ted Ray in a play-off for the 1913 U.S. Open, Bobby Jones's

Grand Slam performance in 1930, and Arnold Palmer's ability to generate fan interest when his charisma and go-for-broke style appeared on television sets in the 1950s.

Like many of the greats of the game, it was a father who introduced Arnold Palmer to golf. Milfred "Deacon" Palmer had worked as course superintendent and head professional at Latrobe Country Club since 1921. One job wasn't enough to pay the bills, so Deke labored in the melt shop at the Latrobe Steel Company, owner of the Country Club. "I will never forget Dad coming home from work at the steel mill," Palmer recalled. "He could barely walk. He almost crawled. He was so tired. And he had scars all over him from where the molten steel splashed on his body."

Father wanted son to be a golfer, and he gave Arnold a set of cut-down clubs when he was four. "The first set was mixed, no specific brand," Palmer recalled. "When I was twelve, I took my mom's Patty Berg two-wood and used it until high school. Then I used a Hagen driver and the old First Flight irons. Later I got a set of MacGregor irons, and then Wilson's, which I used when I went on Tour."

In 1954, the muscularly built Pennsylvania native won the U.S. Amateur, beating Robert Sweeny, one up. That's when Gene Littler, the 1961 U.S. Open champion, proved he was a prophet as well, telling anyone who would listen, "That's Arnold Palmer. He's going to be a great player someday. When he hits the ball, the earth shakes."

That ability was apparent during the 1954 Amateur at the Country Club of Detroit. Palmer was relentless, and years later he would call the triumph his most memorable achievement in golf. "The one I most revere is the Amateur title," he remembered fondly. "It was the turning point. Everything came from that. I had been in the service for three years, and when I came out I didn't know what I was going to do. I was sort of looking, searching, not knowing. Winning the Amateur changed all that."

Jack Nicklaus's first recollections of Palmer were from 1954: "I was coming off the course after playing in the Ohio Open in Sylvania, and it was pouring down rain. There was one guy out on the practice tee, hitting them, drilling them, about waist high. I didn't know who he was, but someone said, 'That's Arnold Palmer, the defending champion.' I said, 'Man, oh man, is he strong.'"

Palmer's charging style, one that triggered a go-for-broke attitude on the golf course, was evident in his private life. At the Shawnee Country Club, a revered A. W. Tillinghast course in Shawnee-on-Delaware, Pennsylvania, the Fred Waring Four Ball was an annual event. A beautiful young woman named Winnie Waltzer was in charge of the luncheon program and placement of players and guests. She asked a girlfriend about Arnold Palmer, and the giggling reply perked Winnie's interest. She sat next to Arnie herself, and seven days later Palmer asked her to marry him. The marriage is still going strong over forty years later despite Arnie's shenanigans, including one instance in 1955 the night after the Masters.

The couple was pulling a small mobile trailer, which was their home away from home. The 1952 Ford hardtop Palmer drove had trouble on a steep mountain in western Pennsylvania. Without hesitation, Arnie turned to Winnie and said, "We've got to lighten the load. You'll have to get out and walk." And she did.

Arnold Palmer's first victory on the PGA Tour was the 1955 Canadian Open. In 1988, he won his final Senior Tour event, marking a span of thirty-three years in the victory circle. Along the way, he won eighty-nine times, sixty on the PGA Tour, nineteen internationally, and ten as a senior.

Galleries took a shine to Palmer from first glance, and the famous Army began to form. For Palmer to assume center stage, he needed foils, and it was first Gary Player and then Jack Nicklaus who provided the excitement. The Big Three became better known than the president of the United States, though Dwight D. Eisenhower kept his name in the news by hanging around Arnie as much as possible.

If two victories and one defeat define the image of Arnold Palmer's career, they would be the 1958 Masters, the 1960 U.S. Open, and the 1966 Open.

The 1958 Masters was significant, for it was the first of Palmer's seven professional Major championships. "The 1958 Masters will always be special," Arnie observed. "I loved Augusta and wanted to win there so badly. Putting on that first green jacket meant more to me than anything."

That Masters was also the first coming of Arnie's Army, the boisterous squadron that followed his every shot, cheering their idol as their King strode the fairways at the course Bobby Jones and Alister Mackenzie built. "The galleries were incredible," Palmer recalled. "They were like family. I was amazed to see many of the same people at tournaments around the country. But at Augusta, they cheered me on, boosted my play. I will never forget how they treated me."

Palmer admitted his golf swing was basically whiplash in style, but a masterful putting stroke made up for it—especially at Augusta, where the hole always seemed to get in the way of Arnie's ball. "If I ever needed an eight-foot putt and everything I owned depended on it," the immortal Bobby Jones once commented, "I would want Arnold Palmer to putt it for me."

Though his persona as the hard-driving, pants-hitching, chain-smoking, devil-may-care, never-play-safe warrior captivated competitors and fans alike, Palmer cemented his seat on the throne in the 1960 U.S. Open at Cherry Hill. He began the final round an also-ran, but then electrified the gallery by driving the first green. Seventeen holes later, Palmer had outlasted Ben Hogan, the antithesis of the charismatic Palmer, and Jack Nicklaus, the upstart twenty-year-old who would soon be the challenger for Palmer's throne. "It was the greatest championship in the history of the game," Palmer stated. "I won, but with Hogan and Jack in the hunt, well, that was what golf was all about."

Those two victories were Palmer's finest, but his stunning defeat in the 1966 U.S. Open at Olympic left an everlasting effect on him. The stage had been set for Palmer to win his second Open title, and that seemed assured when he built up a seven-stroke advantage over Billy Casper with just nine holes remaining.

Palmer forgot about Casper and concentrated on shooting 36, which he knew would permit him to break Ben Hogan's 1948 record of 276 at Riviera. But bogeys instead of birdies befell Palmer, and when he could manage no better than 39, Casper's brilliant 32 brought the two dead even. Palmer lost the play-off the next day, his heart broken from Sunday's final round.

"Olympic," Doc Giffin, Palmer's press secretary for what seemed like centuries, said, "has been an open wound for years." Palmer put a different spin on it, recalling, "People don't remember that Billy played some great golf. It just wasn't my bobbling. And I had to make that downhill three-footer on eighteen to tie."

Casper's win was devastating, and Palmer never won another Major championship. "I think it kicked the wind out of Arnie," Casper said later.

Regardless of that defeat, Palmer's legacy lived on. His most telling images were his facial features, the chiseled cheekbones, the squinty eyes trying to follow a shot, and the cocked head. When Palmer finished his swing, the club stood still in the air while Arnie imparted the proper body English and then presented either the best smile God ever created or a scowl that must have made his golf ball cringe.

Former Tour professional Jerry Barber told reporters, "Arnie grabs the course by the throat and literally shakes it to death." "Palmer tried to force the course into submission," Jack Nicklaus recalled.

While Palmer's record was outstanding, it was his love affair with the fans that would be his legacy. "Arnie was a superhero," the wife of a fine amateur recalled. "And super sexy. When he looked at me I felt like I was naked."

Tiger Woods and other heroes of the future owe him a debt of gratitude every single day. As Woods said, "Arnold Palmer is golf. I still get goose pimples every time I'm around him." Jim Colbert added, "Arnie's a lot like Muhammad Ali. A great champion, a man of the people."

After Arnie passed fifty, he brought the same hell-bent-for-leather golf game to the Senior Tour. In his debut, he won the PGA Seniors' Championship. The crowds at every stop increased tenfold, and Palmer treated them to superb golf well into his early sixties.

When Arnie was felled by prostate cancer in early 1997, the world was shocked. But it was true, and golf fans everywhere included their fallen hero in every prayer. Surgery was successful. One of the first interviews Arnie gave was to Jim Kelly, the polished ESPN broadcaster whose professionalism and enthusiasm for the Senior Tour played a big part in its success. "I sat with Arnold in Orlando," Kelly recalled. "He talked to me like my brother, or my dad, or my best friend. I nearly cried because it was so special. Arnold asked me if I'd had my PSA [the exam to detect prostate cancer] checked, and I shook my head no. 'Promise me you'll do it,' he demanded, and when Arnold speaks, Jim Kelly listens. Him talking to me was so special because when I was a youngster I would go to the putting green and be Arnold Palmer. He also unhitched his pants and showed me his scar. I left with a tear in my eye. What a wonderful man."

Within months of the surgery, the Palmer smile was back on the Senior Tour. Prior to that, Arnie had played in the Bay Hill Classic at his home course in Orlando, where Tiger Woods was making a much ballyhooed appearance. But the story was Palmer, and reporters flocked around him again. "If I play in a tournament, I'm still foolish enough to think I can win," Arnie said.

During the 1997 season, Palmer was seldom a contender, unable to master the golf course for three consecutive rounds. Every once in a while, the magic of the fifties and sixties reappeared, as it had in Park City when he'd beaten new rookie Johnny Miller head to head. But age and cancer had taken their toll, and Palmer was philosophical about when it might be time to call it quits.

"I can't imagine not playing competitive golf," he lamented. "But the handwriting's on the wall. One of these days, I may just lay the clubs down and head home. I can find a damn good game at Bay Hill or anywhere I go. And I'm certainly not going to embarrass myself. But I love the game and the competition. That's what keeps me going."

20

THE MATCH BETWEEN THE ARNOLD PALMER/TIGER WOODS team and Tom Lehman/Davis Love III at the Palmer Gala was a skins game, better-ball competition, and Arnie flashed some of the old magic, attempting to keep up with his young playing partner.

A select crowd of 6,500 fans was treated to a special day that saw the competitors joke and tease while trying to make birdies for charity. At the end of the day, their efforts tossed $750,000 dollars into the Latrobe Hospital Fund, which already had a Palmer wing or two. The match also boosted visibility for Arnie's prize possession, The Golf Channel, still struggling to hit the big time.

At the first tee, Lehman, the 1996 British Open champion, set the stage by assuming a boxing position in front of Woods and Palmer. He punched his fists through the air, got a good laugh from Tiger and Arnie, and then unleashed a drive down the first hole with a mighty swing.

After all four players teed off, Lehman asked Palmer a curious question as they strode down the fairway. "Ever top one off the first tee?" Tom queried.

Palmer, attired in a pink golf shirt with a red Palmer umbrella emblem on the pocket, paused before answering, "Can't say that I have. I've hit them out of bounds though," he said with a pensive look.

Woods holed a ten-footer for birdie on the first green for a skin. Palmer's brow unfurrowed and he exchanged high fives with the young phenom. On the second tee, Lehman called out, "Lucky, lucky, lucky," at Woods, who enjoyed the banter.

Woods's one-iron launched the ball 260 yards down the center for his next tee shot. After that, Palmer wound up and swung so hard it appeared he might have opened the incision from his surgery. The ball nestled in the fairway a good thirty yards behind Tiger's ball. "Must have caught that one in the neck," Woods said, laughing.

Commentators on The Golf Channel referred to Arnie as "Mr. Palmer." The others, however, were Tom, Davis, and Tiger. But the crowd yelled, "Go, Arnie," trying to urge his ball into the hole on every putt.

Unfortunately, it didn't go in, and Woods's ball was unruly as well. Tiger was in the trees so much Davis Love III razzed him that instead of the "I'm Tiger Woods" commercials he made for Nike he ought to bring out one that was titled "I'm in the Woods." At day's end, the Lehman/Love team had reeled in $15,000 while Palmer/Woods could only muster winnings of $3,000.

It didn't matter. The Golf Channel promoted its venue, and Tiger, Tom, and Davis paid their respects to the grand master of golf. Arnie appreciated it. "To have these guys give their time to come here for me is something very special," he said. Tiger Woods saw it a bit differently, saying, "Arnold Palmer *is* golf. I'd travel to the end of the earth for something like this."

Arnie made an appearance at the Pittsburgh Senior Classic at Quicksilver Country Club on Labor Day weekend, but it wasn't a memorable one. He played badly and finished far down the leader board at +7. Like everyone else in the world, Arnold mourned the loss of Princess Diana of Wales, killed in a tragic car accident in Paris. Her charm and smile, like Palmer's, had made Diana beloved by millions.

With defending champion Tom Weiskopf on the sidelines due to what Senior PGA Tour official Phil Stambaugh labeled "other commitments" and Hale Irwin tending to his golf course design business, Dr. Gil Morgan continued his pursuit of Irwin's lead in the money standings. Ten events remained until the season-closing Energizer Senior Tour Championship, and Morgan needed to make up nearly $250,000 to catch his rival.

Mediocre opening rounds of duplicate 71s made winning impossible, but Gil charged on Sunday, finishing with a 66 to finish at eight under. Morgan moved $50,600 closer to Irwin.

The other Morgan, Walter, found his putting stroke and duplicated Gil Morgan's 66. That catapulted him into third place, putting nearly $80,000 in his pocket. It solidified his standing in the top thirty-one, necessary for a 1998 season exemption.

The duel for the championship came down to over-fifty rookies Hugh Baiocchi, twice a bridesmaid in 1997 due to losses in play-offs, and Bob Duval, father of David, dubbed the "best professional not to win a tournament." Grandfather Hap was also a club professional, marking three generations of Duvals in the golf business.

Bob Duval, a nervous sort who was continually in motion even while waiting for a fellow competitor to play, had tournament officials ready to engrave the Pittsburgh Classic trophy with his name as he led by three strokes playing the fifteenth hole. But an ugly pushed tee shot found water, a double-bogey six resulted, and the game was on. Baiocchi played a difficult bunker shot from 150 yards to within five feet of the hole on eighteen and holed the putt for birdie, finishing at ten under. Duval limped home to tie, and then the two players marched around the play-off holes as if they wanted to play another full eighteen.

Besides wanting to bank the $165,000 first-prize booty, both players knew a win meant Q-School exemption for the 1998 season. Baiocchi had less at stake since his top-twenty standings on the money list bode him well. Duval, the former Florida State Seminole and head professional at Timaquana in Jacksonville for nearly ten years, hadn't been so fortunate and was only in the tournament by pure luck. His 70 during the Monday qualifying round had made him fifth alternate, and when Orville Moody withdrew during the Pro-Am, Duval was in.

Duval was a favorite of the animal lovers in the gallery with his shaggy-dog head cover. It was dubbed "Buddy" after his chow at home. Buddy, Jr., a less bleached version of the mutt, was in the car, having proven unlucky. "He's on probation," Duval explained.

Over the first five holes of the play-off, Duval, one of the long hitters on the Senior Tour, and Baiocchi, who had not had a bogey in thirty-six consecutive holes, both had chances to win. They failed, causing Duval to ask Donna Caponi, the former U.S. Women's Open champion turned Golf Channel commentator, "What time does it get dark in Pennsylvania?"

On the sixth play-off hole, the sixtieth of the week, Duval found a bunker with his tee shot and blooped his wedge shot short of the green. His chip was long and on a slope, leaving himself a nearly impossible seven-footer. Baiocchi "lagged" his fifteen-footer to gimme distance for par, and when Duval's effort to tie slid by the left edge, Baiocchi proved that the third time was the charm in a play-off by winning his first championship. "You can't imagine what this means to me," he explained after receiving the trophy. "It's truly a dream come true, especially after those two play-off losses."

Baiocchi's turnaround had come earlier in the year during a round with Lee Trevino. "The last round at Charlotte, I played with Lee and shot sixty-eight," he said. "Before that I had been trying too hard. Lee was encouraging, and that sixty-eight really boosted my confidence. I knew I could play with these guys."

Hugh Baiocchi, the latest first-time winner on the 1997 Senior Tour, wasn't a factor until late in the tournament at the Bank One Classic in Lexington the following week. Another rookie, Walter Hall, the Raleigh, North Carolina, native, took command in the first round with 66 and eventually posted a top five finish. Veterans Jay Sigel and Bruce Summerhays took shots at the lead as the tournament progressed, but on Money Sunday, the duel in the final holes was between Isao Aoki and Vicente Fernandez.

The battle for the championship at Lexington, being played for the final time in the Kentucky horse country after fifteen years of hosting the tournament, turned at the sixteenth, where Aoki duck-hooked his drive into swampland. He holed a testy eight-footer for bogey, but Fernandez, nicknamed "Chino" by his fellow competitors, birdied the sixteenth and seventeenth to give him a one-shot lead. His rounds of 67, 69, and 67 provided his second win on the Senior PGA Tour. Aoki was second, tying Buddy Whitten, another rookie struggling to keep his card.

The Argentinean, whose fellow countryman Roberto De Vicenzo was his hero, credited the return of his putting stroke—he had been number one in putting in 1996—with the difference. Fernandez, who'd been born with one leg shorter than the other, became the fifth foreigner to capture a victory on the 1997 Senior PGA Tour.

While Fernandez was ecstatic about his putting stroke, other players lamented their games. John Schroeder finished well, but complained, "I haven't putted well or driven well. Every week I have nine bad holes that cost me."

Bobby Stroble believed most of his game was in good shape, but he experimented around the practice green using a sand wedge to chip the ball. After several good shots, he commented, "Seems to work. Could be the difference."

Jim Albus, beset by injuries that had kept him from performing up to his standards, suggested he had no excuses. "I'm healthy," he explained as his caddie, son Mark, picked up his practice balls. "Ready to play well."

Bud Allin, a winner earlier in the year in the American Express Invitational, was desperately attempting to find the swing that had made him a champion. "Yesterday for about four holes," he said, "I had it, that something I had down in Florida. I got off the track, but I'm starting to play better." Bob Duval, fresh off good performances in several tournaments, said the difference in his game was confidence. "Early in the year, I wasn't ready to play well," he explained. "I hadn't competed on Tour like all the other guys. Then I started to score better, and play more offensively than defensively. That's what has gotten me going."

Simon Hobday was scratching his head at his poor play and wondering when it would end. "If you're going to play with me," he explained to Mike Hill, "you'll have to downgrade your game."

For Hubert Green, his nearly $400,000 in earnings didn't mean he was pleased with his performance. "Hell, I'm thirteen thousand dollars short of paying for the sand we've used down in Florida for my new house," he said. "So my game has to get better. And it is, I'm *this* close to playing really well. I just wish the Tour was starting now instead of winding down."

Green and Allin realized they had to play better if they wanted to qualify for the lucrative Tour Championship in November. Positioned at twenty-eighth and twenty-ninth on the money standings, respectively, the two veterans of the game realized it might take as much as $500,000 in earnings to earn a spot at Myrtle Beach. "That's the key to the season," Allin said. "That's my goal now."

The Bank One Classic had come on a weekend when the world mourned the recent deaths of Princess Diana and Mother Teresa.

Chi Chi Rodriguez's thoughts were with Mother Teresa. "I idolized that woman," he whispered, wiping a tear from his eye. "She was a humble woman who spent her life looking after the unfortunate. We had our picture taken together about fifteen years ago. I still carry it in my suitcase. Her physical body may be gone, but her soul and spirit will continue to live. What a wonderful lady."

Rodriguez said Mother Teresa had misjudged him when they

met. "The first thing she said was, 'You are rich, why don't you share with the poor.' As she was talking, I already had a check ready for her. I said, 'How do you know that I don't share with the poor?' She looked down and said nothing. She knew she had misjudged me. We talked for a long time. Something I'll never forget."

BOOK V

HALE VERSUS GIL

21

"MOVE OVER, HALE AND GIL," LARRY NELSON WARNED. "THERE'S A new challenger in town."

Ironically, the venue for Larry's statement was Augusta, site of many fine Nelson performances. This time, however, it was Augusta, Missouri, where Nelson took aim at the elite on the Senior Tour.

A slight, balding man at 5'9" and 150 pounds, Nelson was a likely choice to threaten topflight players like Irwin and Gil Morgan. The Vietnam veteran, winner of two PGA championships and a U.S. Open crown, won ten times on the PGA Tour.

As he approached fifty, Nelson looked back with mixed emotions on his professional career. His performances had been outstanding, but his pride had been hurt on at least two occasions. "I never got my due for winning the Open," he explained. "I guess I just wasn't the proper type of champion, not having come up through the ranks the traditional way, with lessons, and a big-club background. Some writers don't want to say anything nice, and I guess I was a victim of that."

Nelson also felt slighted when the captain for the 1997 Ryder Cup team was announced. With a record of 9-3-1 in competition, Nelson was told he was the natural fit to lead the team in the fall matches in Valderrama, Spain. But then Tom Kite got the nod, leaving Nelson with a broken heart. "I can't argue against Tom, of course," he said. "But the honor would have been nice."

Nearly a year before Nelson's debut at the Boone Valley Classic on the Senior PGA Tour, he began preparing. He beefed up his upper body and began practicing the short game that had bode well for him during his twenty-plus years on the PGA Tour.

More than anything though, it would be the Nelson mind that would test his senior peers. "I still can't outdrive them," he lamented, "but I'll get the job done somehow." To show he could, Nelson entered the Greater Milwaukee Open on Labor Day to test his game against the flatbellies of the PGA Tour. A final-round 72 spoiled three previous scores in the 60s, but Nelson proved his game was rounding into shape for the Senior Tour.

Nelson's debut at the Boone Valley Classic was highly anticipated, but an announcement in Lexington, Kentucky, overshadowed
all play. Larry Gilbert, riding high after his triumph in the Ford Players Championship, revealed he had lung cancer. "The doctors say
they caught it in the early stages," Gilbert said. "They predict I'll be
back playing in no time." He became the third member of the over-
fifty gang to be stricken with cancer.

After presentation of a birthday cake topped with a giant golf ball on
Wednesday by Boone Valley Classic officials, Larry Nelson carved out
a 69 in his first round as a Senior Tour player. That was three shots
from the lead held by Rocky Thompson, who swore, "I've taken four
lessons from four different people, and they all worked. I had to because I've been suffering from some physical problems this year—a
problem called 'bad swing.' I saw a video of my swing, and I threw up
right there in the hotel room."

One golfer had his mind on the wrong sport during the first
round. Walter Morgan shot an uncharacteristic 77, but who could
blame him? Before the tournament, Morgan was declared the official
Boone Valley fishing champion when he caught not only the biggest
bass—two pounds fourteen inches—but the largest blue gill—fifteen
ounces. "Unfortunately, I played like I fished," Morgan joked. "Big."

Vicente Fernandez wished he'd left the fish alone. After his first
round, the champion at Lexington celebrated with a bowl of gumbo,
unaware that jumbo shrimp were in it. The next morning, his entire
body was swollen, and he was forced to withdraw. "I first learned I was
allergic to shellfish way back in 1976," Fernandez said. "Chi Chi and I
were having supper, and fifteen minutes later I started swelling up and
they rushed me to the hospital. I almost died. Spent five days there. I
blamed the whole thing on Chi Chi, but it was really the shellfish."

While Fernandez was receiving medication to shrink his body,
Hale Irwin strove to erase a bad memory from a year ago. In the 1996
Boone Valley Classic, Irwin had putted like a beginner in the final
round, permitting Gibby Gilbert to tie him. When Gilbert prevailed
in the play-off, Irwin slunk away, embarrassed by the loss in front of
the hometown folks.

Despite distractions stemming from his unofficial post as host
for the tournament and time spent assisting with the Hale Irwin Children's Hospital Program, Irwin tied for the lead with David Graham.

For many players in St. Louis, time was getting short in their quest to make the top thirty-one list. Of the eight qualifiers at the Q-School in 1996, only Bob Dickson seemed assured of an exempt position for 1998. Will Sowles, David Oakley, Dennis Coscina, Buddy Whitten, and Dick Hendrickson all had squandered their opportunity to keep their playing cards. "The only saving grace would be a win," Oakley lamented.

Those on the bubble included Bob Duval, settled in thirty-fifth place, and Frank Conner, in thirty-fourth. John Schroeder, Brian Barnes, John D. Morgan, Mike McCullough, Terry Dill, Larry Laoretti, and Bobby Stroble needed superb play to make the elite exempt field.

Staying in the top thirty-one for the year also affected play in the lucrative season finale—the Energizer Tour Championship. Conner and Duval had an outside chance, along with Kermit Zarley and Bruce Crampton. Heading into the Boone Valley Classic, Bud Allin, a winner in Florida but a disappointment since, occupied slot number thirty-one. Dave Eichelberger—whose game had picked up in recent weeks after he improved his lining up of shots—Jim Dent, J. C. Snead, and Hubert Green—still battling his ineffectiveness to drive the ball far enough to be competitive—needed strong finishes in the final seven events to ensure they'd play in Myrtle Beach.

All of those players yearned to hit the leader board in St. Louis, but Hale Irwin captured the headlines. In addition to winning in his hometown, he wanted to rid himself of Gil Morgan, who had closed to within $185,000 in the money earnings race. When the final round began, Irwin would find out if he could beat his rival, for they were paired in the last threesome along with David Graham.

History was on the side of Irwin, who had won all five times he led or shared the lead heading into the final round in 1997. But Morgan had something to prove to Irwin, and he expected to prevail. "Hale's playing great," Doc said. "But so am I."

Through the first twelve holes, Irwin managed to stay ahead of Morgan. They played like two boxers fighting for the middleweight crown. Each took his shot, only to be rebuffed by play that was superb under pressure. Their titanic test provided Senior Tour fans the best drama since the Graham Marsh/John Bland confrontation in the U.S. Senior Open.

Irwin was first to strike, creatively handling his ball, which had nestled itself in an old divot on the thirteenth fairway. Positioning the ball back in his stance, he blistered a low nine-iron shot over water to within ten feet of the flag. When he confidently holed the putt, he led by two. But Morgan was up to the challenge, holing his birdie try at fourteen to climb back within one. "Not so fast," he said. "The game isn't over yet."

Irwin responded like a gunfighter, knocking his approach shot at fifteen close to the cup. "Take that, Gil," Irwin said, his lead restored to two.

The two combatants continued their duel at sixteen, showing off their respective skills in the "Show Me State." Irwin drilled an iron shot to within five feet, but Morgan lasered his inside it. Both made their putts, and Irwin's lead was two with two holes to play.

Morgan needed the victory. First prize was $195,000, second $81,000 less. If Morgan won, he was within $100,000 of Irwin, but a loss upped the margin to more than $250,000, with only seven events to play.

Morgan gave it his best shot, birdieing the last hole to finish at −14, which beat every player in the field except one. Irwin was not to be denied, and he proved it with a razor-sharp three iron to the seventeenth green, leaving him with a comfortable two-putt birdie that sealed the win. "Hale was just too good today," Morgan said. "Just too good."

Though he meant the remark with respect, Morgan's comment was a vast understatement. For fifty-four holes, Irwin had recorded no bogeys. Not even close to one. His driving was precise and long, reducing the already short-length Boone Valley Country Club to a driver and wedge practice range.

Irwin's putting stroke had been steady all week, but it was the iron play that separated him from the others. Jim Colbert had surmised earlier in the year that Irwin might be the best iron player on any Tour in any part of the world, and no one could quarrel with the suggestion. "I took two weeks off to let the air out of the balloon," Irwin said. "And to pump it back up. I was just winging it in the first round, but then my game came together. Winning at home is what it's all about. My iron shots were the difference. They put me in great position all week."

Regarding the chase for the money title and the Player of the Year honors that went with it, Irwin was nonchalant. "Chasing the number one money winner is not going to rule my life," Irwin said. "I'll play out the season on my own terms."

Others in the field had no such discretion. Of those fighting for exempt spots, either for the 1998 season or the Energizer Tour Championship, Mike McCullough had fared best at Boone Valley, finishing in the top ten. Bob Duval made a good showing, while

Bobby Stroble and Frank Conner kept their hopes alive. Brian Barnes, still fighting the effects of season-long injuries, finished at +8, and measly winnings did nothing to improve his position.

Those players had long left the course when Hale Irwin was accepting congratulations for his seventh win on the 1997 Senior Tour. The trophy ceremony was an emotional one, but it was the moment just after Irwin knocked in a three-inch putt on eighteen to clinch the win that remained the week's most vivid image of the Joplin, Missouri, native.

Irwin stood patiently while David Graham putted out. There for all the world to see was the Irwin grin, admittedly a sheepish one, but an honest reflection of the genuine side of the champion, a side that surfaced too seldom. It was the same face-wide smile that Irwin had exhibited when he'd captured his three U.S. Open Championships. No false facial expression, no smart-aleck tone, just the pleasant side of a private man never comfortable in the public spotlight. Just a superb athlete whose competitive drive matched an inner spirit that made him one of the great players of all time.

22

On the first tee at the Comfort Classic at the Brickyard in Indianapolis in mid-September, the amateur with thinning hair and a paunch that made him look pregnant stepped up to the ball, hands shaking, heart at full throttle. Dressed like an American flag, he waggled too many times and then unleashed a whiplash swing that made Chi Chi's look as if it were in slow motion.

The ball careened off the club face, banged against a metal garbage can, narrowly missed several spectators who ducked for cover, and zinged away toward the electronic scoreboard positioned on the adjacent eighteenth hole. Nonplussed, the amateur picked up his tee, lowered the bill of his Auto-Zone cap in hopes no one would recognize him, and sauntered off whistling a happy tune as if he'd just made a hole in one.

From the beginning, Pro-Am competition was the lifeblood of the Senior PGA Tour. Without the thousands of amateur golfers who paid big bucks to play with the heroes of the game prior to nearly every scheduled event, the Tour would be nonexistent. And hundreds of worthy charities would have empty coffers instead of receiving millions of dollars during the Tour's twenty-year span.

The format was standard. Fifty teams, made up of four amateur partners and a Tour professional, played on the Wednesday and Thursday before a tournament. On many occasions, there was also a MasterCard Senior Series Pro-Am held on Tuesday. All together, eight hundred to nine hundred amateurs a week competed in the thirty-four events holding Pro-Ams.

Amateurs' cost to play ranged from $2,500 to $3,000 per spot per day, with discounts given for purchasing two-day ducats and foursome packages. Simple arithmetic revealed that more than $2 million found its way into each event. Of that, more than 20 percent was earmarked for such worthy organizations as Big Brothers/Big Sisters, the Dyslexia Educational Foundation, and Christina's Smile, headed by Dr. Robert Garza, which provided free dental care for over two hundred needy children during the Comfort/Brickyard Classic.

The remainder covered a portion of the million-dollar-plus

purse that was offered to seventy-eight professionals every week. National sponsors supplied the difference, with local corporations, large and small, taking a smaller bite out of the pie. In certain events such as the Comfort/Brickyard Classic, the principal sponsor, Comfort Inns, also ponied up significant dollars to ensure television coverage.

For the amateurs and the corporations, the Senior PGA Tour was the ultimate win-win situation. Companies gained publicity for their products, and their CEOs and CFOs were able to hobnob with Senior Tour players and other hotshots in the corporate world. Being involved with the charities improved the image and provided table talk for the next year.

The amateurs cherished memories of playing with Arnie, Chi Chi, or someone else they idolized. They might shoot 120, but the memory lingered, especially if they could hit just one shot that drew a rave from one of the greats of the game. For weeks, months, and years afterward, the shot would become even greater. A five-footer to save par by a twenty-seven handicapper with two strokes on the hole would become a curling, deadly quick thirty-footer as time enhanced the memory. "Arnie couldn't believe I made it," the player would expound. "He said it was one of the greatest putts he ever saw."

For the hefty entry fee, often paid by a corporation for a customer or worthy executive, the amateur reaped a gift package sent from heaven. The goody bag varied, but at the Comfort/Brickyard Classic, the list was outstanding. When the amateur pulled his automobile up to the gift-package tent, his trunk was stuffed with an Ashworth merino wool sweater, pullover, and golf shirt, spanking-new brown and white golf shoes, a shoe bag, Hunter etched beer glasses, and a sleeve of Titleist golf balls. All were encased in a beautiful black tote bag with COMFORT/BRICKYARD CLASSIC emblazoned across the side.

On the eleventh hole, the amateur players and their professionals posed for the camera. When they completed play, the picture had been mounted in a wooden frame for posterity.

Perhaps the biggest perk of playing in a Senior Tour Pro-Am was competing on a golf course set up for championship competition. The atmosphere mesmerized first-timers who spied the bleachers, corporate tents, television camera stands, ESPN/ABC banners, and clicking electronic scoreboards dotting the course. Would-be Walter Mittys loved the experience, for even the rank amateur could easily fantasize himself into the world of the professional athlete, poised for competition against the best Senior Tour players in the world.

"It's a chance at competition and to give some money to charity," businessman Vince Danile, a close friend of Jim Colbert's, admitted. "I play in seven or eight a year. Playing with Jim, with Palmer and Trevino are the highlights of my life. And Trevino remembered me the next year."

Danile also cherished the friendships he made through the years. "When Graham Marsh won at Park City, we celebrated with some fine port. I told them, 'Life is too short to drink cheap wine.' I've gotten to know most of the pros. For a ten handicap like me, that's very special."

The amateur also remembered a lesson or tip he had received from the professional. Whether it occurred or not. After one event, an eighteen handicap told a member of the press that Graham Marsh showed him a new grip to use with short wedge shots. The reporter just shook his head. Graham Marsh was in Asia and wasn't even competing that week.

What the amateur could not control was the selection of the professional to lead his foursome. Before the event, a blind draw was held. Amateurs in the know were well aware which professionals were cherished as partners and which ones would make the experience similar to a visit to the dentist.

The amateurs had many favorites, but the most coveted partners were Arnold Palmer, Chi Chi Rodriguez, Lee Trevino, John Jacobs, and Jim Colbert. These professionals and most of the others realized the significance of the pro-ams and treated their playing partners with courtesy, readily helping with a shot or a putt.

Others, such as Bruce Crampton, Dave Hill, J. C. Snead, and Walter Zembriski, made amateurs cringe when the announcement was made that they had been drawn. Oftentimes their sourpuss demeanor meant a torturous day, and the amateur had to suffer through a round simply hoping he wouldn't do something to trigger an outburst from the huffy professional who felt he was doing him a favor to come out and play.

Crampton was the worst of the worst. His remarks to amateurs, officials, and especially volunteers forced a suspension early in his Senior PGA Tour career. At one tournament, over seventy-five complaints about him were received. When amateurs at the Comfort/Brickyard Tournament learned they had drawn Crampton for the second straight year, they prayed for relief. It didn't work. "Crabby" was as pouty as ever.

Dave Hill wasn't far behind. Besides being known for his abrasive behavior and nonstop complaining, he had managed to anger the CEO of Enterprise Rent-A-Car, the principal sponsor of the Boone

Valley Golf Classic, by bad-mouthing the event to a man who had worked tirelessly to produce a quality affair. Then Hill withdrew, leaving everyone hoping he might crawl into a hole and stay there.

Every professional who competed was required to play at least one Pro-Am day. Those down on the money list played both. After he shot a course-record 63 in the final round at the Comfort/Brickyard Classic, J. C. Snead told *Indianapolis Star* reporter Phil Richards, "I need the money to move up the list. I don't want to have to play *two* Pro-Ams next year." One observer heard the remark and said, "Don't you wonder what J.C. will be like when *he's* eighty-five? He's the ultimate grouch now."

Anecdotes about pro-ams were legendary. Bob Murphy's caddie, Mark Huber, recalled a certain CEO with PaineWebber who attempted to drive his cart under the ropes. "He got the rope tangled in the golf bag," Huber remembered. "It pulled the post out, and it went whistling past my face over my cart. The guy didn't ask how I was, just said, 'Well, at least I didn't break any clubs,' and took off on his merry way."

Willie Miller, Jim Colbert's longtime caddie, remembered when he and his boss simply stood in amazement at what they saw during a Pro-Am in Milwaukee. "There was a lake fifteen yards in front of the tee," Willie laughed, "and this guy hit the ball three times and never got it to the lake. The shots all came off the toe with a 'beek' sound. Jim looked at me and said, 'Well, I've never seen *that* before.'"

Johnny Mac, Chi Chi Rodriguez's caddie, nearly lost his life in a Pro-Am. "Two amateurs were by the green, one in front and one behind," he recalled. "I held the flag for the guy in front, who was clearly away. Just as I yanked it, the golfer in back skulled his shot and the ball hit me square in the head. I saw stars as I fell to the ground."

Larry Ziegler recalled shots by amateurs he didn't think were possible. "One time a guy topped a three-wood, but actually spun the ball backwards. Another clod topped it, caught the ball, put it in his pocket, and walked away like nothing happened."

John Bland's memories of Pro-Am partners centered on their nervousness. "They're so excited to play, many get to the course at five A.M., when it's still dark, to practice. For the first few holes, they fidget and fuss, but then they're all right."

Bland recalled one instance when a fellow professional assisted in a ruse with a buddy of theirs. "The CEO of a very large company was scheduled to play with [Scottish golfer] Sam Torrance, who had a bit of a reputation as a tough one," Bland said. "Before the match, the CEO's friends primed him, telling him how Sam was quite vicious and would get upset at the slightest thing. By the time they got to the first tee, the CEO was shaking like a leaf. He proceeded to whiff his tee ball. Torrance walked over to him, grabbed him by the throat, and said, 'Don't you ever hit a shot like that around me,' quite gruffly. The CEO was petrified, about to die until Sam let him in on the secret. Meanwhile, the guy's friends were crawling on the ground laughing."

Many professionals had horror stories to tell. Will Sowles and Bob Dickson marveled at the play of their amateur partners. "In Kansas City," Sowles recalled, "we bogeyed the first hole and I'm thinking 'Oh, no.' We played the last seventeen holes *twenty-three* under par. By day's end we had eight twos and a one on the card. At the fifth hole, every player made eagle except me. Guys were holing field shots from everywhere. It was the most amazing thing I'd ever seen. Next day, Bobby Nichols had that group and only got it to fifteen under. I told him he hurt the team."

In the Pro-Am competition at the Comfort/Brickyard Classic, Dickson explained, "I had the best team I ever had in twenty-nine years. We parred two holes and still shot twenty-three under. I just tried to stay out of the way. Those guys were unconscious."

There is no golf course in the world like Brickyard Crossing. And no better example of the genius of Pete Dye. He took flat acreage and molded it into a jewel of Americana in spite of the presence of high-tension power lines, railroad tracks, and rusted chain-length fences against a backdrop of a gigantic water tower and the famed Indianapolis Motor Speedway, home of the Indy 500. What Dye built was a one-of-a-kind golf course complete with rolling hills, huge mounds, and a meandering creek bulked with leftover remnants of the crash wall at the Speedway.

The par-three seventh hole was a devilish Redan-type design. Golfers standing on the tee during play in the Comfort/Brickyard Classic had to concentrate more than usual to ignore the sounds of race cars as they buzzed by on the two-and-a-half-mile oval track. During a stint at the practice tee after the Pro-Am, Walter Morgan, the ever-present stogie sticking out of his mouth, kept wincing every time a race car zoomed by. He turned to Eddie Cheever, the famed Indy racer standing nearby, and just shook his head. "Man, those things are loud," he proclaimed.

The sounds Walter heard were students of the Richard Petty Driving School, where the king of stock car racing held court with would-be drivers hoping for fame and fortune. Mixed between their laps, Indy cars sped around the track testing tires.

Pete Dye's unique golf course, with four holes inside the famed oval racetrack, and the smooth operation of the tournament by Speedway president Tony George reaped rewards for the event. Forty-three of the top forty-five Senior Tour players were in the field, including Hale Irwin and Gil Morgan, who resumed their duel for the money earnings lead for the year.

Other contestants had less heady goals. For club professional Rollie Schroeder, head professional at the Speedway for twenty-five years, the chance to compete with the big boys was a dream come true. Given a sponsor's exemption, Schroeder said, "To play with these guys every year is so special. I've looked up to them all my life. The first year I remember standing on the tee with Chi Chi, Arnold, and Miller Barber. I thought, 'What am I doing here?' "

Four of the eighty-seven golfers who attempted Monday qualifying for the Brickyard had smiles on their faces. Tony Perla, whose win of eight bucks from Jack Nicklaus during a practice round for the U.S. Senior Open in 1996 was a treasured memory, led with 68, along with Fritz Gambetta, in the field for the first time since being cast aside by Cincinnati club professional Bob Hauer's sixty-foot putt at the Kroger Classic.

At 69, along with Bobby Mitchell, a successful Tour player in the 1970s, was Harry Toscano, the rebel suing the Senior PGA Tour for its policies about entry into tournaments. Scuttlebutt was that if any Tour player was paired with the outlaw Toscano, he might withdraw.

Left with the decision as to who played with whom was PGA Tour official Gene Smith. "There are three categories we use for the first-round pairings," he explained. "We pair together nonwinners on either the PGA or Senior PGA Tour, players who have won, but not in the past five years, and those who have won on the Senior Tour in the last five years."

Once the pairings were posted, the squabbling began. The PGA Tour trailer was besieged by complaints from certain players, mostly those on the fringe whose egos were out of control. They demanded to know the reason for being paired out of their group. "We have to explain that sometimes the numbers don't quite work out," Gene said. "I won't name names, but some of the guys really give us hell."

The exception to the rule was Arnold Palmer. Officials paired Arnie wherever they wanted, often to accommodate television. Nobody griped about that.

That didn't mean the Senior Tour was without its petty jealousies. Many of the same fringe players, most of whom had played on the PGA Tour, exhibited animosity toward the club professionals and the foreign contingency.

"The club professionals and the foreigners are looked upon as being outsiders, not a part of the fraternity," a Senior PGA Tour official said. "It's ridiculous, but that's the way they see it. Especially those who are sliding down the all-time money list. They're jealous as hell of those guys."

Gene Smith paid little attention to the angry ones, but when he completed his pairings for the first round of the Comfort/Brickyard Classic, Rollie Schroeder, ever the gentleman, gained the honor to play with Harry Toscano along with Bob E. Smith. Toscano wasn't competitive and fell back in the field after the first round.

While many of the Tour's bubble group were intent on improving their position, Brian Barnes decided to take a lesson to improve play. For the better part of two hours, he stood on the practice green with U.S. Senior Open champion Graham Marsh, who chastised Barnes's setup with his flop-shot play, saying, "Brian, you can't chip from that position."

Over and over the tall, meaty Brit, who, along with his caddie, Phil, had taken to a Slim Fast diet to lose a few pounds, practiced flop shots to the green. Bruce Summerhays joined the discussion, and the three professionals bantered back and forth as Barnsey attempted to pick the club up more cleanly and produce high floaters that would stop instantly. Meanwhile, Nick DePaul, Marsh's caddie, practiced *his* wedge work and penciled in the *USA Today* crossword puzzle while lamenting, "Graham needs to practice his own short game. He doesn't do that enough."

When play began on Thursday, Barnes managed a 70, but Marsh's flop-shot tips spelled no relief for Barnsey's sick game. Though he wore a blue and red plaid golf shirt for luck, he limped home to rounds of 73 and 72 and finished tied for forty-second. Winnings of $4,515 didn't aid his cause. The Q-School, looming just two months ahead, was becoming more and more of a reality.

First-round play had marked the return to the Senior Tour of Arnold Palmer. Fresh from a visit to the Mayo Clinic and a check of his progress after surgery, the King was in a feisty mood. "They told me I didn't have to return for a year," he said, while inquiring about the condition of Larry Gilbert, stricken with lung cancer.

Palmer, toting head covers with "The Deacon" stitched on them in honor of his father, wasn't aware that the deadly disease had afflicted another member of the Tour family, Larry Ziegler's caddie, Eddie Stankus. Although given only a 10 percent chance to live through surgery scheduled for the following week, Eddie stood bravely alongside his boss, cracking jokes and having a good ol' time. "He may not make it," Ziegler said of his caddie and friend when Eddie walked away from the practice tee, "but we're going to laugh all the way through this tournament." When Eddie returned, Ziegler was ripe with barbs: "Oh, Eddie Wonder is back, Stevie's brother."

Eddie returned the volley. "I was feeling better before I had to watch this," he laughed as Ziegler smacked balls down the practice range. "Larry's swing will make anyone sick." Ziegler did make Eddie feel better in the tournament's final round, perhaps the caddie's last on the Tour, shooting 69, his best score in weeks.

The talk on the practice tee before the first round wasn't of golf but of the incredible experiences the players had while touring the Indianapolis Motor Speedway the day before. Tournament officials had set it up for the professionals to drive the famed oval along with instructors from the Richard Petty Driving School at speeds between 115 and 140 miles per hour. "I've never had so much power under my foot," exclaimed Homero Blancas. "Wait until I tell my dad I lapped at 131 [miles per hour]," John Morgan exulted. "I could go around there about a hundred times," said Bob Duval, who claimed to hit a speed of 143.6. "Do they have a senior circuit?"

Dave Stockton not only hit the track, and loved it, but watched his wife, Cathy, daughter, Tammy, and son, Ron, blaze around the Motor Speedway. "I've never been that nervous before," Cathy said after her drive. "It was awesome," chipped in Tammy.

Arnold Palmer didn't take a spin, but bantered with veteran Indy-car driver Eddie Cheever. "Were you out there making noise?" Arnie asked upon spying Cheever behind the eighteenth green. "No, I drive the faster ones with no roofs," Cheever explained.

Pretournament favorites for the Comfort/Brickyard Classic crown were Hale Irwin, Gil Morgan, and John Bland, searching for his first win of the season in spite of winning nearly a million dollars. Irwin was spotlighted in one of the day's two featured pairings, one that saw him play with Jim Dent and Chi Chi Rodriguez, who bounded onto the first tee with raised hands, inviting applause that pumped up the crowd.

Beside the basketball player–sized Dent, Rodriguez looked like a dwarf, but there was no mistaking the Chi Chi smile. Even though

Irwin had won seven times and more than $1.7 million in 1997, the Cheech was clearly the player the spectators came to see. He was armed with a new weapon, a cut-down 27-inch Ping putter that he nicknamed "Little Bertha." It even had its own compartment in Cheech's golf bag: the umbrella hole.

"I putted so bad last week at St. Louis," Chi Chi explained as he hunched over the tiny wand, "that I decided to try this. I used one thirty years ago in the army and won the post championship. I'm so close to the ground now I can kiss it if I make a good-sized putt."

The leading money winner on the Tour had shaken his head when he saw the new putter. "Hale told me that now I can do a knife dance instead of a sword dance," Rodriguez explained. "And of course I only have thirteen and a half clubs. I've got room for more."

Little Bertha behaved itself in round one, although Rodriguez had to take nearly a full swing for any putt over twenty feet. Cheech's final score was 70, and he was delighted with the half club. "I can roll the ball so smooth the green doesn't know what's happening," he said.

The 11:50 tee time group was a very special threesome. John Bland, his Cheshire cat smile apparent, had been paired with Gary Player and Arnold Palmer. "I picked out a new shirt and pressed slacks for this," Bland, not known as one of the great dressers on the Tour, explained. Numerous other professionals applauded the effort, and John was quite resplendent in a green-and-white-striped shirt with cream-colored trousers to match his straw Taylor Made hat.

"Remember to say that Arnie and Gary are playing with *me*," Bland kidded. "Not the other way around."

Player was nonchalant about the pairing, telling the crowd, "I'm playing with a rookie," referring to Palmer. Arnie spouted back, "South Africa's ganging up on me," to the delight of those bunched around the first tee. Moments before, he had been besieged by autograph seekers on his way from the practice tee, where fans had huddled around him. Even though Hale Irwin, Gil Morgan, Raymond Floyd, John Bland, and Graham Marsh were also practicing, Palmer had the crowd. "Arnie can miss a putt and I'll hit a perfect shot and he'll get more of an ovation when he taps in than I will," Larry Ziegler observed.

Watching Palmer sign autographs impressed Bland. "Palmer, and Player, too, they are such gentlemen with the crowds," he said. "They set a standard for all of us."

Player was dressed in black and gray to match the strands of hair sneaking out from under his cap. It had a black knight, the logo for his golf company, imprinted across the front.

Player hit first and rocketed a drive down the middle. "The PGA tells me I'm the only golfer to have won professional tournaments in five decades," he said, forgetting that Sam Snead had done likewise. "And I'm determined to win in the year 2000 and beyond."

Earlier in the week, Player had promoted the Comfort/Brickyard Classic on the radio, telling the audience stories about his travels around the world. "The moment I get on a plane, I can fall asleep," he began. "So on a flight from L.A. to Japan, I laid down in the aisle and slept all the way across the ocean. When we neared landing, the stewardess came by and asked a woman who was sitting nearby knitting, 'Is he all right?' 'No, miss,' she said, 'I think he's dead.' "

After Player bowed to the applause of the spectators on the first tee, Arnold Palmer slashed through the ball, sending it soaring against the threatening gray sky. An eruption of whistles and applause followed; the crowd had seen the King hit a tee shot one more time.

When round one was completed, a native of Rhodesia/Zimbabwe stole the headlines from the South Africans. Simon Hobday, who later labeled his round "a miracle," led with 65, puffing away on cigarettes while chattering nonstop about the round straight from heaven. "I've been driving the ball bad, hitting my irons bad, and putting bad," he explained. "Today, something happened. I wish I knew what it was." He didn't, and a 76 followed by 70 left him shaking his head.

Next to Hobday after round one was John Morgan, who supplemented his earnings on the South African and European tours as a market gardener, one who grows crops for sale at the market. He shot 66, two better than Al Geiberger, whose lucky marking penny with an angel cutout, which he bought in a Hallmark store, had brought home a satisfying round.

Some were reluctant to admit it, but many on the Senior Tour relied on more than just a superior golf game for the battle at hand. Superstitions ran rampant as each player volleyed for that extra oomph that might make the difference between winning and losing.

Emphasis was placed on the proper golf ball to play, but, more important, the number on that ball. "We never play a number four," Bob Murphy's caddie, Mark Huber, explained. "Tried that and we had a couple of seventy-fours or seventy-fives. That was the end of the fours. I give them to ESPN cameramen."

J. C. Snead avoided balls with threes, believing they could mean three putts. Sandy Jones, caddie for Bunky Henry, had her own method: "We play ones for the first round, twos in the second, and threes in the third." Willie Miller, who would officially "retire" as Jim

Colbert's caddie later in the year, said they avoided sevens and eights. "No high numbers, bad luck," he explained.

Miller said he found trouble on one occasion when he caddied for Jim Dent. "Jim hated number fours," Willie said. "So I separated them all out. At the seventeenth hole, he topped the last one that wasn't a four into the water. I handed him a number four and he tossed it back and I said, 'Jim, that's all we got.' He hit his drive all right, but then his second plugged under the lip of a bunker. That's the last time I ever did that."

One caddie in Europe nicknamed Spanish Dominic decided to help himself to a few practice-range balls. He deposited them in his player's bag and then unknowingly provided the golfer with one that he hit on the first tee. In the fairway, Dominic noticed the markings on the ball and called it to his boss's attention. "I hope you stole enough golf balls to get us around," the angry player remarked, aware that they couldn't change the type of ball or the markings on it during the round, per tournament rules.

Marks on golf balls were distinctive. Rocky Thompson, who avoided number threes, as did Gil Morgan, saw Dick Hendrickson's wife dab a single red dot over the number on the ball. Rocky did that too, shot 67, and has used a red dot ever since.

Chi Chi Rodriguez saw numbers as important in another way. "You know that twenty-seven-inch putter I have," he explained. "It works because anything with a seven in it is lucky."

Many players coveted lucky ball markers. Bruce Summerhays used distinctive coins that had proven worthy. David Graham used two English coins given to him by a friend. Bunky Henry had tried that without success. "I had a friend who gave me a lucky ball mark. I used it every day. Missed every putt. Threw it away."

U.S. Senior Open champion Graham Marsh believed in another superstition. "Never use another golfer's broken tee," he explained, unwilling to say why.

Marsh didn't believe Chi Chi Rodriguez's theory about the importance of color of clothing. "Red is a bad color," the Cheech said. "I'm hyper enough without being around red. Gray and dark blue are the best colors. Hogan, Snead, and Venturi always wore gray. And they played their best when they did." Told that Arnold Palmer was wearing gray that day, Chi Chi predicted, "He'll have his best round of the tournament." Arnie didn't cooperate. He shot 74. Rodriguez added, "If I draw a pairing where a partner is wearing red, I ask them to go change. And by the way, green is the best color on Sunday. The color of money." Bob Murphy agreed, saying, "Not only is it the color of money, it's the luck of the Irish."

Al Geiberger backed up Chi Chi's observations. "If I wear a certain-color shirt or pants and play well, then great. They stay in play. But if I play bad, they go in the closet. Many times I've almost run out of equipment in a bad week."

Geiberger believed his parking spot during tournaments was critical. "I watch where I park the car both at the hotel and the course," he reported. "If I play well, I'll go back to that same space. If not, I'm out of there looking for a different one."

Placement of equipment was on the mind of caddie Sandy Jones. "The clubs have to go in certain spots," she said of her superstition. "In the same compartments every time. The driver gets its own little home, the putter with the three-wood. And so forth. That's very important."

Geiberger's lucky penny vaulted him to a tie with Hale Irwin at 68, one ahead of Bob Murphy. Murphy still had visions of the recent safari he and wife Gail had taken along with Bob Charles, Gary Player's wife, Vivienne, and family members to Africa. "I was too dumb to be scared. But the animals were astounding," Murphy said. "When we landed, there was the biggest elephant I ever saw on the runway taking a dump. I said, 'Are we in the right place?' And the lions were big, too. We saw a cheetah kill, something Gary told us later never happens. It was an amazing trip."

In the opening round David Graham was amazing, firing 67. Ray Floyd, seeking his first win in twenty-three appearances since the 1996 Players Championship, shot 69. Gary Player had 71, but the exuberant crowd that followed his threesome had a day full of memories to take home.

Saturday's second round saw dark Indiana skies and sweater-weather temperatures greet the competitors. Players with early tee times were bundled up as if it were December instead of September, but that didn't prevent low scoring across the board. Dana Quigley, who had opened with a sterling 66; Gil Morgan, fighting back after a mediocre Friday round of 71; David Graham; Bob Murphy; John Morgan, the former mathematics teacher; and newcomer Larry Nelson fought for the lead.

The resurgence of good play was good news for Floyd, who had seen few bright spots with his game. "I took six weeks off this summer," he explained. "Didn't play competitively, just with the family. I realized how much I missed the game. I'm ready to play well again."

In many ways, the fact that Floyd was still playing at all was remarkable. By all accounts, the PGA Tour party boy of the 1960s
should have been committed to a mental institution, his brain drained
of any semblance of sanity by a wide variety of alcoholic beverages and
late-night escapades.

Despite being a mercurial wonder who played superb golf almost
from the time he picked up a club at age five, Floyd nearly destroyed
himself through one bad habit—women—which led to another—
drinking. "If there is anything better than women," Floyd bragged in
the mid-1960s, "I don't know what it is. I like women and partying,
and I'm not ashamed of it. It doesn't affect my golf, and I have
tremendous recovery power. All I need is six hours' sleep. It's not like I
turn into a pumpkin at midnight."

And he didn't, amazing his fellow competitors with topflight
play even after a night on the town. Like Walter Hagen before him,
it was as if Floyd could step off the dance floor, or out of the bed-
room, or back away from the bar, and then fire ten birdies on the
way to a 64. All that while golfers like Gary Player and others were
sipping fruit drinks and exercising until their bodies were dripping
with sweat.

What amazed most challengers was that Floyd played golf part-
time, as if attendance at Chicago Cubs games, dates with starlets, or
bets that he could drink anyone under the table all came before golf.
"We all wondered what Raymond could do if he stayed away from the
booze and the girls and got eight hours' sleep," one professional observed, unaware that the jolt to his lifestyle would probably have
caused him to shoot 80. When a reporter asked Floyd what color his
eyes were as he yawned his way to the tee in the mid-1960s, he
replied, "Red."

Floyd differed with those who believe his ability is God-given.
"I've worked hard," he stated, though the grooved swing that won
four Major championships and twenty-two victories on the PGA Tour
seemed to follow him from the crib.

It took Floyd six years to win his first Major, the 1969 PGA
Championship. Later he added a Masters victory, one in the U.S.
Open, and a second PGA Championship. Natural talent prevailed
even when mixed in with a Party Now–Practice Later attitude. And
the girls . . . There seemed to be more Floyd groupies, enticed by the
blond locks and the mischievous smile, than Arnie had in his Army.

At the Masters one year, a buxom woman with little to cover her
attributes showed up with a badge that read "Mrs. Raymond Floyd."
Her skimpy attire didn't meet Augusta National standards, and she

was escorted to the nearest bus stop. Next day, a beautiful redhead appeared with a badge that read "Mrs. Raymond Floyd." Since she had less on than the blonde, the authorities sent her packing as well.

If there was one defining moment in the Floyd golfing legacy, it occurred at the 1976 Masters. Sans blonde and redhead, Floyd played golf like few before him or since. Floyd devoured Augusta by firing a seventeen-under-par total to tie Jack Nicklaus's record. It was finally eclipsed in 1997 by Tiger Woods.

"It was one of the great feats of golf," Tom Weiskopf recalled. "It was unbelievable how aggressive Raymond played." Aggressive enough to win by eight shots over Ben Crenshaw. Jack was eleven back.

By his own admission, that week Floyd was unconscious, telling reporters, "I tried to birdie every hole. If I don't play that way, I don't make birdies, and if you don't make birdies, you don't win."

While Floyd's long game that week was superb, especially with the driver and a new five-wood, his putting touch was so delicate he could have holed the ball on slanted linoleum. The key was great hand-eye coordination, as evidenced by a story former Tour player Ken Still told about Floyd.

"At a Cleveland Indians game, mosquitoes were driving us nuts," Still recalled. "But Raymond kept snagging one after the other with quick, backhanded moves. I think that's why he putted so well. His eyesight was superb, and he had great hands."

Superb putting, especially under pressure, was what Floyd said he wanted to be remembered for: "I would like someone to say, 'Watch Raymond Floyd play golf. He conducts himself as a gentleman.' But along with that I want to be known as the greatest putter who ever lived. Maybe that won't be my epitaph, but I'm at least in the top ten."

That lofty standing certainly was evident when Floyd was matched against the great concentrators in the history of the game. He gave the word "focus" new meaning, channeling into a zone that few others in sport have known. Jack Nicklaus could do it, Ben Hogan to be sure, but Raymond dived into a semiconscious cocoon that separated him from other mortal beings.

At the 1986 U.S. Open at Shinnecock Hills, Floyd's stare was emblazoned on his face from start to finish. He was forty-three years old at the time and aware that he might be contending in a Major championship for the final time. On the back nine, securely in the hunt, he bounded off one green and right past a pretty spectator who mouthed a word of encouragement and waved to him. He ignored her like a stranger. It was wife Maria.

Floyd shot 32 on that back nine that day and conquered the course. Even though he'd lost some of the physical aspects of his game, he'd beaten the underlings with his wits. By blocking out distractions that impeded others, Floyd used his mind to overcome adversity and will himself on to victory.

The gifted ability to concentrate, manage his golf game under pressure, and consistently exhibit a superb short game bode well for Floyd when he hit the Senior Tour in 1992. He served notice he was serious by winning three times, and joining the million-dollar club two years later. Entering the 1997 season Floyd had compiled thirteen Tour victories, including five Majors. Only the Senior Open had escaped his clutches.

"He's still the best chipper on the face of the earth," Rocky Thompson pointed out. "And you always think he's going to make a putt."

That reputation was tarnished during the 1996 season when Floyd posted only one victory. He had continued to dominate the Senior Skins' game with his artistry in the early part of the year, but bad putting drove him nuts. "I'm just not making anything right now. I planned on playing less and better, but if you can't make the putts it won't matter," he predicted as the 1997 season began to unfold.

Through four-fifths of the season, Floyd had not counted a victory nor had he contended on many occasions. Heading into the Comfort/Brickyard Classic, the all-time money winner active on the Senior Tour with over $10 million in total career earnings stood twenty-sixth on the 1997 money list with just over $400,000.

"If I can't win out here, I'm history," he said midway through the 1997 season. "You won't see me out here when I'm playing like a dog."

Armed with a new spirit, Floyd started working on his game. A final-round 67 at the Boone County Classic in St. Louis and a sizzling 64 in the Brickyard Pro-Am on Wednesday had set the stage for the opening 69 and a flawless 66 in Saturday's second round. Along with David Graham and Bud Allin, who professed to have no understanding of his golf game just minutes before teeing off on Friday, Floyd trailed leader Larry Nelson by one.

Of the leaders' rounds, Allin's was the most mysterious. "I didn't have a clue yesterday or on the practice range today," the skinny veteran with the shock of white hair admitted. "But just before I hit the first tee, I remembered a swing thought from last year. I liked it so much I told my mom about it then, but I gave up on it. I can't tell you what it is, but I just thought about that one thing all day." Pressed by a reporter for his "secret," Allin continued to be evasive. "It'll all come out in my book," he said in reference to a manuscript he'd been writing for twenty-odd years.

Whatever *it* was produced five consecutive birdies from holes two through seven. "I hit a good solid shot at number two, then another couple at three. 'Hey, I might have something here,' I thought. And I carried it through the round. Normally, I'm always fidgeting with my swing, as much as twenty-five, thirty times a round. But today, I found something. I hope it comes back tomorrow."

Asked if his method of changing his thought process with nearly every swing wasn't contrary to what golf instructors preached to their students, Allin smiled. "I'm no golf guru," he said. "Hell, I changed my putting stroke this morning, too. Went wristy for the first time in twenty, maybe thirty years. I was a whole new golfer out there."

Lurking two shots behind Allin, Graham, and Floyd was Dr. Gil Morgan, still hopeful of speeding past Hale Irwin before the Senior Tour season was over.

Three shots behind Morgan and Bob Murphy stood Chi Chi Rodriguez with his magic miniwand in tow. "I'm adopting the putter," the Cheech said. "It's becoming like one of the family."

Tied with Chi Chi was Al Geiberger, who fired a 72 in spite of bad news. "I lost my penny with the angel last night," he explained while diving into his pocket for another one. "But luckily I bought a bunch of them. While the one is missing in action, I'll try this one." The loss produced a round four shots worse than opening day, and Geiberger went to his hotel room in search of the original lucky penny.

Stationed at 148 was Arnold Palmer with a second straight 74. "My golf game's not very good," he explained. "There's not any single part that excels. Right now it's a struggle."

No matter, said the fans. After Arnie completed his round, hundreds of admirers ringed the area behind the green, nearly toppling him over as he tried to make his way across a footbridge to the clubhouse. Palmer barged into the thicket of worshipers, patiently signing hats, scorecards, programs, dollar bills, T-shirts, and even a golf ball or two. Nonetheless, the King wasn't happy with his golf game as he walked toward the practice tee for an hour-long session. "I'm too old for this shit," he'd exclaimed at the ninth hole. "Too damn old."

Practicing provided hope. Minutes before he played in the early-morning cold weather on Sunday, the King proclaimed, "I'm going to play like the Palmer of old, not the old Palmer," but his round was spotty, resulting in twin 38s that produced a disappointing 76. Palmer left for the airport and his second favorite passion, flying, where his brand-new multimillion-dollar Citation 10-550 whisked him back to Latrobe.

Meanwhile, the front-runners, neither of whom weighed more than 150 pounds dripping wet, were jockeying for the lead. Larry Nelson and Bud Allin looked like half-pints compared to 6'1" Ray Floyd, but they kept pace in the early going. Allin recorded two birdies in the first three holes.

Unlike Floyd and Nelson, who had captured seven Major championships between them and were set financially, Allin still was struggling at age fifty-two years and eleven months to guarantee the nest egg necessary when golf no longer could provide him a living. He also needed to win as much cash as possible to solidify his position on the top thirty-one money list, as well as the top seventy all-time money list, another standard that could keep him exempt in coming years. "I need the cash, that's for sure," Buddy said on the practice range.

When Allin birdied the twelfth hole on top of Floyd and Nelson, the lead was still two. Allin, seeking his second win of the season, kept playing well. His closest pursuers were Jim Dent, David Graham, and Larry Nelson. Floyd, seeking professional victory number thirty-six, couldn't keep pace, ending his chances for a victory he had predicted that morning. The movable parts of his swing never meshed, and he fell out of the hunt. On the final two holes, Floyd produced errant shots, one ending up in a slithering creek. He finished fifth.

At fourteen, David Graham earned a par that was significant to the outcome, though it got lost in the next day's headlines. After depositing his tee shot in a heinous greenside pot bunker, Graham's blast ricocheted off the bunker face in front of him and nearly hit his leg on the return flight into the sand. Nonplussed, the Aussie lofted a soft shot to within five feet and holed the curling putt to keep within striking distance of Allin and Nelson, playing behind him.

Through fifty-three holes of the tournament, Allin led, but the dramatics at eighteen overshadowed everything that had come before it. Graham, playing with Bob Murphy and Gil Morgan, neither of whom were thrilled with Graham's methodical, almost agonizingly slow style, played the hole perfectly. A long drive preceded a crisp wedge shot to within six feet on the mounded green. The putt was true, and Graham was now tied with Allin and one ahead of Larry Nelson.

Though he had battled with true grit seldom seen on any golf tour, batting away his foes like a gladiator intent on saving the fair maiden, Allin finally succumbed to one bad swing in the 66 he would card that Sunday. Believing he had a one-shot lead on Graham and wanting to avoid the creek bed on the right at all costs after recalling a horrid shot the year before that barely cleared the ledge adjacent to the creek, Allin came over the top of the ball just a smidgen and darted it off the tee into the heavy left rough. From a flier lie in the hollow, he smacked a five-iron on a low trajectory toward the green, but the golf gods were most unkind and the ball scampered onto a downslope in the rough to the left of the green in a near-impossible grassy lie.

Allin gave it his best effort, but the ball bounded out of the rough, down a slope, up a mound that appeared to have a small elephant buried beneath it, and then down the side toward the hole, just behind the slope. The ball had no brakes to stop it and rolled into the short rough over the green some twenty feet from the hole. After Larry Nelson singed the hole for a birdie to tie David Graham, Allin made a valiant attempt to hole his chip shot for par, but the ball was left and long. To his credit, he made the testy four-footer coming back, ensuring himself of a tie for second with Nelson, which earned Bud a much-needed $84,000 for himself and wife Carol, a nervous wreck after the near win. The money moved him eight notches up on the magic list to the twenty-third spot.

Graham banked $157,000 for victory number three of the year. He sported a smile that made his bulbous nose seem invisible, and gave partial credit for the win to another Senior Tour player.

"Lee Trevino shares part of this," he exclaimed. "After one round we played, he told me my putting stunk. He made me put more of my weight on the left side and changed my left-hand position. The results today were magnificent."

"I played my heart out," spouted Bud Allin. "It just wasn't quite good enough."

Finishing six shots back of the leader was Gil Morgan, who birdied the last hole to tie with Murphy and John Jacobs. His paycheck for a week at the office was $37,800. That was $26,425 more than the check of Hale Irwin, who shot 68, 73, and 70. The gap between the two would-be players of the year was now $239,402.

Geiberger's lucky penny, which he found, produced a so-so final round of 71, but his attention was quickly diverted to the Texas Open where son Brent had finished runner-up and won over $100,000 more than his father. Chi Chi and his wonder putter managed 72. That in spite of a nip of Bee Alive Queen's Nectar before the final round that made one spectator suspicious. "A fan saw me drinking the nectar.

Thought I was hitting the booze," said Chi Chi, who had thrilled the crowd at eighteen with a little Spanish two-step after hitting a superb shot out of the rough and onto the green.

Setting a course record with 63 in the final round was J. C. Snead, who finished in the top ten. Playing partner John Paul Cain summed up his feelings. "Who did you think you were out there, Hale Irwin?" he kidded.

Of those in the hunt for the top thirty-one list, Bob Duval, with a final-round 66, made the most headway. Bobby Stroble had another good showing, moving to forty-seventh. Frank Conner, Mike McCullough, and John Schroeder failed to improve their precarious positions.

Graham Marsh and John Bland didn't contend, but their earnings made them the fifth and sixth Senior Tour players to top the million-dollar mark. With his first-prize check, David Graham had become the fourth.

Six events remained before the season's full-field closing Tour Championship in Myrtle Beach. There were only six more chances to play well enough to be exempt for the 1998 season, when the riches of the Senior PGA Tour would reach new record heights. "You need a four-to-six-week run of hot play out here a year," Bunky Henry, one of those hoping for a miracle win, observed. "That's what it takes. That's what we're all searching for."

Talk about bad timing. On the weekend of September 26, the Emerald Coast Classic, the thirty-third full-field stop on the Senior PGA Tour, was played in Pensacola, Florida. With the exception of Arnie, all of the top-name players on the Tour competed. The weather cooperated, the play was superb, the drama was everything spectators yearned for, and the champion was a popular one who thrilled the crowd with spectacular shot making.

Problem was, few noticed. The Ryder Cup was being played across the Atlantic, six time zones away in Valderrama, Spain.

Senior Tour competitors were captivated by the event, for many of them had experienced the thrill of representing the United States or Europe in the every-other-year match-play event. On the foreign side, Tony Jacklin, though not a contestant at Pensacola, had the most vivid memories. Besides having competed on seven teams with a record of 13-14-2, Jacklin captained the Europeans from 1983 to 1989.

In 1987, his savvy with the pairings and cheerleading efforts led to an embarrassing loss by the United States at Jack Nicklaus's Muirfield course, the first loss ever on American soil. Jacklin's experiences challenged that of Englishman Brian Barnes. His two wins in one day over Jack Nicklaus in the 1975 matches were his most prized memory in six trips to the competition. Twenty-four other Senior Tour players had competed for the United States.

Only Hale Irwin had earned consideration by captain Tom Kite to be a member of the 1997 squad. His superb play on the Senior Tour and in Major championships throughout the year kept him in contention, but in the end, Kite chose Fred Couples and Lee Janzen. Chi Chi Rodriguez believed Kite was crazy with those choices. "He needed to pick Tom Watson and John Daly," the Cheech surmised. "Watson has the experience and having someone on the team like Daly who can hit the ball a mile past everyone is intimidating."

Irwin, who sported a 13-5-1 record as a member of five Ryder Cup squads, Larry Nelson, 9-3-1, Arnold Palmer, 22-8-2, J. C. Snead, 9-2-0, and Hubert Green, undefeated in three appearances, had been the most successful of the Senior Tour members. Ironically, Ray Floyd, with a 12-16-2 record, had been a disappointment.

Though it had occurred nearly thirty years ago, in 1969, Jack Nicklaus's decision to concede Tony Jacklin's three-footer in the matches to provide the Europeans with a 16-16 tie was still the subject of controversy. Nicklaus gave the putt in the spirit of sportsmanship, but J. C. Snead, for one, still burned at the mention of Jack's act. "If I'd been a player on that team, I'd have drop-kicked his butt into the bunker. He had no right to do that."

All who competed in the Emerald Coast Classic kept one eye on the matches in Spain, especially when Europe battled the United States to a three-three tie the first day while leading one of the two matches suspended by darkness. "The matches are about bragging rights," Floyd explained. "And it's two years until you get another shot. Losing in 1995 was tough to take. I think our boys will bring back the cup."

They didn't. Though the United States rallied on the final day with superb play, they came up short and lost the Ryder Cup for the second consecutive time.

"I knew we were in trouble when I saw Tiger putt that ball into the water on seventeen," Lee Trevino explained. "It was going so fast it could put a dent in your car."

Meanwhile, there was a golf tournament being played at Pensacola. Trevino was the defending champion, having won a five-way play-off in 1996, but his chances of winning a tournament for the seventh consecutive year further diminished when he finished far down the leader board.

Another golfer searching for his first win in 1997 was Isao Aoki. Though he stood seventh on the money earnings list with nearly a million dollars, he had failed to enter the winner's circle in twenty-two events. That meant there had been few opportunities for Aoki to enter the media room, something reporters *didn't* regret. Few showed up, for the experience of having questions funneled through an interpreter (most times Aoki's caddie, Andy Wada) to a man who spoke enough English to earn a teaching license boggled the mind.

Aoki's refusal to conduct his own press conference was part of his aura, designed to perpetuate the mystical image of the man they called "Tower" in Japan because of his six-foot height. He could have been called "The Leaning Tower" because his outside-in looping swing and backward lean sometimes made him look as if he might fall down.

The most lasting image of Aoki, who learned the game while a caddie in junior high school, occurred in 1980, when he nearly stole the U.S. Open trophy and packed it back to Japan. At the end of fifty-four holes at Baltusrol, Jack Nicklaus and Aoki, who would accumulate nearly sixty victories worldwide, were dead even.

In the final round, Nicklaus led Aoki by two shots after nine holes, but precision iron play and a deft putting stroke kept Aoki close. His main weapon was a tin-colored putter, which he positioned with the back of the heel to the ground. That meant the toe was up, a very unconventional style, but necessary ever since Aoki's first set of clubs, given to him by a U.S. air force officer, were too long for him.

To adapt, the reserved Japanese golfer crouched low over the ball, his hands at knee level. The results at Baltusrol had been astounding; Aoki had used but fifty putts over the first thirty-six holes. He finally lost to Nicklaus in the final round, but Aoki had made his mark in America.

While holing out a wedge shot to win the 1983 Hawaiian Open brought him fame, being best known for finishing second to Nicklaus in the Open long irritated Aoki. He was determined to drown out that memory when he joined the Senior Tour in 1992. The Japanese hero responded to the challenge by winning the Nationwide Championship that year and then added five more wins as 1997 began.

"Aoki's got six gears," Lee Trevino quipped. "He's like an eighteen-wheeler. And he can change gears anytime he wants to. He's an awfully good player."

Aoki truly loved to shadowbox with the press. Most times he avoided them, and, when cornered, spit out a few words that frustrated a reporter looking for a quote. At the Bank One Classic in Lexington, a Golf Channel analyst learned what a handful Aoki was to interview. Two questions that drew unintelligible answers cut the discussion short, and the reporter walked away shaking his head, his eyes rolling. Aoki wasn't bothered, though. He left the area behind the eighteenth green with a huge smile on his face, certain he had bamboozled another member of the press.

At the Emerald Coast Classic, Aoki opened with a mediocre 71, and then, like one of the supersonic jets that took off from Pensacola's nearby naval base, he blitzed the field with a Senior PGA Tour record 60, breaking the mark held by five golfers.

Three consecutive birdies early in the round stoked Aoki's fire. Two more on the front side gave him a 30. He duplicated that score on the back nine, firing five more birdies. "I start to think about shooting fifty-nine after sixteenth hole," Aoki said in broken English. "The difference I go back to my old putter, the one I use for twenty years." Told that it looked like an old Acushnet Bullseye, Aoki smiled as he mumbled some Japanese words to his interpreter. "He say it not Bullseye, but 'Top Secret,'" the interpreter explained, leaving reporters to wonder whether the brand name was Top Secret or the name of the putter was a secret.

Two chances on the seventeenth and eighteenth holes to duplicate the 59s recorded by Al Geiberger and Chip Beck fell short. But that didn't keep Aoki from enjoying his performance. "I play very well," he remarked. "Now I see if game stay together for tomorrow."

It did. Gil Morgan sought to wrestle away the Emerald Coast Classic crown, but Aoki fought his way to a 65 and tied Morgan, who shot 64, his twenty-third consecutive sub-par round, one away from the record held by Bob Murphy.

As the sparring partners teed it up in the play-off, Aoki's confidence was high. The 60 and the final-round 65 were fresh in his mind. At the first play-off hole, Morgan's approach iron ended up on the back edge of the green. Aoki, who nearly holed his approach shot, stopped the ball four feet from the pin. Using the trusty putter that had holed putts in sixty of his sixty-eight wins worldwide, he drilled his ball into the cup for the victory to win the $165,000. He became the sixth foreign golfer to win on the Senior Tour in 1997, joining David Graham (three wins), Graham Marsh (two wins), Bruce Crampton, Hugh Baiocchi, and Vicente Fernandez.

The play-off defeat for Gil Morgan was costly. If he had prevailed, the difference in money earnings between him and Hale Irwin, who finished tied for third, would have been $105,000. That would have eaten up all but $140,000 of Irwin's lead. As it was, Dr. Gil's second-place check totaling $96,800 brought him within roughly $200,000 of Irwin with six events to play.

Of those scrambling to hit the top thirty-one list, Bob Duval, who finished tied with Irwin for third, made the biggest move. By winning $60,500, he climbed into twenty-ninth spot. Hubert Green now occupied the bubble spot, just ahead of Gibby Gilbert, Dana Quigley, and Kermit Zarley.

Though he finished far down the leader board at Pensacola, Gary Player left hundreds of children with a special gift: a fun look at golf and words of wisdom about the game he loved. At a pretournament clinic, Player performed his bag of tricks, hitting golf balls with clubs turned backward, turned upside down, and with the toe of his clubs. "These kids need to see that golf can be fun and learn a bit about the history of the game at the same time," Player exulted. The children agreed. One looked over at Aoki being interviewed and said, "He might have won, but I love Gary Player."

Player's clinic, Aoki's course-record 60, and his play-off victory over Gil Morgan in Pensacola brought sunshine to players stunned by the news that the cancer that had struck Senior Players Championship winner Larry Gilbert spread into his bloodstream and was inoperable. The cigar-smoking champion from Lexington took the news with the same bulldog manner he exhibited on the golf course, saying, "I now have a bigger battle ahead of me, but I am a fighter and I do not give up."

Isao Aoki hadn't forgotten his friend, even though he was celebrating the victory by climbing over the million-dollar mark for the 1997 season. "I was very happy today," he explained. "But would be happier if Larry Gilbert was back."

23

AFTER BOGEYING THE FIRST FOUR HOLES AT A TOURNAMENT IN MEM-
phis, Raymond Floyd turned to his caddie, aptly nicknamed Golf Ball,
and asked the distance to the fifth green from their position in the
fairway. Golf Ball dutifully retrieved a scrunched-up yardage book
from his pants pocket and proclaimed the distance to his hot-under-
the-collar boss. Floyd called for a seven-iron, took a practice swing,
and lofted the shot toward the putting surface.

The dimpled sphere blasted up into the sky, dead on line, but
the ball could only wave at the pin as it flew past and landed twenty
yards beyond the green. Floyd stood there in disbelief, then glared at
Golf Ball, who was trying to hide behind the golf bag. "Let me see
that damn yardage book," the huffy former U.S. Open Champion demanded. "Are you sure it's for Memphis?"

Without a pause, the caddie responded meekly, "Memphis? I
thought we were in Fort Worth."

Golf Ball was part of a fraternity, a close-knit group of wander-
ing nomads who trekked from city to city with one goal in mind: to
share in the riches of the PGA, LPGA, and Senior PGA Tours. If
behind every good man there was a good woman, as the old saying
goes, then behind every good golfer on Tour, there was a caddie who
carried the huge bag, cleaned the clubs and balls, knew the yardage
distances as if they were playing their home course, selected the
proper club when requested, marked the ball with a Magic Marker,
read the break in the greens on occasion, held the flag when necessary,
and took the abusive language for an errant shot that had to be his
fault.

The caddie also shined shoes, arranged airline flights, booked
dinner reservations, picked up laundry, stored valuables, set up dates
with adoring females, and provided advice on clothes. Though slavery
was outlawed, caddies were the closest thing to a servant, but they
served by choice, not by force.

The evolution of the caddie toward prominence could be
traced to Herman Mitchell and Angelo Argea. In the early 1970s, the

kinky-haired Greek and the broad-shouldered black man became television stars while laboring for Jack Nicklaus and Lee Trevino.

At one point, their star quality actually outshone their masters', something neither Jack nor Lee was crazy about. That didn't keep Jack from assisting Angelo with the fair sex. During the height of his popularity, Jack helped his tall, willowy caddie pick out women for Angelo to ask out for an evening of frolic.

Herman Mitchell was a wise-cracker like his boss. Once, when asked by Trevino, "What lies behind that bunker on the right side?" Mitchell answered, "Double bogey, double bogey, and double bogey."

With all due respect, the caddie, by nature, was a rather strange human being, an oddball of sorts. Nicknames said it all. Over the years, such characters as Six Pack Jack, Cricket, Rabbit (who'd be struck by a car during the 1997 season and sidelined for six weeks), Port-O-Let (full of shit), Penitentiary Larry, Speedway, Goofy Allen (who was also known as the King of the Parking Lot), Pine-Cone, Little Round Jerry, Shitty, Harley-Davidson Man, Clone, Big Brian, Pat the Crook, Johnny Mac, Parnelli (always on the highway), Big Red, the late Squeaky, House Dog, Dog Patch, Golf Ball, and The Green River Killer (LPGA Tour), among others, roamed fairways, roughs, and multiple watering holes across the world. Others in "The Caddie Nickname Hall of Fame" included those in Europe: the Shield (kept the media away from his player), Wobbly (his knees shook), and perhaps the most infamous caddie, Cornflake, thought to resemble a serial killer.

Many times spectators wondered what was happening. When an official in Jacksonville asked for Mule, Dog, and Bear to appear at the caddie bin, a fan asked, "What have you got here, a bunch of animals?"

If only those caddies with the wondrous nicknames could have been linked up with professional golfers who also had an alias. Think of the possibilities: Piranha, Merry Mex, Karnac, Ohio Fats, Golden Bear, Smokey the Bear, Gentle Ben, Moose, the Hawk, Iceman, Light Horse, Chicken Hawk, Lay Up, Concentration Henry, The Haig, The Squire, Little Poison, Big Momma, Great Gundy, Wonder Woman, The Walrus, Mechanical Man, The Machine, Radar, Buffalo Bill, Champagne Tony, The Spy, Mr. X, and Deadman.

Television announcers would have a field day. "In this threesome we have the Walrus with his caddie, Harley-Davidson, Gentle Ben and his sidekick Penitentiary Larry, and Chicken Hawk with Port-O-Let," and so forth.

Many times caddies picked up nicknames they didn't warrant.

Playing with Simon Hobday, Bob Murphy heard Hobday's loyal min-
ion called all kinds of names. "What's that caddie's first name?" Murphy asked his own caddie, Mark Huber. "I don't know," Mark replied.
"Well, it must be f_____ c____," Bob proclaimed, "because that's
all I've heard all day."

Caddies came in all shapes, sizes, and nationalities. And from all
walks of life. Don Ryan was an English professor at Murray State who
left Tishomingo, Oklahoma, every summer to toil on the Senior Tour.
Ken Harms, who bagged for Hubert Green in 1997, was a former
PGA assistant professional in Pennsylvania. His fiancée was talented
LPGA player Emily Klein.

Both genders were represented, as well as family members and
friends of Tour professionals, who dented the market for the vagabond
caddies attempting to make ends meet. At every Senior Tour event,
there were twenty-five to thirty prospective caddies searching desperately for a loop. Many went empty-handed and headed for cars packed
with their worldly belongings, hoping their luck would improve and
they'd hit pay dirt with a player who broke through and won a big
check.

Sandy Jones, a pert brunette with a bubbling personality, was one
of those. While not approaching the all-time record set by Goofy
Allen, the "King of the Parking Lot," who had caddied for *seventy* different golfers on the Senior Tour alone, the thirty-year-old Jones
switched mounts nearly as often as there were tournaments. A native
of Minnesota, she began caddying in 1995 after working as the pro-
shop manager at Brackett's Crossing Country Club in Lakeville. A ten
handicap, she met Walt Zembriski at the Burnet Senior Classic in
Minneapolis. A week later she was caddying for the former steelworker in Indianapolis.

"I liked the people, the fact that my office was outdoors," Jones
explained. "And the excitement. But it was the other caddies, the fact
that we were all free, had fun together, drank together. It was like a
family; that appealed to me."

Jones nearly quit her new career shortly after it began. Sexual ha-
rassment problems with Zembriski resulted in a lawsuit, later dropped.
But Sandy kept going, caddying for a series of players, including Jerry
McGee, Butch Baird, Homero Blancas, Jim Colbert, Bob Duval, and,
for most of the 1997 season, Bunky Henry.

When no job was available, Jones helped out Jim Kelly and Andy
North in the ESPN truck during telecasts, marking down changes on
the leader board. "There's no security to what I do, but I understand

that," she explained. "I don't know what's going to happen from week to week, but that's the adventure of it. I'm a good caddie and getting better. And I love the lifestyle."

Unlike Sandy Jones, Roy Bland, the younger brother of John, never saw the fruited plains of the United States until the Bland brothers assaulted the Senior Tour in 1996. "John and I hooked up in 1991, just in time for the Dunhill Cup," Roy recalled. "We may be brothers, but we're friends as well. We get a bit harsh with one another once in a while, but it's quickly forgotten."

Forty-seven-year-old Roy Bland was a golf course superintendent before turning to caddying. "That was at the River Club in Johannesburg," Roy recalled. "Helps me a bit with the greens, although courses in America are so different. Overseas they're not in as good shape, and golfers have to play all sorts of funny shots, bumps, and so forth with the mounds and everything. With the weather, the wind, the bounces, it's a different game."

The Bland combination had been successful, utilizing a regimen before each tournament. "I'll check out the yardages, maybe buy a yardage book from a local, then walk the course," Roy explained. "Then it's practice round on Tuesday, one day of the Pro-Am, and we're set. Making sure the yardages are right is my job, not John's. That's what he pays me for."

Both Sandy Jones and Roy Bland constantly used "we" when referring to play. "Caddie and golfer are a team," Sandy said. "When we do something great, we do it together. When things go bad, that's the way, too. I feel awful when I mess up on the yardage, and I know my player feels bad when he screws up a shot. We laugh and cry together."

Mike Hill's son Mike, Jr., who often caddied for his father, made the point after his dad hit a shot that was less than desirable. "We hit our wedge as hard as we could," he explained.

Caddies also felt they knew when a victory was due. "We could feel it coming," Willie Miller said. "No herky-jerky feeling in my stomach. A real calm. Like it was meant to be."

Roy Bland put it another way. "We live or die as one," he said. "One for all and all for one." Roy Bland's finest moments came when brother John was in contention. "That's what it's all about," he explained. "Coming down the stretch. Head to head. May the best man win. When one shot makes the difference."

Mark Huber had seen that moment time and time again. Caddie for Bob Murphy, he was one of the lucky thirty to thirty-five Senior

Tour caddies with a regular mount. Caddying had been big business for him, for Murphy had constantly been a top ten money winner since his debut on the Senior Tour.

"Caddies out here normally make five to six percent of the players' winnings, sometimes eight to ten percent," Huber said. "Ten percent if there's a win. In addition, some caddies make endorsement money. Murph made me a deal with Callaway, and some years ago I wore a shoe for a company that paid me. And I get expenses on unusual trips overseas or to the Caribbean at times."

Huber figured $35,000 to $40,000 was his break-even number, and a percentage of Bob Murphy's earnings over the past few years (nearly $4 million) had permitted him to start a rainy-day fund. "I'm one of the fortunate ones," he said. "Lots of caddies out here make the minimum. Some just get fifty bucks a day or three fifty for the week, with no percentage or bonus, even for winning."

Mark Huber's ascent to the Senior Tour was a long way from his home of Havana, Illinois, where he was raised in a jail cell. His father was police chief, later sheriff, and their home was attached to the jail. In the late 1980s, Huber's brother Dan was caddying on the PGA Tour, and Mark decided to try his luck.

Nearly ten years later, Huber had traveled the land, putting 295,000 miles on a 1991 Toyota Previa van that once was driven by Lee Trevino before he switched to his Cadillac. Huber's mileage was minuscule compared to the nearly 750,000 miles Tom Wargo's caddie, Larry Reinfeld, had on his 1978 red Chevy van, which had lived through three engines, six windshields, and nearly fifty new tires. Wargo's opinion of his caddie's treasure: "It rides like a tank."

Like Reinfeld, Huber loved the solitude of the highway, though he missed wife, Cathy, and daughter Cassie. "My first job was with Phil Blackmar, then Mike Nicholette," he explained. "I met up with Murph at Hilton Head. His regular caddie was sick. He said, 'You need a job? You know how to caddie?' I said, 'Sure,' even though I really didn't. Murph said, 'All right, I'll pay you five hundred dollars for the week, or five percent of my winnings, or a hundred and fifty and all the beer you can drink.' I said, 'You better pay me five hundred dollars because you'll lose money on the other deal.' "

Huber made $500 that week since Murphy missed the cut. "Big Lee Trotter was Murph's regular caddie," Mark said. "And when he came back, I caddied for Woody Blackburn. We also missed the cut. I kept caddying, working for CBS on the side, then Lee and Bob broke up at Westchester and Bob said, 'I want you.' "

Murphy was bothered by arthritis, and Huber's earnings were scarce. "He dropped out of some tournaments, had to withdraw from others," Mark recalled. "So I caddied for Doug Tewell, Tom Purtzer, Curt Byrum, Brad Fabel, Gregg Twiggs, and Larry Rinker. Murph and I kept in touch, and when he decided to come out on the Senior Tour in 1993, we hooked up again."

They had instant success. Murphy won at Birmingham, where Huber recalled, "Bob played so well all I had to give him was water," and at Indianapolis, Bob, Mark, and Murphy's biggest fan, wife Gail, became a formidable threesome. Counting the scintillating play-off win over Jay Sigel in the Toshiba Classic in March, there had been eleven trips to the winner's circle.

Huber's work ethic with Murphy symbolized those on the Tour. "I give Bob all the information he asks for," Mark explained. "I know all the yardages, and sometimes I'll even draw little maps on score-cards to show where the trouble is or how the wind direction will af-fect a shot. Sometimes Murph won't ask me anything; other times he wants to know it all. If he's in between a seven- and eight-iron, and asks me what do you think? I'll tell him and add, 'Hey, there's plenty of room past the pin,' or something like that. Most times, though, I just try to stay out of the way."

Little things meant a lot, Huber believed. "I had to learn how to keep my hands free when I've got the golf bag at the tee. I hold the strap in between my legs. I also learned from Squeaky Medlin about how to caddie when it's raining. He told me to stick the dry end of the towel in my pants and let the wet end stick out. My hands are still free, and the player can wipe off the club or let me do it."

Huber watched Murphy's swing closely. "When he hired me, there were three rules. He said, 'One, be on time, two, no hangovers on tournament days, and three, if you ever fall asleep during my back-swing, I'll fire your ass.' I haven't so far. But I do know his swing. It's an athletic move, the hesitation, like a pause at the top of a windup with pitching. It needs to be smooth, never rushed, and I watch to see that he's doing that."

Huber took care with his own body language. "I try not to get too excited," he said. "Murph doesn't need a cheerleader. He once told me, 'When I see you come to the tee, I shouldn't be able to tell whether I made a bogey or birdie by the look on your face.' "

That face, according to Huber's estimates, would appear at thirty Senior Tour events in 1997, plus five of what he called "Made for TVs." Figuring three rounds in each of the thirty events, and four rounds in five other events, that meant Mark had lugged the golf bag and driven the cart for approximately 130 rounds. Added to at least one Pro-Am for thirty of the tournaments and his weekly walk-the-course routine, the total neared 200. With eighteen holes in each round, Huber had toiled nearly 3,600 holes. That's approximately 800 miles per year, based on each round being a walking distance of almost four miles.

Those miles he'd walked hadn't been without incident. At The Legends in Palm Springs in the mid-1990s, Huber's bonehead play almost cost him his job. "Jim Colbert was Murph's partner," Huber remembered. "At number eight, an official told me Bob's ball went over a mound. Like an idiot, I drove the cart over the hill. As I went by, I felt a thump on the tire. I stopped and said to a spectator, 'Did I run over the ball?' 'With both tires,' he replied."

Before talking to Murphy, Huber sought out Colbert. "His ball was wedged in a bramble bush, and he was on his hands and knees trying to figure out what to do," Huber said. "Almost in tears, I told him, 'I ran over Murph's ball.' Colbert looked up at me and said, 'What?' I said, 'I ran over Murph's ball.' Jim replied in a brisk voice, 'I f_____ heard you the f_____ first time. I've got an unplayable lie, and you've run over my partner's ball.' "

The penalty for Huber's handiwork was one shot. "Murph wasn't real pleased," Huber noted. "But Jim saved my butt. He got relief from some sort of burrowing animal hole, knocked his ball on the green, and made a thirty-footer for birdie to bail me out. At the next tee, Murph asked me for a ball. I said, 'You got one.' Colbert said, 'Give him another one; that one has too many f_____ tire tracks on it.' "

Despite that faux pas and others, Huber loved his work. "I do this because I can be associated with a professional athlete," he admitted. "I wanted to play professional baseball, and I guess this is my vicarious relationship with sport. Besides, being around Murphy is very special. He has such integrity, honesty, and a great competitive desire."

How long would Huber, at age forty-one, continue? "If Murph's health isn't good or he decides he's had enough, that will be it for me. I'll miss the family of friends, but one day it'll be time to move on."

Huber was one of the caddies who cared about others, often providing memorabilia for worthy causes. John Sullivan, the current caddie for Hale Irwin who also labored for Johnny Miller and Jack Nicklaus, gathered up hats, golf balls, and other souvenirs signed by the players to benefit a family in North Carolina whose son had a kidney transplant and couldn't afford the medical bills. All of the caddies joined in a special tournament set up by Tom Wargo in Centralia after the Boone Valley Classic. Dubbed "Caddies for Kids," forty of the bag toters raised nearly $25,000 in a "Caddie-Am" to benefit the Special Olympics and a home for abused children.

At times, the caddies themselves felt abused. Often when their player hit a bad shot, or misclubbed, they were blamed. Angelo Argea called Jack Nicklaus's punishment "The Look," when the Golden Bear stared him down with his icy-blue eyes. Bruce Devlin once bloodied his caddie's nose by throwing a club down at the ground after a bad shot and having it ricochet back in the caddie's face. Veteran Ed Furgol threatened to beat his caddie to a pulp after a round in which he purposely kept dropping clubs during Furgol's swing.

Mark Huber said such incidents were rare. "Most players realize how important the caddie can be," he declared. "And treat us as a professional at what we do. And they should. Look at all the successful players. All have a top-notch caddie, one who relishes being in contention on Sunday, when we have to perform under pressure just like the player does."

At The Vantage Championship in Clemmons, North Carolina, that caddie was John Sullivan, Hale Irwin's trusty ally. "The Clone," as he was known, continued his superb work, and so did his boss, firing a first-round 64 in search of his eighth victory of the season. With $1.5 million in prize money up for grabs, all the contenders were present, hoping to put the skids on Irwin's stampede toward winning $2 million for the year.

Irwin was bothered by a sore shoulder caused by inflammation in a biceps tendon, but he was playing golf at a level that no longer limited discussion as to whether he was the finest player on the Senior Tour. With seven victories, including the PGA Seniors' Championship, more than $1.7 million in earnings, and competent showings in two Major championships, talk now centered on whether Irwin, at age fifty-two, might not be the best player in the world.

Some sportswriters scoffed at the idea, pointing out that Irwin was winning on short courses against inferior competition when compared to the Tiger Woodses, Greg Normans, and Colin Montgomeries of the world. But on average, the Senior PGA courses were only fifteen to twenty yards a hole shorter, and pin placements for the season had been the toughest in the history of the Tour. And Gil Morgan, Larry Nelson, David Graham, and his fellow seniors were providing Irwin with top-notch foes every week.

When Irwin trotted out a superb course-record-tying 62 at The Vantage in the second round, the talk about his superiority heightened. "He's playing as well as anybody in the world," Larry Nelson suggested. "And he has all year." "Is Irwin too good for this Tour?" sportswriter Lenox Rawlings queried.

Comparing Irwin to Woods, Norman, Montgomerie, and the rest of the so-called youngsters might have seemed ludicrous to many, but Tom Kite, captain of the Ryder Cup team, certainly hadn't thought so. "Hale Irwin deserved serious consideration based on his record on the Senior Tour and in the Majors," Kite had said. "He's still one of the finest strikers of the ball in the world, and that competitive spirit is second to none."

During Irwin's week at The Vantage, one in which it was announced that Bruce Devlin had become the fourth Senior Tour player to be diagnosed with cancer, his play elevated to new heights, but it was his performance at clutch time that impressed those who believed Irwin was the world's best player.

Unable to make a birdie for fifteen holes, Irwin told caddie John Sullivan, "We better start making something happen." And he did. A birdie at sixteen sparked his stretch drive. After a par at seventeen, Irwin came to the par-five final hole realizing he needed a birdie to win. It was then that he pulled off a shot that sent shivers through the boisterous crowd and reminded golf experts of his true greatness.

A perfect drive left him with 245 yards to the green, but a mere five-yard opening between greenside bunkers set up a challenge most golfers would have avoided. Undaunted, even after watching Dave Eichelberger, who had leaped into the fray with a final-round 62, unload a tying birdie, Irwin pulled a three-wood from his bag and unleashed a rhythmic swing that catapulted the ball high into the air.

The shot was memorable even in flight. On the Senior Tour, only a handful of players hit the ball with the ecstasy Irwin displayed. The ball exploded off the club face and jolted into the air on a high crescent path before beginning its dip. Then the tiny sphere floated down from the sky like a burned-out meteor in slow motion. One, two bounces, and then it rested comfortably on the green, just twenty-five feet from the hole.

The huge crowd seemed frozen for a moment before the noise crescendoed back from the green to Irwin's position on the fairway. The clatter was deafening for a shot that would become one of the more memorable in Senior PGA Tour history. Even Irwin got excited, lofting his club into the air as he waved to the boisterous crowd.

"Off the deck like that, that's about as far as I can hit that club," Irwin proclaimed later. "I wouldn't say it's the best three-wood shot I ever hit, but it certainly is the best shot of the year."

Two putts later, Irwin was the champion. He decided a repeat performance of his memorable 1990 U.S. Open jaunt around Medinah's eighteenth green was in order as he high-fived several fans in the gallery after holing the final two-and-a-half footer.

The first prize of $225,000 permitted Irwin to become the first golfer to earn over $2 million in a single season. Even Tiger Woods, who had jump-started the season with mercurial play, was still $50,000 and change short of the mark.

That represented quite a milestone in golf. Arnold Palmer had astounded golf fans when he won more than $100,000 in 1963. It took seventeen years for Tom Watson to cross the $500,000 barrier. Eight years after that Curtis Strange won more than a million dollars. Hale Irwin had doubled that in 1997.

"When I started out as a professional, I didn't know if $200,000 was attainable," Irwin stated. "To put another zero there is amazing." Irwin's opponents left the course shaking their heads, while Sullivan prepared to cash another big check.

Talk on the Senior Tour now centered not on whether Irwin would win the money title and Player of the Year, but his assault on a seemingly untouchable record: Peter Thomson's nine wins during the 1985 season. "Right now it's like the carrot in front of the horse," Irwin spouted. "And I happen to like carrots."

That boast, which came on a weekend when the golf world mourned the loss of 1965 PGA champion Dave Marr to cancer, might have ruffled the feathers of golfers such as Gil Morgan, who finished fourth at The Vantage despite his twenty-sixth consecutive sub-par round, breaking the record held by Bob Murphy, but facts were facts. Even the return of Jim Colbert, who announced he would play the final four events of the year, didn't seem enough to dent the chances of Irwin setting records others only dreamed about.

At the trophy presentation, Irwin expressed his true feelings about comparisons with Tiger Woods without saying a word. Asked if he was pleased that he had beaten the golfer thirty-one years his junior to the punch in passing the $2 million mark, Hale flashed that wry smile of his that clearly expressed satisfaction.

So who was the better player? Who had the better year, at least to date? Asked if comparisons between him and Woods could be made, Irwin begged the question. "I don't want to say that one or the other [of our records] is better," he explained. "We're simply in different arenas."

While all the hoopla at The Vantage had focused on Irwin's eighth victory of the year and the passing of the magical $2 million mark, there was another statistic that was even more astounding. Gil Morgan may have been under par for twenty-six consecutive rounds, but Irwin was a mind-boggling *eighty-five* under par for the last twenty-one rounds he had played.

"Know what the difference is between a coconut and John Bland?" Simon Hobday once asked. "You can get a drink out of a coconut."

So explained the personal side of John Bland, defending champion at The Transamerica, held at Napa, California. It also provided insight on the state of his golf game as he competed in his second full year on the Senior PGA Tour. "I never try anything that's against the basic nature of my game," Bland explained. "I weigh the risks carefully and never play carelessly. I play right to left, and if the pin's tucked in the right side, most times you'll see me play to the left and take par."

Bland's frugal ways and conservative nature fit his quiet demeanor. But his ready smile and gentle storytelling made him one of the most popular golfers on any professional tour, among competitors, spectators, and tournament officials alike.

After "Blandy" won his first try at being a member of the over-fifty gang at the London Masters, several good friends held a farewell dinner for him. He was about to embark on a trek to America to seek fame and fortune on the Senior Tour, and longtime competitors and friends such as Tony Johnstone and Frank Nobilo wanted to wish him well. Or roast him.

"You are simply not good enough to play on the Senior Tour, Mr. Bland," fellow South African professional Johnstone had proclaimed, according to John. "You will be eaten alive out there and be back here with your tail between your legs inside of two weeks. My advice is to cut your losses and stay here in Europe with your mates."

When it was his turn to retort, Bland, a competitor on the European Tour for seventeen years, was in rare form. "You are nothing more than a lowlife," Bland said in his noticeable accent, a smile on his face. "You have no class. The only reason I speak to you is because you have a lovely wife." Bland also made a vow that evening that if successful on the Senior Tour, and he confidently believed he would be, he'd share his wealth with those who doubted his chances at success.

The winner of the 1978 South African PGA wasted little time in proving Johnstone wrong, but it had been a long journey from his homeland in the Knysna Cape area of South Africa to the courses in America.

He and brother/caddie Roy, three years younger, were born in Johannesburg. Their father was a golf course manager but didn't play the game. "Gary Player was the inspiration to all of us," John Bland recalled. "He was a wonderful competitor, an idol of mine. He played at such a high standard and with such grace. His play opened the door for guys like me and Hugh Baiocchi and even Ernie Els, who won the Open again this year. We were all influenced by Gary."

Bland was a club professional for two years, then began playing as a competitive professional when his kids were out of diapers. In 1977, a decision had to be made, and the choices were clear. Either he stayed in Europe and played the Tour or opted for the United States as David Frost and later, Nick Price, chose to do. "It was make-up-your-mind time," Bland said, "but there was so much excitement in Europe. Tony Jacklin, Seve, Nick Faldo, Ian [Woosnam], all of them. They were winning Major championships in America. I got caught up in all of that excitement and chose the European Tour."

Bland's decision was one he never regretted. "There was tremendous growth at the time on the European Tour. Europe had the best players, maybe not the depth of the Americans, but the best. At one time, the Europeans were ranked 1-2-3-4. And the money was increasing. In '77 they put up one million pounds in prize money. By 1990, there was more than twenty-two."

Travel time was another determining factor in Bland's decision to play in Europe. "I could leave London on Sunday night and be in South Africa on Tuesday to see my family. If I'd gone to America, the time-zone difference would have made it impossible."

After Bland won his first tournament in 1970, big things were expected. But lack of confidence held him back. He played in the shadow of Gary Player and others, never quite hitting the big time, though he was a consistent player from an early age.

"Gary Player and I go back thirty years," Bland, ten years younger than his colleague, recalled. "I won a state junior and got the chance to play with him in a charity event. That was the first time I met him."

Player remembered the meeting. "John never missed a fairway back then, just as he doesn't now."

Statistics backed up Player's words. "Before we came over here to the Senior Tour," Roy Bland pointed out, "John and Colin Montgomerie were always one-two in hitting the fairways, flip-flopping position. Colin's now number one over there, and John is first on the Senior Tour here."

Besides being able to hit the tee ball straight, Bland had one other great attribute: He could putt with the best of them. "I've never known a South African who was a bad putter," Tony Jacklin observed. "Bobby Locke through Gary Player and now John. I think it's because they grew up on very grainy greens and you had to make solid strokes to have any success."

Bland's driving and putting excellence offset other deficiencies. His swing was functional, not outstanding, his iron play adequate. His short-wedge game and chipping ability, along with the deft putting, were his saving grace.

Bland's record in Europe and around the world was outstanding. He won more than twenty tournaments, including the Benson and Hedges International Open, and one with an auspicious name, the Martini Open. He led the South African Order of Merit four times and played in the 1975 World Cup and on two Dunhill Cup squads.

The 1991 matches were special, for the South African team was playing in an international event for the first time. South Africa had been banned from competition due to the country's apartheid policies. "We were the first team to come out and play," Bland explained. "Gary [Player] was captain, and it was a bit of history. We won that year, too."

Bland had fond memories of the European Tour. "I especially miss the great cities of Europe," he said. "Madrid is my favorite city in the world. The old city there. And Prague is very special."

As he approached fifty, Bland began working harder on his game, but the win at the London Masters was the corker. "I knew when I won there that good things were ahead," Bland said. "My confidence level was strong, and I really looked forward to playing in America."

To do so, Bland wrote to five tournament sponsors seeking a chance to play in the late months of 1995. Only The Transamerica replied positively. There he set the Senior Tour on its ear by nearly winning, but Lee Trevino put on a charge and left everyone else in the dust. Bland's fifth-place finish portended well for the coming weeks. He shot 68 in the "four-spotter" at Los Angeles and shocked his Senior Tour competitors when he won the championship. "That was the key," Bland recalled. "In the last few holes, I was a bit nervous, but then I thought, 'Damn, if I can win this thing, no qualifying school where a thousand guys play for eight spots.' So I stepped it up a notch and won. Good gracious, that was wonderful."

Bland, representing the Fancourt Golf Club in South Africa, also didn't forget his promise to Johnstone and others. He sent them all dollar bills, and on the one to Johnstone, he scribbled, "Lowlife."

Competitors on the Senior Tour jokingly called for his banishment. "Okay," Hale Irwin said, "he played too well. Deport him."

Jim Colbert added, "You've got to go, John. Send him home."

The victory meant Bland was exempt for the 1996 season. With Team Bland in order (wife Helen and brother Roy as caddie), the wily South African stung the Tour with superb play that garnered him four wins and more than $1.5 million in prize money. Johnstone kept receiving his shares. "I'd be playing in a tournament," he remembered. "And some guy would come up with a dollar bill and say, 'It's from John.'"

For years the two had played practical jokes on each other. Johnstone wanted to meet South African President F. W. De Klerk. When Bland, a longtime friend of the president's, introduced Johnstone, his nemesis, according to Bland, told De Klerk, "Listen, I do not agree that you have screwed up the country as John has been telling everyone over in Europe."

Bland's Senior Tour play earned him Rookie of the Year honors and friends across the land. While others were practicing, John was telling a story, joking with fans, enjoying his newfound life. "If you had to ask me what life on the Senior Tour is all about, I'd have to say it's like heaven on earth. I'm a fifty-one-year-old kid on a never-ending adventure, and I love every moment. At the 1995 Senior Open, I got to play with Arnold Palmer. Even made a hole in one. It doesn't get any better than that."

Bland's wry sense of humor stretched to PGA Tour officials who marshaled the courses. They were used to seeing the famous "Bland Salute." "No matter where I am on the golf course," Gene Smith explained, "if John sees me, he'll take his right hand, extend the middle finger, and slowly rub it against the bridge of his nose. And he doesn't care if a national television audience is watching when he does it."

While the future appeared rosy, Johnstone still warned those who trusted Bland a bit too much. "He may be a wonderful player, frighteningly good, but he's the worst driver of an automobile who ever walked the face of the earth," his friend explained. "At last count, he had destroyed fourteen cars. In Johannesburg, he reversed a new one and dropped it off a five-foot ramp. The bumper was buried in the concrete."

Roy Bland agreed, saying, "We went out in the speedboat one time and John was heading us right toward a sandbank. He braked, held on, and I went flying across the water."

Regardless of his lack of prowess with vehicles, John Bland proved he could play with anyone. Though 1997 had not produced a victory, he continued to be in contention nearly every week. The second-place finishes at the U.S. Senior Open to Graham Marsh and to Gary Player at the British Senior Open had left their mark though. "Especially the Senior Open loss," Bland said. "The Senior Open and the Senior British Open are the two real Majors of the year because they're open to anyone who qualifies. There were twenty-five nations represented in the Senior British Open. And there are no advertisements on billboards or around the course. I like that."

Bland still felt he was playing better than ever. "I've had seventeen top tens in twenty-nine events," he pointed out prior to defending his title at The Transamerica in October. "Three seconds and two thirds. Hale and Gil are setting the standard, but I'm pleased with my performance."

And he was pleased that more foreign golfers were on their way to the Senior Tour. "Peter Townsend, Peter Oosterhuis, Bernard Gallagher, Christy O'Conner, and José-Maria Canizares are all good players. And more will be coming. Seve and the rest."

At The Transamerica, Bland, who once shot 59 and had eighteen holes in one to his credit, played, in his own word, "awful." A second-round 77 sent Bland reeling, and he never recovered.

The champion was gray-haired Dave Eichelberger, who outlasted Jimmy Powell and DeWitt Weaver. The win for "Ike" was his third on the Senior PGA Tour. It was a sweet one for a golfer who once played in twenty-two straight events on the regular tour without making the cut.

Bob Duval, whose final-round 69 moved him up the leader board and ever closer to making the top thirty-one, didn't win, but his son David did, at the Michelob Championship in Virginia. "That will take the monkey off his back," Dad beamed proudly, aware that David had finally recorded his first PGA Tour victory.

Frank Conner made the biggest jump of those needing late season finishes to keep exemptions and get into the show at Myrtle Beach. A final-round 67 advanced him to a tie for second, and he sneaked into the top thirty-one. Bobby Stroble, Tony Jacklin, Bob Wynn, John Schroeder, Mike McCullough, and Brian Barnes all failed to improve their positions.

Legends at The Transamerica played more exhibition golf than competitive golf. Arnold Palmer never broke par, but dazzled the crowd. Lee Trevino's shot making was mediocre, and Johnny Miller, making his second start on the Senior PGA Tour at a course just five miles from his home in the Napa Valley, finished twenty-third. "I looked at the hole when I putted," Miller, who had shot 64 and 65 in practice rounds, admitted. That was the same technique that worked for him when he'd won in 1987 at Pebble Beach.

Miller's post-round comments provided explanation for his inability to contend. "I didn't have a lot of fire in my rounds," he reported. "I was real good for nine holes and that's all I ever play with my kids. Then I say to myself, 'Do I really have to play another nine?' " That comment didn't endear him even to the hometown fans, especially those who passed by "See Johnny Play" signs tacked to posts and telephone poles along the route to the tournament.

The exception to the rule among the golden oldies was Chi Chi Rodriguez, whose luck with his miniature Little Bertha putter produced a top ten finish. "Cheech gets a bit more speed with that sword dance of his now," ESPN's Andy North surmised as he watched Rodriguez's ritual after he had holed a fifteen-footer for birdie.

Dave Eichelberger's smile at the trophy presentation was nearly as wide as Chi Chi's putter was long. And the check for $120,000 would come in handy, too, since wife D.C. was back in Hawaii expecting twins. "I was really scrambling out there," he admitted, "experimenting with my grip and stance. Then I decided I better bear down and get on with it. Those twins are on the way, and I'll be needing the extra cash."

His voice was not as deep nor as loud, but when Jim Colbert teed the ball up at the Hyatt Regency Maui Kaanapali Classic, the thirty-sixth full-field event on the 1997 Senior PGA Tour, and announced "I'm *baaack*," the strong, boisterous tone was similar to that of Arnold Schwarzenegger. Like the actor, Colbert, fit and ready after prostate cancer and arthroscopic surgery on his knee, was ready to terminate the opposition in the final four events on the Senior Tour.

The 1995 and 1996 Player of the Year, absent from the Senior Tour for four months, had served notice his competitive juices were still flowing when he joined the PGA Tour's Nick Price and LPGA competitor Kelly Robbins to win the Gillette Tour Challenge in Hamilton, Bermuda, the Tuesday before The Transamerica in Napa. Colbert had contributed three birdies to the effort, and each player took home a cool $150,000 for eighteen holes' worth of effort. Teams that included Bob Murphy and Walter Morgan finished in the runner-up position. Hale Irwin's group was fifth, one shot ahead of Dr. Gil's team.

At Maui, Colbert had several goals in mind: "I want to see where my game stands," he pronounced. "I've been playing, but not competitively. I know stamina will be a problem, but I'm ready to see how I do out here. Can I win? Of course, but that's not likely this week. Especially with Hale playing so well."

One player Colbert hoped to challenge was Bob Charles, the winner of the Kaanapali Classic in both 1995 and 1996. He led Jim by a hundred thousand dollars and change on the all-time money list for the PGA and Senior PGA Tour. Both trailed Lee Trevino.

Colbert didn't add much to his winnings total in Hawaii. A second-round 66 added his name to the leader board, but a disastrous 76 on Sunday proved he wasn't quite ready for prime time.

Bob Charles was enjoying yet another superb season when he came to the beautiful beaches of Hawaii. Charles was playing better than ever, and the reasons were apparent to him.

"All right, here's my secret," the sixty-one-year-old former sheep farmer from New Zealand began. "Now listen closely. Besides visits to the fitness trailer and my own exercise and stretching regimen, the key is broccoli, and more broccoli. And of course carrots and cauliflower, plus other fruits and vegetables. That's why I feel as good at sixty-one as I did at fifty." So said the only southpaw ever to win a Major championship (British Open). His win in Hawaii in 1996 had been the willowy veteran's twenty-third on the Senior PGA Tour to go with a dozen other world senior crowns, including the 1993 Senior British Open.

Charles's reasons for continuing to play despite hitting the sixty mark were simple ones. "One, I love the game of golf," he explained. "Two, I love the competition. Three, I love picking up a check. And finally, I keep wondering what the hell I'd be doing with the idle time if I didn't play golf."

The most lasting image of Bob Charles, married to Gary Player's sister, Verity, appeared at the 1963 British Open. He and Phil Rodgers came to the last hole even. After their approaches to the green,

Rodgers had the advantage, though their recollection of the moment differed. "Phil said my putt was seventy feet and his was seven," Charles remembered with a chuckle. "Well, mine was actually about forty-five and his was fifteen. I hit mine to about five feet, and then Phil hit an awful-looking putt that was wide and two feet short. He putted out. The ball hit the cup, spun around, and dropped in. To my amazement, he pulled off his cap, and put it over the hole. The reserved English crowd didn't know what to think. After he re-moved the hat, I made mine." Charles then prevailed in the play-off the next day.

When Charles turned fifty in 1986, he shook up the Senior Tour. Ten years later he had won more than $7 million. Five victories in the over-sixty MasterCard Seniors in 1996 previewed great things to come in 1997, and the old left-hander didn't disappoint, dominating the events with eight victories. At $18,000 a pop, Charles had a regu-lar retirement fund coming in nearly every week.

Andy North believed he knew why. "Bob Charles is always under control," the former U.S. Open champion explained. "He doesn't try to do anything he shouldn't because he knows his game so well."

His goal is to win the New Zealand Open in 2004. "That was my first win," Charles explained. "I'll be sixty-eight then, and it'll be the fiftieth anniversary of that victory."

Entering the 1997 event in Maui, Charles and others in the over-sixty gang had the beaches of Myrtle Beach, South Carolina, on their minds. Though there were no MasterCard champions competition in Hawaii, two events remained before the top sixteen qualified for the Energizer Senior Tour MasterCard Championship the first week in November.

Of the over-sixty gang, Charles and Chi Chi Rodriguez made the biggest splash in Hawaii. Charles, who had recorded four eagles on his way to victory in 1997, charged toward the leaders in the first two rounds, but his putting stroke wasn't bold enough and left the ball short of the hole on several occasions. Down the stretch he commit-ted the unpardonable, double-bogeying the 122-yard, par-three sev-enteenth, where twenty-one other golf balls had found the drink. He settled for 72 and finished fifth.

In the second round, Rodriguez, carrying his dinky putter as if he were readying himself for a baton-twirling competition, was paired with Charles and Hale Irwin, but Chi Chi felt he had an advantage over the competition. That came after a phone lesson with his brother Je-sus, a teaching professional in Puerto Rico.

"My brother told me I wasn't standing upright enough," the winner of twenty-two events on the Senior Tour explained on the practice tee. " 'Stand up straighter to the ball, quit bending over so much,' he said. 'Your posture is bad.' "

Rodriguez saw improvement right away. "When I don't stand up straight, I never get the club back far enough," he said. "Hit the ball too low. Now I'm hitting it long and straight. Besides, when a man named Jesus talks, I listen."

Armed with a new stance and continued success with his midget putter, Chi Chi bounded into contention and stayed there. "Little Bertha is behaving herself," Rodriguez said. "It keeps me from having the yips. I used to be known as the daylight putter because my ball never saw the darkness of the hole. That's all changed."

Chi Chi finally finished in the top ten for the second consecutive week. He was so pleased with his trip to the magical shores of Hawaii he decided to purchase property overlooking the ocean where the North Pacific humpback whales hung out.

Bruce Summerhays jumped out in front after two rounds at thirteen under, ready to add a second win to his one at the Saint Luke's Classic, but talk centered around Hale Irwin and his chances to tie Peter Thomson's record of nine Senior Tour wins in a single season. Most players felt the chances were excellent. Irwin, who represented the nearby Kapalua Resort on Tour, knew the tricks of playing in the tradewinds as well as putting on grainy greens where the key was to position the ball so that putts could be hit down-grain.

Early in the week, Irwin had gone pheasant hunting, but in the second round, the catch had been birdies. He bagged six to go with five on Friday, and his 67-63 total brought him to within one of Bruce Summerhays, whose son Brian was the caddie choice for the week.

At the 155-yard, par-three seventeenth, Hale Irwin hit another shot that epitomized his dominant play on the Senior Tour. Facing a left-to-right wind that gusted to thirty miles an hour and caused the palm trees to bend, Irwin spanked a six-iron that bore low in the wind and settled after one bounce to within a foot of the hole. No other player in the field had that shot, could hit the ball that solidly on a low trajectory. No wonder North proclaimed Irwin "the best iron player in golf right now." The fact that Irwin was hitting a remarkable 75 percent of the greens in regulation backed up his claim.

North could easily have added best putter as well. While Irwin's new rival, Tiger Woods, was struggling with his putting touch at Disney World in Orlando, Florida, Irwin seemed to be making everything he stroked. He was averaging 1.738 putts per hole, better than all but five of the players on the PGA Tour.

The final round was a study in contrasts. Summerhays, the lifelong club professional and former golf coach at Stanford who never played the PGA Tour, against the great champion, Hale Irwin. Predictably, the match was no contest. On the island about which Mark Twain remarked, "I went to Maui for a week, and stayed five," Irwin took command at the sixth, where he made birdie and Summerhays chopped his way to triple bogey. If there was any doubt of the outcome, Irwin drilled a twelve-footer at fifteen and walked off the green chortling "I love you, I love you" to his putter as he kissed its sole.

That birdie positioned Irwin at thirteen under, and his three rounds of 67-63-70 blew by the field by three. The win was worth 127,500 coconuts. Summerhays and Mike Hill finished tied for second.

Irwin's feat meant his ninth victory in twenty-one events, his thirteenth in less than three years on the Senior Tour. Fifty-two of his sixty-seven rounds had been under par. And Peter Thomson now had a partner alongside his name in the record books.

"Now I can think about ten," Irwin remarked. "I'll probably play the Ralphs Classic in L.A. and then the Senior Tour Championship. We'll see what happens."

What most of his competitors hoped was that he'd decide to stay on Maui, do more pheasant hunting, and leave them alone. Hale Irwin had other ideas as he and wife Sally, ever ready with the victory kiss after the triumph, flew home to plan their daughter Becky's wedding. "It's been fun. A great run," the champion proclaimed. "Now I want to win number ten."

With two events remaining before the Energizer Senior Tour Championship, several golfers needed to either snag a tournament championship or cash a big check at the Raley's Gold Rush Classic in El Dorado Hills, California, the third week of October. While the rest of the world readied themselves for Halloween, seventy-eight players hoped for more treats than tricks as they tried to slip up the leader board so they could compete in two weeks for the riches in Myrtle Beach.

Near the magical thirty-first spot were Gibby Gilbert, Hubert

Green, J. C. Snead, Jim Colbert, Bob Dickson, Jim Dent, and Dana Quigley. Larry Gilbert, in the top ten money earners all year, wouldn't compete due to his spreading cancer, but according to Tour rules, no substitute would be named. That meant thirty golfers would vie for the Senior Tour Championship.

The Raley's Tournament was also important to John Schroeder, Bobby Stroble, Brian Barnes, Terry Dill, Larry Laoretti and Tony Jacklin, all still attempting to break through and win or collect enough winnings to warrant an exemption for the 1998 season. Entering the thirty-seventh full-field tournament, Bob Dickson needed a strong finish to the year since earnings of nearly $500,000 only earned him a twenty-ninth-place ranking.

One golfer who didn't have to worry about entrance into the big show or keeping an exemption for 1998 was Dave Stockton. He'd been building up cash reserves all year long, standing ninth on the money list. Not surprising for a golfer with two PGA Championships in his pocket.

When Stockton joined the Senior Tour full-time in 1992, it was merely a matter of time until his unshakable mind-set provided a victory. It came at the Senior Players Championship. Competitors knew for certain Stockton would drive them nuts with his chipping and putting skills as he had done in the sixties and seventies.

"I knew he'd win out here," Bob Murphy said. "Stockton has never seen a putt he didn't think he could make."

Twelve more Senior Tour victories came Stockton's way, though he hit a dry spell of thirteen months before breaking through at the 1996 U.S. Senior Open. At Canterbury in Cleveland, Stockton massacred the field in the first three rounds, opening up a seven-shot lead. Hale Irwin made a charge on Sunday, but Stockton prevailed by two.

While Stockton didn't compete in the Raley's at Dorado Hills, Gil Morgan, still believing he had a glimmer of hope to catch Hale Irwin in the money standings, did. But an ugly first-round 74, when the swirling winds led to scores in the eighties by Don Bies, Billy Casper, Walter Zembriski, and Jesus Rodriguez, Chi Chi's brother, took its toll and he never contended.

At the end of the second round, former San Jose State golfer Bob Eastwood assumed command of the tournament. Seeking his second title on the Senior Tour, after having been awarded victory when heavy rains washed out the final round at the Bell Atlantic, Eastwood opened with 67 and 69 and then threw two birdies at the field in the final four holes on Sunday to record a 68, good enough for a two-shot win.

The win for Eastwood was special, for it came in front of family and friends who rooted him along. Son Scott was his caddie, his mother, Elva Jane, led the cheerleaders in the gallery, and hunting and fishing buddies lent their support. "I got very emotional, all choked up," a teary-eyed Eastwood said after the victory. "To win here is really something."

24

WHEN THE RALPHS CLASSIC OPENED IN LOS ANGELES THE LAST week of October, all eyes were on Hale Irwin. His superb play in 1997 had recalled Chi Chi Rodriguez's comment when Lee Trevino had dominated the Senior Tour with seven wins in 1990. Asked by a reporter how Lee was playing, the Cheech responded: "We have the PGA Tour, the LPGA Tour, and the Lee Trevino Tour."

The same could be said for Irwin, for his domination had been every bit as impressive as Trevino's. Bruce Summerhays said it best after Irwin's win in Hawaii: "Hale is playing the best golf of anybody in the world right now. If he were playing on the regular Tour consistently, he'd win again—he's that good."

Critics saw the matter another way. *Golf World*'s John Hawkins, the latest naysayer predicting the doom of the Senior Tour, wrote a column entitled, "How Good Is Great?" While he praised Irwin as being the "best player in the world over twenty-one years old," during two weeks in which Tiger, named PGA Player of the Year, failed to defend championships won in 1996, he ridiculed the remainder of the over-fifty gang, writing, "There isn't much competition out there right now, not when a three-time U.S. Open champion in excellent physical condition shows up to play a bunch of three-star generals from the 1970s and all the latest graduates from Pro Shop U."

The "ouch" felt by Senior Tour members could be heard all the way to California, especially by golfers who knew John Hawkins hadn't bothered to regularly visit their venue to see firsthand of what he wrote. Others were hurt by remarks labeling the Tour the "Geritol Ball" and "Grecian Gardens."

Reporters such as Hawkins appeared to have little sense of history, unable to comprehend what the Senior Tour was all about. If he had mingled with a crowd at an event, or spent time with the players, he'd have realized that the seventy-eight golfers who competed every week presented golden opportunities for fans to see true heroes of the sport. He'd have understood that whether they watched Hale Irwin win, Gil Morgan challenge, Arnie tee it up and shoot 76, Lee chatter his way around to a similar score, or Chi Chi perform his sword dance just one more time, the golfers of this generation were the links to the past and to the future. Important links, ones to be treasured, not ridiculed, because somehow a great player like Irwin had dominated.

Senior Tour members let articles like the one by Hawkins slide by, but in private they were incensed. "John Hawkins is an idiot, but we've known idiots ever since the Senior Tour began," one player explained. "I feel sorry for guys like him. They have no idea what golf is all about, especially out here."

Irwin, for one, didn't believe the article worth comment. Besides, a win at the Ralphs Classic would be number ten, permitting him to break Peter Thomson's record. That was far more important than addressing the comments of the naysayer.

Irwin was trying to become immortal, but others on the Senior Tour knew their week on Wilshire Boulevard in Los Angeles was make-or-break time. Of the eight qualifiers at the Q-School one year earlier, only Bob Dickson was in position to retain his card. He was positioned precariously in the number thirty spot and desperately needed a good showing at the Ralphs. His Q-School compatriots, Buddy Whitten, Dick Hendrickson, Will Sowles, David Oakley, Mike McCullough, John Morgan, and Dennis Coscina required a miracle win or they would return to the seventy-two-hole torture chamber in late November in Ponte Vedra, Florida. Of that group, McCullough had been the most successful, earning nearly $360,000.

Of all the golfers on the top thirty-one bubble, Bobby Stroble, the affable 6'1", 230-pound Georgia native had come the furthest in his quest to play with the best of the best on the Senior Tour. Earlier in the year, an incident had reminded him that the struggle continued.

The husky black golfer had held two Styrofoam cups of steaming hot coffee in his hands when he departed the players' lounge at the Crandon Park Golf Course in Key Biscayne, Florida, site of the Tour's first event in January. "Hey, pal," a security guard warned, "if you're going to take two cups, then we won't let you come in here again."

Though the warning could have irritated him, the fifty-one-year-old Stroble, heading to the practice tee before the first round of the Royal Caribbean Classic, just smiled to himself and moved on. He'd been mistaken for a caddie before, and he knew the guard meant no harm.

The episode was symbolic of Stroble's life since no one ever knew what to make of him. His rotund build, sleepy eyes, and disheveled manner made him appear more like a caddie, an old football lineman, a limousine driver, or about any other occupation except his current one: a golf professional who had blazed onto the Senior PGA

Tour and whipped up nearly $500,000 in earnings during his rookie season in 1996.

That performance was more outstanding since just three years before, the avid fisherman was playing out of the trunk of his Chevy Impala and sleeping in the backseat at least four nights a week. "If you really want to see what pressure is," he explained, "try doing it when you're playing a two-hundred-dollar nassau with automatic two down presses against three guys packing guns and you've got three dollar bills in your pocket."

The Bobby Stroble rags-to-riches story began in Tampa, when his uncle took him to the exclusive Boca Grande Country Club where he caddied. Soon Stroble was playing in the late afternoon with the other caddies and showing a sense for the game that became addictive.

By the time Stroble neared the legal drinking age, his handicap was dropping a digit a month. It settled at six just as Uncle Sam came calling. Bobby was sent to Vietnam, where the military attached him to the Ninth Infantry Division of the Republic of Vietnam. "I don't talk about that much," he said. "I saw some buddies killed, and I did my share, too. Only difference between my buddies and me is pure luck."

Destiny awaited Stroble when he reported to Fort Hood, Texas, after being overseas. There he met Ol' Sarge, Orville Moody, the army champion. Moody helped Stroble hone his golf game, and by the time the twenty-four-year-old left the service in 1968, his handicap was plus one.

Professional golf was Stroble's goal, but he failed miserably in two tries at the Q-School until finding success and gaining his card in 1976. He lost it in 1977, regained it in 1978, and then lost it a year later. Eight years of chasing his dream against younger competitors produced less than $5,000 in prize winnings.

To keep food on his family's table, Stroble became the greatest hustler to hit the golf trail since Lee Trevino. While Trevino was astounding the world by winning Major championships, Bobby was taking pigeons for every dollar in their pockets, becoming a hustler extraordinaire.

The game plan was simple. Stroble snuck into an unsuspecting town. He'd scope out the golf courses, then appear at the practice tee in his rumpled JC Penney duds armed with a herky-jerky swing and a wristy putting stroke that made *him* look like the proverbial pigeon. At the proper time, he'd flash a wad of bills, never letting those foaming at the mouth see that a hundred on the outside was hiding a pack of ones.

"I'd show up at the practice tee wearing a tennis sweater and gym shoes," Stroble recalled, holding back laughter. "My bag was taped together, and my clubs looked like they hadn't been cleaned in months. If somebody didn't bite, want to play, then I'd just show up on the first tee, show some cash, and say, 'Can I join you guys?'"

The unsuspecting prey never caught on. "Lots of those guys would say, 'We bet and we play from the back tees,' and I'd just nod and get some action and then go from there. Five, six thousand could change hands if I played it right."

Stroble admitted there were times when he had no gas money, none for a hotel room or for a good meal. "There were lots of rock-bottom days, but I just kept going and tried to improve and win some cash to keep above water," the hustler said. "Playing with no money in your pocket makes you play better."

That was an understatement, since Stroble left a trail of legendary stories across America that didn't seem true. Through the years, he beat Payne Stewart and Russ Cochran in the Missouri Open with a final-round 67, Tom Lehman in a play-off in Minnesota, Calvin Peete in North Carolina, and others who marveled at his play. "Bobby Stroble could flat play," caddie Larry Jarman recalled. "He shot fifty-eight in Tennessee, with twenty-five on the front side. I was playing in the group ahead of him. You could let Tiger Woods go over there and play two balls and I guarantee, he'd never shoot twenty-five."

The Babe Ruthian performance came in the 1988 Green Turf Open in Knoxville. At the par 70 Whittle Springs Golf Course, Stroble stood on the fourteenth tee *twelve* under par. He'd shot 64 in the first round, and when he made five straight pars to end his second, 64 and 58 won him the first prize of $1,500.

"I'd shot sixty-two with a ball out of bounds in a practice round," Stroble explained. "Then came the sixty-four, the fifty-eight, and sixty-three, and sixty-four in the next tournament. I was unconscious."

Bobby Stroble not only hustled for money and swept state Open crowns, but played tournaments in the Negro Golf Association, labeled by the black players the "NGA Tour." They held twelve to fifteen events across the country. "We called it the Peanuts Tour, 'cause they had no money up," said Stroble. "But it got me competition, and that's what I needed."

As he neared fifty, Stroble, with a belly that threatened to hide his golf shoes from sight when he addressed the ball, readied himself for the Senior PGA Tour. He played two years on the Hogan/Nike Tour and in 1995, led the Senior Series, the Nike-like Tour to the Senior PGA Tour, in earnings with nearly $90,000.

At the Q-School in 1995, Stroble finished runner-up and gained his card. Exempt for the 1996 season, the journeyman with the nerves of ice recorded nine top-ten finishes, nearly won at The Transamerica, and established himself as a contender every week. "Bobby Stroble will be out here a long time," Calvin Peete said. "A long time."

"I've done some choking in my life, and that will continue to happen," Stroble admitted. "But I'm gonna win one of these days. And maybe another fifty-eight will come along one day."

Brimming with confidence, Stroble thought 1997 was going to be his breakthrough year. But a balky putter and nonexistent short game meant more bogies than birdies, and the only top ten finish came his way during the first two-thirds of the season.

Slowly, Stroble began to return to form, and consistent play moved him quietly up the money list toward the magic number thirty-one spot that meant exemption for the 1998 season. With six tournaments left before the Tour Championship, the good-natured Georgia native stood forty-seventh, $140,000 away from number thirty-one. During the next few weeks, Stroble stayed in the hunt, but heading into the Ralphs Senior Classic he needed a victory to keep from a return trip to the Q-School.

"I hope I can break through," he explained before the Ralphs Classic. "But if not, I'll just regroup and try to play well at the qualifying. And I'll make it and win one of these tournaments. You wait and see."

Hale Irwin let the field at the Ralphs Classic know from his first tee shot on Friday that he was determined to garner win number ten in 1997. He blasted out of the gate with 63 as if to say, "All right, boys, number ten is mine." Larry Nelson, for one, had enough. "If Hale doesn't start easing up, we're going to handicap him."

But Hale fell on hard times at the Wilshire Country Club, where Howard Hughes was once a member. Final rounds of 72 and 73 earned a tie for tenth. Taking his place in the limelight was the returning warrior, Jim Colbert, playing for just the third time on the Senior Tour since prostate cancer surgery.

Colbert opened with a pair of 65s, the second on a day when temperatures soared to nearly one hundred degrees, to lead by three with Money Sunday to follow. "I'm still seeing what I can do since I got back," said Colbert, who became so fatigued at the eleventh hole that he had to ride the entire hole in a cart and eat something before continuing.

The question hanging in the air as round three began was whether Colbert had the stamina to plow through eighteen holes with the same vigor that had sustained him on Friday and Saturday. "There's no way to know until I get out there," Colbert explained. "But at least I'm back in the thick of it."

For nine holes on Sunday, Colbert showed the grit that had made him a champion. Gil Morgan applied pressure early with three consecutive birdies on the front side, and the two were deadlocked playing the tenth. A birdie there by Morgan and a bogey by Colbert sealed Jim's fate, and he faded to tie for fifth with a disastrous 41 on the back side. "The tipoff was at number twelve," Colbert proclaimed. "I hit a perfect eight iron from 141 and came up way short. I'd normally have hit that club about 150. At one point I broke into a cold sweat. I just didn't have anything left. I was so exhausted all I could do was finish."

Meanwhile, Morgan, described by *Los Angeles Times* writer Thomas Bonk as having "a personality as dry as an Oklahoma sidewalk," was parading through the holes with a hot putter that drilled the ball into the hole with regularity.

"I never saw Gil make so many putts," Colbert quipped. And the doctor had luck on his side, too. On the second hole, Morgan's tee ball hit a spectator, keeping it from bouncing into the trees. After dutifully making sure the beaned fan was all right, Morgan calmly made birdie.

Another superb putter, George Archer, fired a 64 that catapulted him into contention at thirteen under par. "My best finish since hip replacement," Archer explained.

Gil Morgan led by two with two to play, but a bogey at seventeen made a par necessary at the closing hole. With his faithful caddie, Mike Boyce, known as "Shitty," loping along beside him, the doctor was up to the task and recorded his fifth win of the 1997 season. His money total of $1,832,000 positioned him $324,000 behind Irwin entering the final tournament of the season.

While Morgan, whose victory caused him to ask, "Can we schedule more events here?" rounded up his clubs and flew to Myrtle Beach and the Energizer Tour Championship, Bobby Stroble made plans to attend the Q-School. His quest for a tournament victory to save his card had started well enough with an opening round of 68, but 72 and 71 on the weekend garnered him less than $10,000. He finished fiftieth on the money list with a smidgeon more than $300,000 in earnings.

Bob Duval didn't compete at the Ralphs Classic, but luck held out and he captured the thirty-first spot on the money list. Quite an accomplishment for a golfer who'd finished fifteenth at the Q-School and didn't expect to play often. His appearance with the elite of the Tour in the Senior Tour Championship was in contrast to the player who had utilized several sponsors' exemptions and five of sixteen successful Monday four-spotters to gain entry into twenty-three events. His thirty-first finish meant an end to those dreaded Mondays and cross-country flights from nowhere to make them. After playing in the Franklin Quest Championship, Duval and wife Shari took the red-eye to Boston, only to find that the airline had lost his golf clubs. A woman at the airline said, "Mr. Duval, don't worry, we can get you a rental set," Duval recalled.

Duval's inability to gain a sponsor's exemption into either Raley's Gold Rush or the Ralphs Classic frustrated him, especially since he'd earned nearly $500,000 on the Senior Tour. At the Ralphs Classic, one of the exemptions was awarded to Deane Beman, who withdrew after an injury. "Hard to understand," Duval said. "Very hard."

The former club professional's ability to stay with the top thirty-one despite being unable to play in both events (he missed by one shot attempting to qualify for each) was his just due after a season in which he battled the odds and won out. Son David made the weekend a total success, winning the Tour Championship for his third consecutive victory, something no one had done since Nick Price won three in a row on the PGA Tour in 1993.

While David Duval's win captured the headlines, he'd exhibited behavior indicating Bob had been a good father. He told reporters, "I was thinking about my dad out there [in the last round]. Having him stay in the top thirty-one was more important than me winning."

The Ralphs Classic spelled doom for players such as Bob Dickson, whose poor play during the final month of the season cost him an exemption; John Schroeder, who finished forty-sixth on the money list; and Brian Barnes, positioned two notches ahead of Schroeder. Mike McCullough (forty-first), David Oakley (sixty-ninth), Dick Hendrickson (sixtieth), Buddy Whitten (fifty-fourth), John Morgan (forty-fifth), Will Sowles (seventy-fourth), and Dennis Coscina (eightieth) failed to retain their exemptions. Others who viewed the 1997 season with disdain were hopefuls Bob Wynn (sixty-fifth), Tony Jacklin (sixty-seventh), Leonard Thompson (fortieth), and Rick Acton (fifty-ninth). There were a fistful of others including Terry Dill and Larry Laoretti, who looked back with regret at poor shots, missed putts, and failed opportunities among the riches of the Senior PGA Tour.

Most disappointed was Bob Dickson, whose game went sour, especially at the Ralphs Classic, where a 71-76-79 result completed a nightmarelike final few tournaments. Earnings of $480,521 positioned him in thirty-second spot on the money list, just $2,080 dollars short of the number thirty-one, meaning he'd either have to return to the Q-School or hope absence of an exempt player would permit him entry. "Three months ago I felt good about my game," Dickson told *Golf World*'s Richard Mudry. "But in the last three months I haven't played worth a flip."

Arnold Palmer limped home at the Ralphs Classic, shooting disappointing rounds of 80, 72, and 75. Though he sported the "Palmer grin" when he left the clubhouse, Arnie was clearly thinking of what lay ahead. His demeanor reminded those who heard his comment "I'm too old for this shit" at the Comfort/Brickyard Classic in September. "Would the King be back in 1998?" they all asked themselves.

Palmer's fellow professionals hoped that retirement wouldn't happen. "He's our Babe Ruth," Jim Colbert proclaimed. Gary Player reflected his feelings another way, saying, "I hope he keeps playing because Arnold's the greatest ambassador to golf the game has ever seen. If I lived in this country, I'd vote for him for president."

Those on the inside looking out after the final event were Bob Eastwood, Hugh Baiocchi, John Jacobs, Bruce Summerhays, Dave Eichelberger, Jack Kiefer, Jerry McGee, Bud Allin, and Frank Conner, all of whom had met or exceeded expectations they had for the 1997 season. Their good play had earned them a ticket to South Carolina, where the top thirty-one money winners would duel for a fistful of cash. Larry Nelson would miss that event, though he had won more than $300,000 in earnings in just six events played.

Frank Conner had earned more than $500,000 in prize money and nearly $50,000 in corporate outings (average fee $3,500) scattered throughout the year. "But my caddie made about $60,000 and I'll have $85,000 to $90,000 in expenses," he explained. "Add the $10,000 more that I spent taking my wife, daughter, and son-in-law to Hawaii with me. No matter, it's been a very good year."

The elite thirty at the Energizer Tour Championship wouldn't include Chi Chi Rodriguez, who finished his year with a seventeenth-place finish at the Ralphs Classic. And with Little Bertha, his twenty-two-inch putter in storage. "I'm going to give it to Tatoo [of *Fantasy Island* fame]," Chi Chi joked. Earlier, he had quipped, "The putter is so short I can pray and putt at the same time."

Making airplane reservations for Myrtle Beach were Jimmy

Powell and Hubert Green, both of whom had played the last round of the Ralphs Classic as if it were a Major championship. The two had finished third and fourth respectively, leapfrogging over Bob Dickson and J. C. Snead into the elite field. Absence of the latter pleased many Tour competitors. "Bump the Grump" had been their battle cry, a reference to J.C.'s disagreeable disposition.

It didn't approach the prestige of either the U.S. Senior Open or the PGA Seniors' Championship, but the Energizer Senior Tour Championship rivaled both The Tradition and the Ford Senior Players Championship for Major status on the Tour. Its purse of $1,700,000 topped the earnings for both of those venues, and since the field was restricted to the top thirty-one money earners on the Senior PGA Tour and the top sixteen MasterCard Grand Masters, that meant more cash to divvy up among fewer players.

First prize carried the biggest pot of the season, $328,000, and dead last still meant $18,500. The Grand Master champion for those over sixty (Charles Coody won by five shots) took home $85,000, with $10,000 provided for the last in line.

One golfer who prized his spot in the elite field was fun-loving John Jacobs. His tie for second place at the 1995 Q-School had ensured him an exemption for the 1996 season, and Jacobs, winner of more long-driving contests in the world than anyone else, took advantage, winning more than $500,000 to ensure his exempt position for 1997.

Heading into the Tour Championship in 1997, Jacobs, brother of Tommy, the PGA Tour veteran and Ryder Cup player, had still not won a title, but consistent finishes had provided over $789,000 in earnings. That was like winning the lottery for the opera and classical music buff from Los Angeles.

Jacobs had been introduced to the game by his brother and attracted attention at age thirteen when he launched the ball more than three hundred yards. "John could hit it so far at that age you couldn't believe it," Tommy recalled. "But he was always happy-go-lucky. Had his mind on a lot of things. Fun things."

"I caddied for Tony Lema when I was sixteen," Jacobs recalled. "Saw how much fun he was having and figured that didn't look like too bad a life." Especially since Jacobs could flat-out play. "I was the best player, by a wide margin, at every level I competed at until the Tour," he said. "And I could compete out there. I just had too many distractions."

A preview came when he entered the University of Southern California in 1964, only to withdraw after *two* days. The army caught up with him two years later, but Jacobs's love affair with golf continued while he was stationed at Fort Hood, Texas—such a love that an unauthorized trip to Mexico for a big-bucks Calcutta match earned him a trip to the stockade for being AWOL.

Ordered shortly thereafter to Vietnam, Jacobs, ever the free spirit, spent time playing in high-stakes poker games and partying with Vietnamese army officials. "Not too many specialists fourth class can say they had dinner with the premier of Vietnam," Jacobs bragged.

When Jacobs returned to the United States, his passion was to play the PGA Tour. But he never found a consistent game, winning just over $100,000 in twelve years after gaining his card in 1968. "Too many ponies, too many trips to Santa Anita, Hollywood Park, and Del Mar, too many girls, too much booze," Jacobs lamented. "My buddies were high-stakes gamblers, jockeys, and trainers who played, not my fellow pros. One day I'd have fifty thousand dollars in my pocket, the next day zilch." Especially after a day at the races. "I got hooked because instead of working hard by hitting balls and practicing my short game, all I had to do was read the *Daily Racing Form* and clock a few horses. Which one made more sense?"

Jacobs's spotty play was also caused by a too-good-to-be-true lifestyle. "Lee Trevino set me up with sponsors, and one of them gave me a free air travel card," he said. "Hell, if I missed the cut on Friday, I'd be in Paris having dinner on Sunday."

By the early 1980s, the gambling bug had been replaced by a desire to play competitively. Unfortunately, the years had warped a promising golf game. Unable to crack the PGA Tour, Jacobs fled the country and found success in Far Eastern tournaments. In the 1980s, the long hitter with the boyish face won the Dunlop International, the Republic of China Open (twice), and the Singapore Rolex Championship. He was the first American ever to lead the Asian Golf Circuit Order of Merit.

"The strangest thing about playing over there was trying to stay clear of all the snakes, gophers, and gila monsters," Jacobs explained. "Ian Baker Finch and I were playing the second hole at Kuala Lumpur. A slimy python was lying there on the edge of the tee. Two dogs were going crazy barking at it. Next thing I know, the python lifts up and spits in the one dog's eye. He takes off yelping. The other dog keeps barking, so the snake struck. No more dog."

Winning in Asia qualified him for the European Tour, and he began competing, especially after falling in love with Valerie, his present wife. "She was my excuse to go to London," Jacobs admitted. "I'd play a little golf, see her, eat some bangers and mash."

Earnings of a few thousand dollars in long-driving contests supplemented his income, but Jacobs became restless for home, wanting to try the Senior Tour. "I finally was at the stage of my life where I wanted a home," he explained. "Valerie loved me, I'm still not quite sure why, but we bought a house in Scottsdale and I began to practice, which was something new for me. I usually just ate breakfast, headed for the course, teed it up, and saw what happened. The 'p' word wasn't in my vocabulary."

Jacobs's second-place finish in the 1995 Q-School opened the door to the Senior Tour, but he didn't play well out of the box. "I'm color-blind," he pointed out. "Everything looks dull. My hand-eye coordination didn't fit too well in Florida because the greens blended in."

Despite the adversity, Jacobs enjoyed a satisfying 1996 season, but at The Tradition in early 1997, he was after something bigger. "I've put more into my game in the last month than I did in my whole life," he explained. "I'm ready to win out here. I may be fifty-two, but I feel twenty-one."

Jacobs almost won, but David Graham eagled the eighteenth at the Southwestern Bell Dominion to nip him by a shot. "That one was like a stake through my heart," Jacobs stated. "David played well, but I had that tournament won and blew it by playing safe. My concentration took a hike, too. That's my biggest problem."

Despite the setback, Jacobs continued his good play. Entering the Senior Tour Championship, he stood twelfth on the money list. He attributed much of his success to his relationship with Valerie. "She helped stabilize things for me," Jacobs said. "Helped me keep my feet on the ground."

Jacobs certainly wasn't the only player on the Tour who felt that way about his better half. Most Senior Tour golfers realized their mates were heaven-sent, willing to put up with the travel, take care of the children for an absent husband, and handle the pressure of dealing with someone whose temperament depended on making three-foot putts for a living.

Especially on Sunday. "I try to keep thinking this doesn't matter," Carolyn Summerhays explained. "But I know it does, a lot." Gail Murphy added, "I take it fairly easy during the tournament, but on the back nine on Sunday, things tense up. That's when my mouth gets dry and I root for every shot. Do a lot of leaning with putts, trying to get them to go in."

Helen Bland said, "I'm very nervous on the inside, a quiet observer, but I try not to show it. I don't talk to John, but he knows I'm there rooting him along." Ruth Anne "Rudy" Schroeder, the wife of Rollie Schroeder, head professional at the Brickyard Crossing, where he competed with the Senior Tour performers, perhaps put it best: "Sure I'm nervous. I want Rollie to play well. We have to live with these guys, you know."

One Senior Tour wife, Maria Floyd, was often tougher on husband Raymond than unruly fans. When he'd miss a putt, she'd exclaim, "*Oh*, Raymond, *oh*, Raymond," as if he were deliberately trying to miss.

Senior Tour wives also had to restrain themselves from strangling smart-aleck gallery members who chastised their husbands. "If someone says something about John I don't care for," Helen Bland proclaimed, "I don't say anything, just give them what I call the look." Carolyn Summerhays admitted she wanted to snap back at someone picking on her husband, but held her tongue. "I just walk away and let it roll off my back," she explained. Gail Murphy tried to do likewise, but every so often she'd give someone a bit of her opinion. "I feel like if it's an out-and-out lie *that* I have to say something," she said. "You can only take so much."

Supporting the golf nomads meant several Tour wives gave up promising careers of their own. Karen Ferree was a club professional, and Willye Dent was an attorney. Many had successful businesses they closed down.

For some, like Gail Murphy, Barbara Nicklaus, Marcia Colbert, Vivienne Player, Willye Dent, and others, the life of a Tour wife had been nearly half a century long.

"Sure, the travel, the uncertainty, all of that made it difficult at times," Gail Murphy admitted. "But being out on Tour with Bob has provided us with a lifetime of friendships, and we've gotten to see the world. I wouldn't trade anything for it."

As always, Gail was just outside the ropes watching Bob compete at the Energizer Tour Championship the first week of November in Myrtle Beach. And hoping Murph and the other players could challenge Hale Irwin when it came to the final few holes on Sunday.

In round one of the championship, her wishes came true. Aided by a trip to an optometrist who informed Bob he needed a prescription change for his glasses, Murphy fired a six-under-par 66 at the lengthy Dunes Golf and Beach Club.

"I'd had trouble lining up putts for a while," Murph explained.

"The first day I put the new glasses on, I saw a difference." Earlier he'd told wife Gail, "Putts are going where I'm looking but not in." Gail had replied, "Then you're not lookin' right."

Lurking two shots behind Murphy, chewing Doublemint gum during his round in sync with his famous hesitation swing, was Hale Irwin. Sandwiched in between them was Hubert Green, who managed a 67 that included a wondrous putting round. "I made everything I looked at," Mr. Green exulted. "Everything."

Three strokes back stood Lee Trevino, winless for the first time in seven seasons. His eyesight was fine, but his golf game sour, the product, he explained, of the absence of the "Trevino shuffle."

"After the Pro-Am, I headed for the practice range," said Lee, twenty-seven times a winner on both the PGA and Senior PGA Tour. "That's when I realized I hadn't been doing the shuffle."

The Golf Channel's Tom Nettles was the first to hear about it. "Lee called me over," Nettles explained. " 'Tom, I've got it, I've got it,' he yelled."

And just what was he talking about? reporters demanded. "In the old days if you look at film, you'll see that I stood over the ball, look at the target, then the ball, and then do a little two-step shuffle before I swing," Lee said. "That allowed me to put the ball back in my stance and in position to shape the shot so the ball headed straight and then fell to the right, landing softly near the target."

Armed with the shuffle, Trevino thought he could win again. "Maybe this weekend," he predicted, "but if not, that's okay, too. If I don't win, it's not like Santa won't come to my house. He'll be there anyway because he visits every day."

Trevino also had a new weapon in his bag, a thirty-dollar putter that had been bargained down from fifty dollars. "I'm a tough negotiator," Trevino said. "Thirty bucks and an autographed ball." He also admitted he still needed to lose a few pounds: "Some people like to smoke and drink. I like to eat doughnuts and chocolate."

When the field of thirty Senior Tour members and fourteen Master-Card Champions (Bob Charles and Jimmy Powell qualified for both divisions) had begun play on Thursday for the four-round tournament, notable absentees were Arnold Palmer, Gary Player, Chi Chi Rodriguez, Larry Nelson, Johnny Miller, and Jack Nicklaus. None had won in 1997 or captured enough loot to earn an invitation.

Another legend, Sam Snead, wasn't entered, but the Slammer

entertained over five hundred fans at a clinic the Tuesday before the tournament. Among those looking on were Bob Duval, Jim Colbert, and Jay Sigel, each amazed at Snead's longevity. "Every swing he takes is the same," observed Sigel. "He can still hit the ball well past two hundred yards." Not bad for an eighty-five-year-old golfer who'd recorded the last of over eighty PGA Tour victories in 1965. There was even a "Sam Snead Restaurant," which featured Snead memorabilia, a few miles down the boulevard from the Dunes course.

Leader Bob Murphy played well in the early going in round two, only to be felled by a double-bogey five at the par-three seventeenth when he hit a full five-iron over the green into a nearly unplayable lie in the bunker. A rebounding birdie at eighteen left him at six under for thirty-six holes in the four-round tournament. But he was three shots back of the co-leaders, Player of the Year favorite Hale Irwin, Rookie of the Year favorite Gil Morgan, and Bob Duval.

Bob Duval? Wait a minute! Was this the same golfer who qualified fifteenth at the Q-School, begged and borrowed his way into a few events, qualified for a few more, and then limped home to nab the thirtieth and last spot for the Tour Championship?

"Well, yes it is, thank you very much," said Mr. Duval, whose sleepy eyes belied a fierce competitive spirit. "I know Hale and Doc are the big boys, but I deserve to be here, too."

Talk about a storybook finish to a magical year on the Senior Circuit. If the underdog Duval could win the Senior Tour Championship on the heels of son David's three consecutive titles on the PGA Tour, including the Tour Championship, the Duval family might be arrested for stealing. Adding $328,000 to David's take of $1.3 million in earnings meant the dual Duvals would bank more than $1.7 million for a month's worth of effort. Imagine the Christmas gifts!

The elder Duval's quest to complete his Walter Mitty year in grand fashion didn't intimidate the longtime club professional. Facing a pairing with Irwin and Morgan on Saturday, he was quite philosophical. "Remember, just being here is still a dream," he explained. "But I've showed I can play. Besides, where would you think I'd rather be? Here, or back at the course searching for Mrs. McDougald's clubs in the storage bin so she can take them on a six A.M. flight?"

No more of that for Bob. In Friday's second round, one he played in chilly temperatures with 1968 Florida State Seminole teammate Hubert Green (Hubie played number one that year, Duval number four), he fired a 66 that featured seven birdies and a deft putting touch with an elongated putter he cradled into his chest to prevent the yips.

Duval had enlisted the assistance of Buddy II, the shaggy-dog head cover banned to the car for poor play earlier in the year. It now joined Buddy I, the bleached-out head cover in Bob's golf bag. "They're talking to each other," Duval quipped.

While explaining that Buddy I covered the driver and Buddy II covered the three-wood, "Rabbit," Duval's caddie, also got into the act. "I talked to Buddy II a bit," he said. "He needs to behave himself."

Duval's newfound celebrity status didn't immunize him from verbal abuse. Bob Murphy yelled, "That's enough, rookie," when he entered the press tent and saw Duval in the hot seat. Duval laughed as he left, but Murphy wasn't through yet. "Don't let that son of yours rub off on you," he bellowed.

Meanwhile, Hale Irwin and Gil Morgan were staging their own private war. "We fed off each other's good play," Hale remarked. "Gil Morgan's a better golfer now than he's ever been. Longer, too. On the par-fives, he's outdriving me by thirty yards. It's 'see ya' time for me 'cause he's way out there."

Gil Morgan's 66 and Hale's 67 ensured they'd play together for the third straight day, along with upstart rookie Bob Duval, who'd joined son David on center stage in the golf world.

While Duval, Morgan, and Irwin took ample time to warm up for round three, Murphy went through a military-like regimen. "I'm up at six A.M. exercising and moving around," he said. "Then Gail uses her elbows on my back for half an hour. After that, I'm in the fitness trailer for an hour. They help stretch me out. Work on my neck, too."

Duval's pre-round exercises paled in comparison, but his play hadn't suffered. "I started playing better when I quit listening to a caddie I had while Rabbit was sidelined. That guy got me to play defensively. Three-woods off the tee and so forth. Then John Bland asked me what I was working on, and I told him my strategy. 'Go hit it as hard as you can and then go chase it,' he told me. So I started playing offensively, and that's changed everything."

The new strategy had produced a valiant effort in the second round, but the pairing with Morgan and Irwin on Saturday brought out the Pepto-Bismol. From the moment Duval awoke to partly sunny skies, he was a nervous wreck. Rabbit tried to loosen him up, and Bob attempted to disguise his stage fright, but it didn't take long for his inexperience to appear.

Duval was so pumped up at the first tee that he drove his ball fifty-three yards past Irwin's and thirty-one yards beyond Morgan's. Then the nightmare began. Duval made four bogies in the first seven holes, to disappear from the leader board.

Meanwhile, the two gunslingers, Irwin and Morgan, were staging their third duel in three days. Morgan was the better of the two in the early going, opening up a four-stroke margin after fifteen holes. But the dogged Irwin came on strong at the finish, birdieing three holes. At day's end, Gil had shot 66, Irwin 68.

Irwin was direct regarding the difference in play. "I played okay and Doc played great," he admitted. "Truth is, I just got dusted. My golf game degenerates a bit with the weather. When it's cold, I'm a bit short going back. Forces me to hit some loose shots."

Morgan, ever the uncomfortable one around the public and press, seemed nonchalant about his play. "I was piddling around out there," he reported. "But I putted *real* well."

For other prominent Senior Tour competitors, one round remained that meant little more than the size of their checks. Jim Colbert, whose last-second heroics at Myrtle Beach in 1996 had been *the* story, John Bland, amazingly winless for the year, Ray Floyd, still fighting inconsistent play, and Bob Murphy, continually in a shouting match with a balky putter, found themselves out of contention, ready to finish off play for 1997 and head for the "Silly Season," where they could pick up hundreds of thousands of dollars at the Diners Club Matches, Lexus Challenge, and made-for-TV events.

One player who'd have given anything to compete on the final Sunday of play was Larry Gilbert. He had stood atop the mountain after winning the Ford Senior Players Championship, only to be stricken with lung cancer two months later. ESPN's Frank Beard spoke for all of Larry's friends on the Senior Tour when he said, "Larry's the salt of the earth, exhibits good character, good morals, and hard work. A real person of substance."

Larry Gilbert was never far from the minds of any of the Senior Tour competitors, including Morgan and Irwin, who approached the first tee in the final round of the final tournament of the year at 11:25 A.M. They were joined by Mike Hill, the jovial brother from the Hill clan who had earned two Senior Tour championships among his career eighteen.

The tension surrounding the match-play confrontation between Morgan and Irwin was apparent from the get-go since the stakes were high. Though Irwin had won nine times and snagged more than $2 million in prize money, Morgan had five wins and $1.8 million in his pocket. Each had won a Major, Irwin the PGA Seniors' Championship, Morgan The Tradition. If Morgan could win the Senior Tour Championship, six wins and more than $2 million might earn him co-Player of the Year honors.

Before the chase for the $328,000 first prize began, Morgan's caddie, Mike Boyce, known as "Shitty," had done his best to ensure his boss would have a good day. "Before the second round, I tried to find a Mobil gas station where I could buy coffee," he reported. "I ended up there, but I took the wrong road. Then we shot 66, so I took that same wrong road again yesterday. Another 66, so which road do you think I took today?"

This caddie knew how fortunate he was. "It's hard to wipe this smile off my face," said Boyce, whose first gig was caddying for an obscure professional named John Topel in 1972. "I earned fifteen dollars a day and 3 percent of any prize money," he explained. Boyce's good fortune had caused Margo, Jim Dent's caddie, to walk up and ask, "How about a loan?"

On the practice tee, Gil Morgan seemed more relaxed than Hale Irwin. At one point, he was crouched down beside the spectator stands inspecting eight-irons laid out with the flanges next to one another. "Yesterday the eight-irons we hit came up about ten yards short," Boyce explained. "Gil wants to see if the loft is off." It wasn't.

If Morgan was the more cheerful of the two, Irwin won the "best-dressed" award. He chose a black-, red-, and gray-checkered sweater, perfect for a forty-five-degree sunny day chilled further with twenty-mile-per-hour winds. Doc was a bit more sedate with a white-on-white ensemble.

After a good-luck handshake from PGA Commissioner Tim Finchem, the Irwin-Morgan-Dave Hill group struck their tee shots on number one. The strong wind put the stops to the fifty-eight-year-old Hill's game, and he disappeared from the leader board as Bob Duval had done the day before.

Morgan, displaying the boyish grin that made him a gallery favorite, birdied first and led by three after number five. Irwin, not willing to give up, cut it to two with a birdie of his own at six. "He's catchable," Irwin had proclaimed earlier. "But I've got to keep pace until the back side. That's when the tournament will be won or lost."

Of the pretenders, only Hubert Green, nicknamed "The Doberman" because of his smallish-sized head and fierce facial expressions, stayed close in the early going. Two early birdies moved him to ten under, six shots back of Morgan and four behind Irwin. He hoped to post a 62 or 63, find the warmth of the clubhouse, and let the front-runners match him, but three bogies midround scuttled those chances.

A final-round 73 was the result, and it tied him with Bob Duval, whose twin-dog head covers resulted in an even-par 72. They finished seventh, one back of Hugh Baiocchi, Jay Sigel, and Lee Trevino, who shuffled his way to a 70. Isao Aoki posted a 67, the finest round of the day, and finished third, worth $154,000.

Entering the back nine, the margin between Irwin and Gil Morgan was three, and Hale knew he was running out of holes. At the par-four tenth, he decided it was time to "push the accelerator," as he liked to put it. Faced with a mid-iron second shot from the fairway to a pin tucked in the extreme front left side of the green, Irwin darted his ball directly toward the target. At the last second, however, he'd gotten a bit quick with the swing, and the result was a pull left that barely cleared the greenside bunker and nestled into the short rough. Morgan had positioned his second shot safely on the center of the green, and as he sauntered down the fairway, Hale Irwin's shoulders dipped just a bit. He'd failed to hit a critical shot when he needed it most, a huge disappointment for one who was trying to break Peter Thomson's single-season record for victories.

When he addressed his ball, Irwin suddenly had new hope. Gil Morgan had a forty-footer for birdie, a difficult one that could easily result in a three-putt. "If I can hole this chip shot," Irwin thought to himself, "and Gil has trouble, a two-shot swing is possible."

Irwin's daring attempt to get himself back in the match-play-like confrontation backfired. His chip was off line and too bold, and when he rimmed the cup with his par-saving putt, bogey was his fate. Doc managed to hole a testy four-footer for par, and instead of gaining one or two strokes, Hale had lost one and fallen four back with eight to play. "Geez," Irwin lamented as he rubbed his eyes while Morgan putted out, realizing the obvious.

The outcome of the 1997 Senior Tour Championship was decided at the eleventh, a severe dogleg par-four that featured a marsh bordering the right side of the hole. Morgan's pulled tee shot bounced onto a downside slope beside the fairway bunker. The awkward lie was nasty, and the marsh now loomed large between him and the green. Meanwhile, Irwin stood in the fairway, trying to pump himself up, determined to make birdie in one last gasp to cut Morgan's four-shot lead. He ripped a six-iron out of caddie John Sullivan's bag, intending to shoot straight for the pin, located to the far right side of the narrow green.

The thinking side of Morgan took over as he assessed his chances with the risky shot that faced him. Mike Boyce went over the yardage twice; "164 plus eight," he repeated. After due deliberation, Morgan, his hair creeping out from under a visor imprinted with Lynx, requested a six-iron. Realizing he was going to hit perhaps the most important shot of the tournament, Morgan surveyed the distance, blocked the watery marsh out of his mind, and straddled the ball. The muscles in his face tightened, and, then, with precision timing, he triggered his forward press, dug the ball out of its resting place, and lifted it on a high arc toward the center of the green. The ball floated for a time against the blue sky as it cleared the marsh and then fell softly on the green. Morgan broke into a self-satisfied grin, flipped his club to Boyce, and then loped down the fairway in his customary manner.

After Irwin watched the result of Gil's effort, he knew nothing less than a spectacular shot would suffice. The three-time U.S. Open champion needed to ignite all of the resources he had and find a perfect swing that would produce a razor-sharp shot kiss-close to the flagstick.

Irwin managed to hit a superb shot on line with the pin, but the ball jumped a bit and ended up eight feet behind and to the right of the hole. Hale stood transfixed in the middle of the fairway as caddie Sullivan replaced his divot. Slowly he started to walk toward the green, his shoulders visibly slumped, an indication that the great warrior knew the inevitable. "That was my last chance," Irwin said later. "I knew he was too out front to catch."

Morgan, whose lag putting had been outstanding all week, easily two-putted, and it was left to Irwin to keep any sense of drama alive for the millions of television viewers and fans lined ten deep. But his putt was meek, and fell to the side of the hole. When he tapped in for par, the difference was now four shots with only seven to play. Irwin glanced at the sky as he left the green, a hitch in his giddy-up apparent as he followed John Sullivan, whose stony face reflected his boss's fate.

"Gil had been playing so well," Irwin said later. "Bang, bang, bang. Really been in a comfort zone. I wanted to push him out of that, but I couldn't. And I knew it after we left the eleventh green."

Morgan's margin reached five at one point, but two late bogies, including one at the eighteenth, permitted Irwin to pull within two. Nevertheless, the triumph, Morgan's sixth of the year, was an overwhelming victory, especially sweet since Hale had defeated him in head-to-head competition at the MasterCard Championships eleven months earlier.

For the second straight year, Irwin's thunder had been stolen. Jim Colbert's shocking putt had devastated him in 1996, and now the good doctor, who announced his retirement from an optometric license that he'd never used anyway, had defeated Hale in their man-to-man match over four rounds in 1997.

Though he would win the Senior PGA Tour Player of the Year Award, Irwin left the Dunes Golf and Beach Club with a sour taste in his mouth. Winning more than $2 million, a Senior Major championship, and a record-tying nine tournament wins should have provided a great satisfaction, but the loss to Morgan had rained on his parade. It shouldn't have. All year long, and especially over a late-season, two-month stretch, there was little doubt that he was the "man," arguably the finest player in the world. His brilliant play was the envy of all who witnessed his mind-boggling performance.

For Dr. Gil Morgan, his victory capped a remarkable season, but he professed future goals. "I can't say enough about how excited I am about my year," he explained. "But I'm still a wee bit behind the guy at the top of the money list. We'll see what we can do about that next year."

Just as had occurred after his win in The Tradition, Morgan had to be told what the first-prize check was worth. He might have mentioned going after the money earnings title in 1998, but that wasn't the reason he played the game. "This is what it's all about," Gil explained. "Days like today when you can see whether you've got what it takes."

"Shitty" Boyce was ecstatic with the victory as well since another big payday meant more time to fish and take it easy near his Florida home. His early-morning journey along the wrong road to the Mobil station for coffee hadn't resulted in another 66, but Doc's 71 was enough to get the job done. "What a trip," Boyce said. "What a year."

So who was the better player, Hale Irwin or Gil Morgan? Opinions differed, but it really didn't make any difference. For in 1997 both Hale and Gil exhibited the qualities of champions, in the tradition of Sam Snead, Julius Boros, Don January, Gary Player, Arnold Palmer, Jack Nicklaus, and Lee Trevino. To be sure, Hale Irwin and Gil Morgan had done themselves proud and, in doing so, thrilled thousands of fans across the country who had one more glimpse of diamonds in the rough.

Bibliography

Ciebman, *Golf Shorts*. Chicago: Contemporary Books, 1995.

Bruce Crutchley, *Golf and All Its Glory*. London: BBC Books, 1992.

Pete Dye, Mark Shaw, *Bury Me In a Pot Bunker*, Reading, MA: Addison-Wesley, 1995.

Nevin H. Gibson, *Great Moments in Golf*. A. S. Barnes and Company, 1973.

Golf Magazine's Encyclopedia of Golf. NY: HarperCollins, 1993.

Steve Hershey, *The Senior Tour and the Men Who Play It*. NY: Simon and Schuster, 1992.

Mark McCormack, *The World of Professional Golf—1995*. Cleveland: IMG Publishing, 1995.

Michael McDonnell, *Golf: The Great Ones*. NY: Drake Publishers, 1971.

Kevin Nelson, *The Greatest Golf Shot Ever Made*. NY: Simon and Schuster, 1992.

Bobby Nichols, *Never Say Never*. NY: Fleet Publishing Co., 1965.

Senior PGA Tour Book—1997.

Senior PGA Tour, The Official Yearbook, PGA Tour, Ponte Vedra, FL, 1996.

Senior PGA Tour Media Guide, PGA Tour, Ponte Vedra, FL, 1997.

Mark Shaw, *Nicklaus*. Dallas: Taylor Publishing, 1997.

Robert T. Sommers, *Golf Anecdotes*. NY: Oxford University Press, 1995.

Various Issues: *Golf World, Golf Week, Senior Golfer, Golf Digest, Golf Magazine, Miami Herald, Las Vegas Sun, Arizona Republic, Chicago Tribune, Indianapolis Star, USA Today*.

Don Wade, *And Then Jack Said to Arnie*. Chicago: Contemporary Books, 1991.

———. *And Then Arnie Told Chi Chi*. Chicago: Contemporary Books, 1993.

———. *And Then Chi Chi Told Fuzzy*. Chicago: Contemporary Books, 1995.

Index

Aaron, Tommy, 6, 48

Acton, Rick, 5, 103, 263

Albus, Jim, 5, 18, 44, 57, 58, 103, 142, 161, 201–202

Albus, Mark, 202

Allen, Goofy, 237

Allin, Brian Thomas "Bud," 5, 17, 21, 41–42, 44–46, 47, 71–72, 167, 202, 209, 226–229, 264

Allin, Carol, 41, 45, 46, 229

Allis, Peter, 72, 170, 174

American Express Invitational, 17, 20, 42, 44–46, 122

Anderson, Willie, 53

Aoki, Isao, 5, 28, 29, 31, 38, 70, 73, 77, 95, 96, 119, 143, 144, 153, 154, 181, 201, 232–234, 274

Archer, George, 6, 19, 33, 72, 180–182, 262

Argea, Angelo, 141, 235–236, 242

Azinger, Paul, 183

Baiocchi, Hugh, 5, 57, 108, 146, 151, 189–191, 199–201, 233, 246, 264, 274

Baird, Butch, 6, 42, 237

Ball, Errie, 51

Ball, John, 51, 100

Ballard, Jimmy, 32, 119–120

Ballesteros, Seve, 30, 53, 140, 190, 246, 249

BankBoston Classic, 175, 177–179

Bank One Classic, 201–202

Barber, Jerry, 195–196

Barber, Karen, 56

Barber, Miller "Mr. X," 6, 18, 54, 56, 64, 137, 217

Barnes, Brian "Barnsey," 3, 6, 22, 23, 76, 83, 88, 112–116, 151, 152, 154, 178, 188, 189, 209, 211, 218, 231, 250, 255, 263

Barnes, Hilary, 113, 115

Bayer, George, 64

Bean, Andy, 98

Beard, Frank, 20, 29, 34, 48, 179, 184, 185, 272

Beck, Chip, 233

BellSouth Dominion, 47

BellSouth Senior Classic, 112

Beman, Deane, 5, 56, 147–148, 150, 154, 263

Berg, Patty, 53

Betley, Bob, 177

Bies, Don "Beez," 6, 20, 255

Billie, Toni, 169

Blackburn, Woody, 239

Blackmar, Phil, 239

Blancas, Homero, 6, 219, 237

Bland, Helen, 168, 248, 268

Bland, John, 5, 12, 16, 34, 57, 62, 64–66, 68, 69, 82–88, 95, 103, 112, 116, 124–133, 139, 140, 142, 150, 153, 155, 160, 170, 174, 175, 190, 209, 215, 219, 220, 230, 238, 245–249, 268, 271, 272

Bland, Roy, 65, 129, 131, 174, 238, 246–249

Bolt, Tommy "Thunder," 53–55, 62–64, 70

Bonk, Thomas, 262

Boone Valley Classic, 208–211, 214–215

Boozer, Emerson, 103

Boros, Julius, 53–55, 82, 164, 166, 276

Boswell, Tom, 159

Boyce, Mike "Shitty," 262, 273–276
Braid, James, 53
Brewer, Gay, 6, 177
British Senior Open, 170–171, 174–175
Bruno's Memorial Classic, 97, 99–101
Byrum, Curt, 240

Cain, John Paul, 6, 146, 150, 230
Calcavecchia, Mark, 183
Campbell, Joe, 177
Canizares, José; Maria, 149, 182, 184, 249
Caponi, Donna, 200
Carlson, Terry, 149
Carner, JoAnne, 53
Casper, Billy, 6, 53, 62, 64, 118, 180, 195, 255
Charles, Bob, 5, 6, 12, 16, 20, 29, 33, 50, 83, 84, 95, 107, 155, 175, 180, 190, 223, 251–252, 269
Charles, Verity, 251
Cheever, Eddie, 216, 219
Chi Chi Rodriguez Foundation, 27
Clampett, Bobby, 90
Clemente, Roberto, 25
Cobra Golf, 39
Cochran, Russ, 260
Colbert, Jim, 4, 11, 13–14, 16, 19, 21–23, 28–30, 32–35, 41, 42, 44–47, 58, 62, 72, 84, 94–97, 101, 103, 116, 119–123, 132, 153, 155, 159, 166, 180, 187, 196, 210, 214, 215, 222, 237, 241, 244, 248, 250–251, 255, 261–262, 264, 270, 275
Colbert, Marcia, 32, 72, 122, 187, 268
Cole, Bobby, 57
Colt, H.S., 170
Comfort/Brickyard Classic, 212–221, 223, 226–230
Conner, Frank, 6, 103–104, 151, 154, 178, 180, 188, 209, 211, 230, 250, 264
Coody, Charles, 6, 88, 104, 265
Cooper, "Lighthorse Harry," 56
Cooper, Pete, 25–26
Coscina, Dennis, 5, 151, 209, 258, 263
Couples, Fred, 118, 231

Crampton, Bruce, 4–6, 28, 106–108, 145, 209, 214, 233
Crampton, Marlene, 107
Crandon Park Golf course, 22
Crenshaw, Ben, 40, 53, 117, 118, 225
Crosby, Bing, 93
Cupp, Bob, 97

Dalton, Red, 182
Daly, John, 90, 117, 231
Danile, Vince, 214
De Klerk, F.W., 248
Demaret, Jimmy, 53–55, 63, 181
Dent, James, Jr., 105
Dent, Jim, 5, 19, 33, 102–106, 150, 209, 219, 222, 228, 255, 273
Dent, Radiah, 105
Dent, Willye, 105, 268
DePaul, Nick, 218
De Vicenzo, Roberto, 53–55, 64, 82, 190, 201
Devine, Dan, 17
Devlin, Bruce, 6, 242, 243
Dey, Joe, 63, 147
Diana, Princess of Wales, 199, 202
Diaz, J., 149
Dickinson, Gardner, 54, 55
Dickson, Bob, 4, 5, 21, 40, 49, 142, 150, 151, 209, 216, 255, 258, 263–265
Dill, Terry, 6, 19, 73–74, 145, 178, 209, 255, 263
Donald, Mike, 90
Douglass, Dale, 6, 20, 88, 91
Dudley, Ed, 25
Duval, Bob, 6, 146, 154, 187–188, 200, 202, 209, 210, 219, 230, 234, 237, 249, 262–263, 270–274
Duval, David, 6, 146, 187, 200, 249, 263, 271
Duval, Hap, 200
Duval, Sheri, 263
Dye, Pete, 95, 147, 216–217

Eastwood, Elva Jane, 256
Eastwood, Robert Fred "Bob," 6, 39, 47, 255–256, 264
Eastwood, Scott, 256

Eaton, Mark, 168
Eichelberger, Dave "Ike," 5, 29, 35–36,
    125, 170, 209, 243, 249, 250,
    264
Eichelberger, D.C., 250
Elder, Lee, 5, 19, 57, 62, 93, 94
Elias, Eddie, 28
Elkington, Steve, 37
Els, Ernie, 37, 54, 118, 246
Emerald Coast Classic, 230–234
Enberg, Dick, 118, 165
Energizer Senior Tour Championship,
    199, 202, 209, 210, 262, 264,
    265, 268–276

Fabel, Brad, 240
Faldo, Nick, 53, 246
Farrell, Johnny, 124
Faulkner, Max, 113, 115
Favre, Brett, 100
Feherty, David, 112
Fernandez, Vicente, 5, 35, 36, 150, 201,
    208, 233
Ferree, Jim, 6, 18, 19, 156, 181
Ferree, Karen, 268
Fetchick, Mike, 108
Fidrych, Mark "The Bird," 18
Finch, Ian Baker, 266
Finchem, Tom, 122, 162, 167, 273
First of America Classic, 187
Fleck, Jack, 62–64, 70
Floyd, Christina, 138
Floyd, Maria, 138, 225, 268
Floyd, Raymond, 6, 12–16, 39, 53, 71,
    90, 95, 137–139, 153, 156, 159,
    166, 189, 220, 223–228, 231,
    235
Floyd, Raymond, Jr., 137–139
Floyd, Robert, 137–139, 189
Ford Senior Players Championship,
    137, 140–144, 265
Forres, Chi Chi, 25
Frank, Barry, 14
Franklin Quest Championship, 163,
    166–169
Frost, David, 246
Furgol, Ed, 242
Furyk, Jim, 20

Gallagher, Bernard, 249
Gallagher, Mickey, 120
Gambetta, Fritz, 150, 217
Geiberger, Al "Berger/Skippy," 6,
    66–68, 138, 221, 223, 227,
    229–230, 233
Geiberger, Brent, 66, 138, 229
Geiberger, Matthew, 67–68
Gentry, Craig, 33
George, Tony, 217
Giffin, Doc, 195
Gilbert, Allen, 143
Gilbert, Brenda, 143, 144
Gilbert, Chris, 143
Gilbert, C.L., Jr. "Gibby," 5, 17, 28–31,
    41, 47, 65, 84–86, 208, 234, 254
Gilbert, Eileen, 31
Gilbert, Larry, 5, 58, 86, 102, 106, 139,
    140, 142–144, 155, 180, 181,
    218, 234, 255, 272
Giles, Vinny, 151, 171, 184
Gillette Tour Challenge, 22–23
Goalby, Bob, 55, 56, 103
Golf Ball, 235
Golf Channel, The, 198, 199
Goosie, J.C., 181
Graham, David, 5, 6, 29, 35–41, 47, 48,
    50, 64, 68, 75, 82, 139, 140, 150,
    153, 208, 209, 211, 222, 223,
    226–230, 233, 242, 267
Graham, Lou, 6, 99
Graham, Maureen, 36
Grate, Frank, 17
Grate, Gaye, 17
Green, Hubert, 3, 5, 6, 18, 22, 23,
    28–29, 56, 64, 65, 68, 76,
    97–100, 162, 180, 184, 202, 209,
    231, 234, 237, 254–255, 265,
    269, 270, 273–274
Green, Ken, 92
Greenwood, Hardy, 157
Grout, Jack, 119
GTE Classic, 36
Gwynn, Tony, 81

Hagen, Walter, 53, 54, 224
Hall, Bill, 148–150
Hall, Walter, 149, 184, 201

Harmon, Claude, 172
Harms, Ken, 237
Harris, Labron, 149
Hartley, Tom, 33
Hauer, Bob, 150, 217
Havemeyer, Theodore, 62
Hawkins, John, 257, 258
Hayes, Dale, 57
Hayes, Ted, 150, 154
Heard, Jerry, 45
Hebert, Lionel, 57, 119
Hendrickson, Dick, 5, 6, 151, 188, 209, 222, 258, 263
Henning, Brian "Bruno," 56–58, 62
Henning, Harold "Horse," 29, 57, 93
Henninger, Brian, 20–21
Henry, Bunky, 146, 221, 222, 230, 237
Hill, Dave, 145, 214–215, 273
Hill, Mike, 6, 64, 119, 202, 238, 254, 272
Hill, Mike, Jr., 238
Hiskey, Babe, 177
Hobday, Simon, 5, 6, 42–44, 130, 168, 202, 221, 237, 245
Hogan, Ben, 54, 60, 61, 63, 70, 140, 161–163, 171, 172, 175, 195, 222, 225
Home Depot Invitational Tournament, 102, 106
Hook-a-Kid-on-Golf program, 49–50
Hoyt, Beatrix, 53
Huber, Cassie, 239
Huber, Cathy, 239
Huber, Dan, 239
Huber, Mark, 123, 215, 221, 237–242
Hulka, Steve, 40
Hutchinson, Jock, 81
Hyatt Regency Maui Kaanapali Classic, 250–254
Hyndman, Bill, 60, 172

Irwin, Becky, 254
Irwin, Hale, 6, 12–16, 20, 21, 32–35, 41, 47, 53, 58, 71, 74–75, 81–92, 95–97, 101, 103, 111–112, 117–119, 123–125, 139, 140, 153, 155, 159, 160, 162, 171, 177–180, 182, 184, 187, 188, 199, 207–211, 217, 219, 220, 223, 227, 229, 231, 234, 241–245, 248, 249, 251–255, 257, 258, 261, 268–276
Irwin, Hale, Sr., 87
Irwin, Sally, 254
Irwin, Steve, 182

Jacklin, Tony, 5, 6, 21, 64, 116, 127, 146, 154, 159, 175–178, 188, 230–231, 246, 247, 250, 255, 263
Jacobs, John, 70, 73–75, 77, 96, 177, 178, 214, 229, 264–267
Jacobs, Tommy, 265
Jacobs, Valerie, 266–267
January, Don, 6, 18, 28, 54–57, 62, 64–65, 161, 166, 187, 276
Janzen, Lee, 231
Jarman, Larry, 260
Johnstone, Tony, 245, 246, 248, 249
Jones, Bobby, 37, 51, 53, 54, 81, 94, 100, 124, 141, 172, 192, 194, 195
Jones, Sandy, 221, 223, 237–238
Jones, Steve, 118

Kaline, Al, 17
Katz, Howard, 14
Kelly, Jim, 96, 196, 237
Kemper Lakes Golf Course, 111–112
Kennemer, Al, 49
Kiefer, Jack, 103, 116, 264
Kite, Tom, 118, 162, 207, 231, 243
Klein, Emily, 237
Knight, Phil, 165
Koch, Gary, 116
Kroger Senior Classic, 144–147, 151, 153, 154

Landers, Freddie, 75
Landers, Robert, 5–6, 75
Laoretti, Larry, 5, 58, 142, 178, 209, 255, 263
Las Vegas Senior Classic, 95–97
Leaver, Robert, 17
Lee, Bill "Spaceman," 18

Legends of Golf Tournament, 47, 53, 54, 56, 63–66, 68–69

Lehman, Tom, 11, 192, 198–199, 260

Lema, Tony, 172, 173, 265

Letterman, David, 18

LG Championship, 35–36, 38

Littler, Gene, 6, 19, 64–65, 112, 193

Locke, Bobby, 53, 118, 129, 247

Lopez, Nancy, 53, 161

Louis, Joe, 103

Love, Davis, III, 192, 198–199

Luigs, Lisa, 107

Lundstrom, David, 150

Mac, Johnny, 215

Mackenzie, Alister, 194

Mangrum, Lloyd, 52

Marr, David, 18, 147, 244

Marriot, Bill, 165

Marsh, Graham "Swampy," 5, 22, 23, 44, 64–66, 68, 69, 103, 123–133, 139, 144, 150, 153, 167, 170, 180, 209, 214, 218, 220, 222, 230, 233, 249

Marsh, Ken, 126

Marsh, Rodney, 126

Martin, Jim, 101

Massengale, Rick, 17, 30, 42, 149

McBee, Rives, 150, 177

McCord, Gary, 112, 166

McCullough, Mike, 4–5, 151, 154, 188, 209, 210, 230, 250, 258, 263

McDermott, Joe, 153

McGee, Jerry, 6, 67, 111, 145, 151, 177–179, 237, 264

McLean, Jim, 30

Medlins, Squeaky, 91, 240

Meeks, Tom, 125

Meredith, Don, 103

Middlecoff, Cary, 52, 53

Miller, Johnny, 5, 6, 41, 53, 87, 88, 98, 131, 140, 159, 161–167, 169, 172, 175, 180, 189, 196, 241, 250, 269

Miller, Willie, 14, 23, 72, 121–122, 215, 221–222, 238

Mitchell, Bobby, 217

Mitchell, Herman, 157, 159, 235–236

Montgomerie, Colin, 242, 243, 247

Moody, Orville, 181–182, 200, 259

Morgan, Gilmer Bryan, II "Gil," 6, 12, 18, 21, 23, 39, 48, 64, 65, 68, 70, 71, 73–78, 82, 84, 85, 95, 97, 101, 111–112, 116, 125, 129, 139, 140, 144, 153, 159, 162, 180, 187–188, 199, 207, 209, 210, 217, 219, 220, 222, 223, 227–229, 233–234, 242, 244, 245, 249, 251, 255, 257, 262, 270–276

Morgan, John D., 5, 102, 103, 151, 154, 188, 209, 219, 221, 223, 258, 263

Morgan, Walter, 5, 12, 22, 29, 33, 102, 199, 208, 216, 251

Morris, Old Tom, 53

Mother Teresa, 202–203

Mowry, Larry, 6, 150

Mudry, Richard, 18, 264

Mullins, Moon, 177

Murphy, Bob, 5, 17, 19, 21–23, 28, 29, 33, 35, 38, 44, 47–52, 58, 64, 72, 88, 94, 103, 112, 115, 119–123, 144, 150, 153, 155, 180, 181, 215, 223, 227–229, 237–241, 244, 251, 255, 268–272

Murphy, Gail, 48, 50, 51, 223, 240, 267–269

Nagle, Ken, 54

Nelson, Byron, 53, 54

Nelson, Larry, 5, 6, 112, 117, 172, 207–208, 223, 226, 228, 229, 231, 242, 261, 264, 269

Nettingham, Earl, 62

Nettles, Tom, 76–77, 269

Newcombe, Dave, 169

Nicholette, Mike, 239

Nichols, Bobby, 3, 6, 19, 72, 216

Nicklaus, Barbara, 141, 268

Nicklaus, Charlie, 141

Nicklaus, Gary, 117, 138

Nicklaus, Jack, 3, 6, 12–16, 19, 27, 36, 38, 40, 47, 51, 53, 55, 58, 60–61, 69–72, 82, 84–91, 93, 94, 98, 100, 101, 104, 106, 113–114,

Nicklaus, Jack *(cont.)*
        117–118, 125, 138–142, 144,
        153, 155, 157–159, 161–164,
        166, 171–173, 176, 180, 189,
        193–196, 217, 225, 231, 232,
        236, 241, 242, 269, 276
Nicklaus, Jack, II, 138
Nicklaus, Jackie, 117
Nicklaus, Michael, 138
Nicklaus, Steve, 138
Nobilo, Frank, 245
Norman, Greg, 37, 39, 40, 53–54, 117,
        140, 162, 164, 242, 243
North, Andy, 12, 14, 167, 179, 237,
        250, 252, 253
Northville Long Island Classic, 180,
        182, 184–186

Oakley, David, 4, 150–154, 188, 209,
        258, 263
O'Conner, Christy, 249
Ojala, David, 146, 154, 188
Olympia Fields Golf Course,
        124–132
Oosterhuis, Peter, 115, 249
Ouimet, Frances, 161, 162, 192

Palmer, Arnold, 6, 11–16, 18–19, 25,
        26, 33, 36, 47, 53, 56–58, 60, 61,
        69, 82–83, 92, 103, 104, 125,
        137, 140, 153–154, 158, 159,
        161–164, 166, 167, 172, 183,
        188–189, 192–199, 214,
        217–222, 227–228, 230, 231,
        244, 248, 250, 257, 264, 269,
        276
Palmer, Jim, 18
Palmer, Milfred "Deacon," 193
Palmer, Sandra, 52
Palmer, Winnie, 193–194
Parks, Willie, Jr., 124
Parry, Craig, 37
Peete, Calvin, 5, 29, 260, 261
Perla, Tony, 149, 217
Peterson, Tom, 141
Pitino, Rick, 100
Pittsburgh Senior Classic, 199–200
Pizarro, Juan, 25

Player, Gary, 4–6, 11, 16, 20, 30, 31,
        36, 43, 47, 53, 57, 58, 62, 63, 70,
        72, 97, 103–105, 116, 125, 127,
        140, 153, 159, 161–163,
        170–175, 194, 220–221, 223,
        224, 234, 246–247, 249, 251,
        264, 269, 276
Player, Vivienne, 172, 223, 268
Player, Wayne, 173
Pott, Johnny, 64, 177
Powell, Jimmy, 6, 20, 108, 249,
        264–265, 269
Prentice, Jo Ann, 52
Presidents Cup, 37, 40
Price, Nick, 37, 246, 251, 263
Purtzer, Tom, 240

Quigley, Angie, 184, 185
Quigley, Dana, 84, 139, 184–187, 223,
        234, 255
Quigley, Paul, 185
Quigley, Wallace, 185

Raley's Gold Rush Classic, 254–256
Ralphs Classic, 257, 258, 261–265
Raphael, Fred, 53–55
Ratcliffe, Noel, 170
Rawlins, Bob, 17
Ray, Ted, 192
Refram, Dean, 187
Rehling, Conrad, 48, 49
Reinfeld, Larry, 239
Rhodes, Ted, 5
Rhyan, Dick, 19
Riber, Burch, 148
Richards, Phil, 215
Rinker, Larry, 240
Robbins, Kelly, 251
Robertson, Allen, 53
Robinson, Jackie, 94
Rocca, Constantino, 94
Rockefeller, Laurance, 26
Rodgers, Phil, 71, 89, 251–252
Rodriguez, Iwalani, 26
Rodriguez, Jesus, 252–253, 255
Rodriguez, Juan "Chi Chi," 3–6, 11,
        20, 21, 24–28, 30, 31, 35, 36, 40,
        42, 47, 75, 82–83, 89, 125, 153,

158, 159, 162, 163, 168, 188, 189, 202–203, 208, 214, 217, 219–220, 222–223, 227, 229–231, 250, 252–253, 257, 264, 269

Rosburg, Bob, 73, 74, 103

Rose, Seymour, 147

Rotella, Bob, 139

Royal Caribbean Classic, 3, 20, 22, 23, 28–31, 42, 48

Rubin, Chuck, 14

Rudolph, Mason, 177

Runyan, Paul, 64, 70

Ryan, Don, 237

Saint Luke's Classic, 189–192

Sanders, Doug, 63, 172

Sanudo, Cesar, 178

Sarazen, Gene, 53, 54, 70, 82, 171

Schroeder, John, 5, 38–39, 151, 154, 178, 188, 201, 209, 230, 250, 255, 263

Schroeder, Kathy, 39

Schroeder, Patty, 39

Schroeder, Rollie, 217, 218, 268

Schroeder, Ruth Anne, 268

Senior Skins' competition, 12–16

Senko, Dave, 64, 73–74, 78

Shaw, Thomas G., III, 6, 71, 167

Shippen, John, 62, 94

Sifford, Charlie, 5, 55, 56, 62, 64, 82, 93, 94

Sigel, Jay, 5, 12, 16, 19, 21–23, 33, 34, 48, 50–51, 100–102, 153, 154, 184, 185, 201, 240, 270, 274

Sikes, Dan, 55

Singh, Vijay, 118

Smith, Bob E., 218

Smith, Gene, 217, 218, 248

Smith, Herb, 23

Snead, J.C., 21–23, 28, 38, 39, 48, 59, 65, 95, 103, 121, 145, 181, 182, 188, 209, 214, 215, 221, 230, 231, 255, 265

Snead, Samuel Jackson, 6, 13, 53–57, 59–65, 67, 69, 70, 82, 103, 140, 161, 172, 181, 221, 222, 269–270, 276

Sneed, Ed, 146

Sorenstam, Annika, 11

Souchak, Mike, 64

Sowles, Will, 4, 151, 188, 189, 209, 216, 258, 263

Springs, Carolyn, 67

Spurrier, Steve, 100

Stambaugh, Phil, 199

Stankowski, Paul, 20

Stankus, Eddie, 219

Starr, Bart, 100

Stephenson, Mo, 104

Stewart, Payne, 260

Still, Ken, 225

Stills, Adrian, 106

Stockton, Cathy, 139, 169, 219

Stockton, Dave, Jr., 138, 142, 168

Stockton, David Knapp, 6, 15, 33, 62, 66–68, 83, 90, 95, 112, 117, 119, 138, 139, 142, 144, 153, 167–170, 175, 187, 219, 255

Stockton, Ron, 138, 139, 168, 219

Stockton, Tammy, 219

Stranahan, Frank, 174

Strange, Curtis, 244

Stroble, Bobby, 3, 5, 42, 167, 178, 188, 189, 201, 209, 211, 230, 250, 255, 258–261

Suggs, Louise, 53

Sullivan, John, 88, 91, 241–243, 274, 275

Summerhays, Bruce, 5, 138, 178, 189–192, 201, 218, 222, 253, 254, 257, 264

Summerhays, Bruce, Jr., 138

Summerhays, Bryan, 138, 253

Summerhays, Carolyn, 191–192, 267, 268

Summerhays, Carrie, 138, 192

Summerhays, Joseph, 138, 192

Summerhays, William, 138, 191

Sweeny, Robert, 193

Tatum, Sandy, 99

Taylor, Dick, 171–172

Taylor, J.W., 53

Tewell, Doug, 240

Thompson, Hugh "Rocky," 3, 66, 145, 181, 208, 222, 226
Thompson, Leonard, 5, 263
Thompson, "Titanic," 73
Thomson, Peter, 37, 53, 54, 127, 179, 183, 190, 244, 253, 254, 258, 274
Thorpe, Jim, 106
Tillinghast, A.W., 193
Tolley, Scott, 83
Topel, John, 273
Torrance, Sam, 43, 215–216
Toscano, Harry, 188, 217, 218
Toshiba Senior Classic, 47, 50–52, 63, 64
Toski, Bob, 55, 119
Tournament of Champions, 11, 21, 35, 48
Townsend, Peter, 249
Tradition, The, 47, 70–78, 265
Transmerica, The, 249–250
Trevino, Claudia, 155, 159
Trevino, Daniel, 155, 159
Trevino, Lee, 3, 4, 6, 12–16, 20, 21, 23–24, 26, 28, 30, 31, 33, 36, 40, 43–44, 47, 48, 50, 53, 57, 58, 62, 64, 71, 74, 87, 97, 98, 102, 106, 113, 119, 122, 125, 140, 153–161, 163, 164, 166, 172, 176, 188, 189, 201, 214, 229, 231–232, 236, 239, 247, 250, 251, 257, 259, 266, 269, 274, 276
Trevino, Olivia, 155
Trotter, Lee, 239
Tryba, Ted, 21
Tway, Bob, 183
Twiggs, Gregg, 240

U.S. Senior Open, 124–133

Vantage Championship, 242–245
Vardon, Harry, 53, 54, 192

Verwey, Jack, 172
Vossler, Ernie, 55, 60, 68, 76, 98, 192

Wada, Andy, 232
Wadkins, Lanny, 98, 162
Wall, Art, 53, 54
Ward, Harvie, 62
Wargo, Tom, 5, 33, 58, 82, 103, 125, 129, 148, 151, 161, 170, 177–179, 239, 242
Watson, Tom, 53, 98, 118, 140, 162, 163, 173, 183, 231, 244
Weaver, DeWitt, 6, 29, 102, 103, 180, 189, 249
Webb, Karrie, 11
Weed, Bobby, 36, 95
Weiskopf, Tom, 6, 16, 57, 113, 141, 145, 155, 164, 172, 183, 199, 225
Wethered, Joyce, 53
Whitten, Buddy, 5, 29, 151, 188, 201, 209, 258, 263
Whittlesey, Merrell, 61
Wood, Dan, 146
Wood, Randy, 149
Woods, Earl, 92, 132, 165
Woods, Tiger, 11, 14, 15, 51, 54, 61, 92–94, 100, 106, 117, 132, 140, 165, 177, 179, 192, 196, 198–199, 225, 231, 242–244, 254, 257, 260
Woosnam, Ian, 246
Wright, Mickey, 53
Wynn, Bob, 178, 179, 250, 263

Zaharias, Babe, 53
Zarley, Kermit "Moon Man," 6, 125, 177, 209, 234
Zarley, Monica, 177
Zembriski, Walter, 6, 105, 145, 182–184, 214, 237, 255
Ziegler, Larry, 18, 19, 33, 167–168, 215, 219, 220
Zoeller, Fuzzy, 162, 183

ABOUT THE AUTHOR

MARK SHAW is a lawyer turned author/journalist whose books include *Testament to Courage*, *Down for the Count*, *Bury Me in a Pot Bunker* (written with Pete Dye), *Forever Flying* (written with R. A. Hoover), *The Perfect Yankee* (written with Don Larsen), and *Nicklaus: A Biography*. Shaw is the host of a daily radio talk show and lives in the art community of Nashville, Indiana, with his wife, Chris, four children, six dogs, eight ducks, and five turtles.